GEOPOLITICS AND THE ANGLOPHONE NOVEL, 1890–2011

Literary fiction is a powerful cultural tool for criticizing governments and for imagining how better governance and better states would work. Combining political theory with strong readings of a vast range of novels, John Marx shows that fiction over the long twentieth century often envisioned good government not in utopian but in pragmatic terms. Early twentieth-century novels by Joseph Conrad, E. M. Forster, and Rabindrananth Tagore helped forecast world government after European imperialism. Twenty-first-century novelists such as Monica Ali, Chimamanda Ngozi Adichie, Michael Ondaatje, and Amitav Ghosh have inherited that legacy and continue to criticize existing policies in order to formulate best practices on a global scale. Marx shows how literature can make an important contribution to political and social sciences by creating a space to imagine and experiment with social organization.

JOHN MARX is Associate Professor of English at the University of California, Davis. He is the author of *The Modernist Novel and the Decline of Empire* (Cambridge, 2005).

GEOPOLITICS AND THE ANGLOPHONE NOVEL, 1890–2011

JOHN MARX

CAMBRIDGE UNIVERSITY PRESS
Cambridge, New York, Melbourne, Madrid, Cape Town,
Singapore, São Paulo, Delhi, Tokyo, Mexico City

Cambridge University Press
The Edinburgh Building, Cambridge CB2 8RU, UK

Published in the United States of America by Cambridge University Press, New York

www.cambridge.org
Information on this title: www.cambridge.org/9781107020313

© John Marx 2012

This publication is in copyright. Subject to statutory exception
and to the provisions of relevant collective licensing agreements,
no reproduction of any part may take place without the written
permission of Cambridge University Press.

First published 2012

Printed in the United Kingdom at the University Press, Cambridge

A catalogue record for this publication is available from the British Library

ISBN 978-1-107-02031-3 Hardback

Cambridge University Press has no responsibility for the persistence or
accuracy of URLs for external or third-party internet websites referred to
in this publication, and does not guarantee that any content on such
websites is, or will remain, accurate or appropriate.

Contents

Acknowledgments		*page* vi
Introduction: The novel's administrative turn		1
1	Fiction after liberalism	19
2	How literature administers "failed" states	47
3	The novelistic management of inequality in the age of meritocracy	89
4	Entrepreneurship and imperial politics in twentieth-century historical fiction	125
5	Women as economic actors in contemporary and modernist novels	170
Postscript: The literary politics of being well attached		213
Bibliography		219
Index		243

Acknowledgments

My work on this book was assisted by the University of California, Davis: the Committee on Research provided several small grants in aid of research and the Division of Humanities, Arts, and Cultural Studies provided start-up funds that helped bring the project to completion. I also owe a profound debt of gratitude to students and colleagues in the Department of English, who were valued interlocutors throughout the research and writing of this project.

I am grateful for the response of audiences at the institutions where I gave talks based on early versions of this work. Special thanks to my hosts at the Wesleyan Center for the Humanities, the National University of Ireland, Maynooth, the Duke University Center for International Studies, and the University of South Carolina Department of English. The response from "WReC" and the participants in the Uneven and Combined Modernisms Colloquium at the University of Warwick convinced me that my book's argument touched a nerve. The Women, Gender, and Sexuality Studies Group at the University of Richmond provided early feedback on a key element of that argument.

An earlier and shorter version of the first chapter appeared in *Contemporary Literature* 49.4 (2008): 597–633. © 2008 by the Board of Regents of the University of Wisconsin System. Reproduced courtesy of the University of Wisconsin Press. An earlier and shorter version of the fourth chapter appeared in *Cultural Critique* 63 (2006), published by The University of Minnesota Press. Thanks to the editors of those journals for permission to reprint material.

I would not have been able to write this book without the good will and sharp questioning of friends and colleagues. Rita Barnard,

Rey Chow, Jed Esty, and Jennifer Wicke read significant parts of the manuscript in various versions on sundry occasions, and I am grateful for their willingness to do so. Ellen Rooney and Khachig Tölölyan offered pointed observations concerning numerous parts of the book's argument as it was taking shape. Because their insights were typically provided during excellent meals, they were all very well received. There is no one I benefit more from while debating the sorts of questions dealt with in this book than Neil Lazarus. I am thankful that he and Tamara Sivanandan have been willing to allow me to show up periodically on their doorstep. The book's citations probably make it clear that Nancy Armstrong's scholarship has profoundly influenced my thinking, but it bears emphasizing that her recent collaborative work with Leonard Tennenhouse has helped me explain how the new (old) Foucault lectures aid in studying novels.

A plurality of readers nudged and badgered me to formulate more clearly the book's intervention into discussions of literature and governance. I received timely advice on the introduction from Timothy Bewes and Peter Kalliney. Rebecca Walkowitz, Saikat Majumdar, Edward Larkin, Weihsin Gui, and Thomas Allen offered incisive comments on individual chapters of the book. The anonymous readers for Cambridge University Press provided the recommendations that allowed me to whip the book into its final shape. I am grateful to Amanda Claybaugh for encouraging me in my argument about failed states and for introducing me to Matthew Hart and Jim Hansen, editors of a special issue of *Contemporary Literature* on the state. The provocations of Barry Faulk and Robin Goodman were instrumental in shaping my thinking at myriad points of the book's composition. Speaking on the phone with Andrew Lewis and Gwynneth Malin has become an essential part of my writing process, and I can only hope that they continue to take my calls. Ray Ryan's confidence in the project was vital and I am thankful for his reassuringly steady hand on the controls at the Press. I rely as much upon Mark Cooper's friendship as his editorial tenacity. Working with him is exactly the kind of pleasure that makes me sentimental about professional relationships. My greatest debt is to Beth Anderson, upon whom I am as entirely dependent on the West Coast of the United States as I was on the East.

Introduction

The novel's administrative turn

This book explains where contemporary fiction got the idea that novels can contribute meaningfully to interdisciplinary debate about governance. Perhaps the most important source, I contend, is the imperial fiction appearing around the turn of the twentieth century. During those years, fiction took an administrative turn, even as resistance movements and increasing competition were leading Britons to anticipate empire's passing. Edward Said describes writers from this era "substituting art and its creations for the once-possible synthesis of the world empires" (*Culture* 189). In so doing, novelists helped forecast a world after European imperialism by identifying problems with empire's administrative strategies and by laying the conceptual foundation necessary to generate new schemes. Twenty-first-century novels have inherited that legacy and continue to criticize existing policies in order to formulate best practices on a global scale.

No one likely will be surprised to hear that many turn-of-the-twentieth-century novels critiqued imperial rule or that many more recent novels critique neoliberal authority. The burden of my argument will be to show how fiction refurbishes government as well as criticizes it. For a case in point, one may turn to such a foundational work as Joseph Conrad's "Heart of Darkness" (1899/1903), which offers evidence that fiction cared as much about salvaging administration as resisting it. The novella famously turns one colonial station manager's complete lack of "restraint in the gratification of his various lusts" into an occasion for considering the broader state of imperial governance (131). Readers are well used to understanding how Kurtz's transformation from paragon of Victorian rectitude into jungle megalomaniac connotes a warning that European empire as a whole was losing its grip. It could be noted more often, however, that by making this logical relation intelligible, Conrad connects the familiar novelistic theme of self-governance to a wider political problem of governing others. "All Europe contributed to the making of Kurtz," and the unmaking of Kurtz signals dire consequences for Europe's ongoing administration of the larger world (117). "No method at all" sums up not only Kurtz's failure to manage his own behavior, but also the absence of a coherent and effective strategy behind empire building in general (138).

In detailing how things went wrong, Marlow also implies what might count as improvement, and he thereby demonstrates the limit of his administrative vision. He is impressed by those few managers who are capable of self-discipline, an apparently short list that includes "the Company's chief accountant," who keeps up appearances amidst "the great demoralization of the land" (Conrad "Heart" 68). Instead of offering empty promises to justify a "philanthropic pretence," Marlow opines that Africa's overseers might better concentrate on concrete tasks like running an efficient supply chain – thus ensuring a pilot like himself has the equipment to fix his steamboat with the appropriate "rivets, by heaven!" (76–83). As Conrad's synecdoche deftly implies, Marlow seems convinced that task-oriented middle management would help organize the muddle Europe has made of central Africa. Conrad's narrator also concludes, however, that a few competent accountants would never be able to reform imperialism on their own. "The conquest of the earth," Marlow lectures, "which mostly means the taking it away from those who have a different complexion or slightly flatter noses than ourselves, is not a pretty thing when you look into it too much" (50–51). Empire can only be redeemed by a persuasive "idea at the back of it," he proclaims (51). Conrad, ever the master at lending ambiguity a sense of expansive implication, nudges his readers to conclude that absent a revamped theory to guide imperial government, reforming imperial practice will be a waste of time.

"Heart of Darkness" may conclude that good government is incompatible with existing rationales for conquest, but it does not reason in turn that Europe should get out of sub-Saharan Africa entirely. There is no hint of a postcolonial future in "Heart of Darkness," in other words, any more than there is an account of social difference to replace the sometimes casual, sometimes deliberate racism propagated by Marlow and company. That said, as Edward Said maintains, by demonstrating the limited conceptual horizon for an empire that cannot check its "tremendous violence and waste," "Heart of Darkness" helps readers to imagine administrative alternatives that Conrad never could (*Culture* 26).

It is certainly the case that subsequent novels proved eminently capable of picking up where "Heart of Darkness" left off. In the decades since Conrad published his narrative, myriad fictions have described small and large shifts in imperial-era practice and policy, thus explaining how colonial systems transformed into postcolonial regimes. In the chapters that follow, I present an array of novels that describe how groups working with and against British Empire paved the way for postcolonial social order and even presaged managerial conditions that commentators typically associate with globalization – including questions of how to oversee and organize mass migration for work, how to grow and profit from multilateral commercial trading operations, and so forth. Among the novels I consider are contemporary historical fictions such as Amitav

Ghosh's *The Glass Palace* (2000/2002) that depict turn-of-the-twentieth-century empire as being every bit as volatile as it appears in "Heart of Darkness." Where Marlow understands such instability as heralding the end of an era, however, characters in Ghosh's work and in a plurality of other novels take the chance to generate far-flung networks of reformers and activists whose collaborative endeavors promise to reinvent the terms for governing around the world.

It would be wrong to suggest that more recent novels like *The Glass Palace* are derivative of "Heart of Darkness," but right to think of them as committed to reimagining the colonial dynamics Conrad portrayed. Where "Heart of Darkness" stipulated an incompetent but all-encompassing colonizing force and a debased, dehumanized colonized population, novels such as Ghosh's portray colonized characters as more various than victims alone and colonial rule as a demonstrably uneven (not to say unpredictable) social condition. As I show in the fuller reading that appears in Chapter 4, *The Glass Palace* is populated with South Asian characters who cut deals, form friendships, and cultivate associations criss-crossing the divide that in "Heart of Darkness" separates colonized from colonizer. Although more recent novels change both the players and the game, they retain the axiom that in "Heart of Darkness" meant a necessary correlation between self-management and political economic control. Where Conrad established a correspondence between Kurtz's lack of discipline and empire's lack of organization, works such as *The Glass Palace* help make it habitual to think of renovating interpersonal connections as a step towards governmental reform.

Through character interaction in contemporary fiction, readers may discover that sentimental attachments afford opportunities to renegotiate the racial hierarchy that structures relations in "Heart of Darkness." In Ahdaf Soueif's *The Map of Love* (1999/2000), which I discuss alongside *The Glass Palace* in Chapter 4, romantic entanglement between ruler and ruled in colonial Egypt predicts twenty-first-century love between a globe-trotting Arab activist and an American traveler to Cairo. Soueif's narrator, Amal, limns a postcolonial world that Conrad's Marlow could not, even as she also conducts research that enables her to reorganize the colonial state that Marlow critiqued. Amal is a writer and scholar, a figure for the postcolonial novelist. She sorts through a chest full of old documents, engaging in historical-cum-novelistic reconstruction that links contemporary geopolitics to colonial antecedents. The past "lies on the table," she thinks, "journals, pictures, a candle-glass, a few books of history" waiting for an author to "tell the story that they, the people who lived it, could only tell in part" (Soueif *Map* 234). *The Map of Love*, like the host of other contemporary works I consider, treats empire as a treasure trove of stories useful for addressing current administrative challenges, which range in such novels from child soldiers to capital run amok.

To treat empire as such a resource is not, I argue, to suggest that Europe or "the West" haunts all contemporary fiction. I do not think that *The Glass Palace* and *The Map of Love* are trapped in the rhetorical bind Rey Chow refers to as "Post-European Culture and the West." In this familiar paradigm, Chow explains, attempts at postcolonial self-writing still bear "imprints of a fraught and prevalent relation of comparison and judgment," in which Europe represents the "referent of supremacy," the precondition for "linguistic and cultural consciousness" (*Age* 89). I argue, rather, that numerous recent fictions retrace the steps that link contemporary to imperial social order less to demonstrate Europe's ongoing authority than to rewrite colonial history and to undo myths of total European dominion. Without ever disavowing the violence of empire, its racism and its rapacity, contemporary fiction provides an alternative to the formulation in which Western authority spawns derivative postcolonial discourse. By offering an account of European domination as never fully complete, always historically delimited, and geographically diverse, these books invite us to shake off the stock formulae of core and periphery, self and other. Their revisionist approach encourages rereading of earlier works of fiction, moreover, as I show in each of my genealogically organized book chapters, which follow Chapter 1. I begin each of these chapters with contemporary fiction, only to reveal precedents in earlier novels.

Through these genealogical chapters, I contribute to a growing body of literary criticism that explains how to interpret imperial anticipations of contemporary cosmopolitanism and global networking.[1] In their introduction to the edited collection *Geomodernisms*, Laura Doyle and Laura Winkiel state their goal as affording "more global and longer histories for modernism" (14). In the opening essay of *Pacific Rim Modernisms*, Steven Yao describes early twentieth-century "interactions among different sites within ... a regional construct [the Pacific Rim] that has received the most attention and elaboration ... as part of the larger discourse of late capitalism" (Gillies, Sword, and Yao 7). In his polemical account of the relationship between postcolonial literature and globalization theory, Simon Gikandi argues that "the discipline of English literature at the colonial university was an important precursor to the theories of

---

[1] This general objective of uncovering precedence for twenty-first-century social organization at the height of British Empire draws scholars as various as the Marxist sociologist Giovanni Arrighi and the conservative historian Niall Ferguson. Arrighi's claim stems from a cyclical theory of capitalism, which leads him to locate precedence for late twentieth-century American financial experiment in late nineteenth-century British imperial financial expansion (*Long* 220). On the other end of the political spectrum, Ferguson finds in British Empire "a form of international government that can work," and that as such yields myriad lessons for the contemporary "experiment of running the world" (*Empire* 362).

globalization" ("Globalization" 651). If previous waves of postcolonial criticism dreamed of putting empire behind us, more recent literary scholarship often seeks to understand the relevance of imperial debate to the questioning of globalization and its attendant social and cultural phenomena.

By specifying how fiction treats governance as a thematic bridge between the global and the imperial, I also contribute to current literary analysis focused on administration. Amanda Claybaugh suggests that the phrase "Government is Good" captures the sentiment behind recent criticism that hopes to save "government from the default academic critiques" and make it "a newly vital topic for scholarship" in the humanities (166). In their introduction to a special issue of the journal *Contemporary Literature* devoted to "Contemporary Literature and the State," Matthew Hart and Jim Hansen catalog existing procedures for weighing "the merits of the state as an analytic paradigm for literary studies in an age of globalization" (495). Some critics detect petitions for specific governmental efforts in recent novels: "the smell of infrastructure" wafts through Jonathan Franzen's *Strong Motion*, according to Bruce Robbins, who hopes that such creative writing rekindles a political passion for public works ("Smell" 25). Other critics understand fiction as calling for a new kind of statecraft: according to Peter Hitchcock, the "wild imaginings" of Nuruddin Farah's prose remind readers that contemporary Somalia needs "more than statistical adjustments and infrastructure plans" ("Failure" 745). Literary study of government is hardly limited to critiquing the bureaucratic *status quo*, moreover. Joseph Slaughter's research into the "mutually enabling fictions" of postcolonial *Bildungsroman* and human rights discourse shows how fiction collaborates with law to help generate the criteria that underwrite non-governmental organizations intervening around the world ("Fictions" 1407). For all of their differences of emphasis and approach, these critics share a conviction held by others including Ackbar Abbas, Rita Barnard, Achille Mbembe, Sean McCann, Michael Rubenstein, Lisi Schoenbach, and Michael Szalay, all of whom demonstrate that literary endeavor in the twentieth century is shaped by and shapes the theory and practice of governance.[2]

At first blush, such scholarly interest in the everyday successes and excesses of governing might appear to ignore more utopian literary representations. Certainly, an emphasis on administrative practice appears contrary to the mode of critical engagement endorsed by Fredric Jameson, who reads modernism with the goal of marrying "a Poundian mission to identify Utopian tendencies with a Benjaminian geography of their sources" (*Singular* 215). "Ontologies of the present demand archaeologies of the future," Jameson declares in *A Singular Modernity* (215). From science fiction to socialist realism to apocalyptic fantasy, there is no denying the proliferation of twentieth-century novels predicated on the possibility of revolutionary social change.[3] But novels of revolution are not necessarily above pragmatic investment in the techniques and strategies of administration. In such works as H. G. Wells's *A Modern Utopia* (1905) and Aleksandr Bogdanov's *Red Star* (1908), Douglas Mao discerns "the utopian author's inclination toward problem-solving by clever engineering," an inclination he contends "is nearly always manifest in some administrative structure that will ostensibly put human life on a new and happier basis" ("Romances" 9). By revealing this managerial impulse, Mao shows utopian fiction to be one particularly visible version of a widespread tendency towards literary governmentality.

---

[2] See Abbas ("De-Scriptions"); Barnard (*Apartheid*); Mbembe (*Postcolony*); McCann (*Pinnacle*); Rubenstein (*Public*); Schoenbach ("Jamesian"); Szalay (*New Deal*).
[3] See in particular N. Brown (*Utopian*) on the modernist and postcolonial disposition towards utopia.

Like some but not all of the critics who attend to fiction's investment in administration, I have found that Michel Foucault's work on governmentality meets the need for an approach as alive to provisional and incremental change as to the wholesale shifts of revolution. Foucault offers what amounts to a centuries' long history of governmental theory and practice in his 1970s lectures at the Collège de France, published as *Abnormal* (2003), *"Society Must Be Defended"* (2003), *Security, Territory, Population* (2007), and *The Birth of Biopolitics* (2008).[4] I spell out what I take from Foucault in Chapter 1, where I also detail the wider stakes of understanding literary practice as a species of governmentality.[5] Foucault's work has the distinct advantage of encouraging us to question the presumed antagonism between humanist and social scientific research on government. Accordingly, my book foregrounds the concerns and contentions literary criticism shares with social scientific research on governmentality by the likes of Partha Chatterjee, Tania Murray Li, Peter Miller, Aihwa Ong, Gyan Prakash, and Nikolas Rose.

By discovering common ground with social scientists, literary critics can equip themselves to keep up with the interdisciplinary research already being undertaken by novelists. In the acknowledgments to *Brick Lane* (2003), Monica Ali thanks Naila Kabeer, a social economist and lead author of the 2009 United Nations World Survey on the Role of Women in Development. Ali writes that she "drew inspiration" from Kabeer's 2002 "study of Bangladeshi women garment workers in London and Dhaka (*The Power to Choose*)" (*Brick* 371). Chimamanda Ngozi Adichie documents her scholarly

---

[4] Important as I think these works are for scholars of twentieth-century literature, they have been equally salutary for critics working in earlier periods. See, for example, Armstrong and Tennenhouse ("Sovereignty") on eighteenth-century literary governmentality and Goodlad ("Pastor") on Victorian modes.

[5] See too my recent essay in *Literature Compass* on what literary scholars might take from Foucault's lectures ("Literature").

inspiration even more thoroughly, providing *Half of a Yellow Sun* (2006) with an Author's Note detailing interviews conducted and a bibliography of works consulted that includes novels and volumes of poetry as well as political science and history monographs (*Half* 433–36). In his acknowledgments to *Sea of Poppies* (2008), Amitav Ghosh notes his "great debt to many nineteenth-century scholars, dictionarists, linguists and chroniclers," as well as a list of more "contemporary and near-contemporary scholars and historians ... too long to reproduce here" (*Sea* 469–70). Novelists conduct research and read widely outside of their discipline. If this is not news, it nonetheless merits notice. Fiction is as likely to collaborate with social science as it is to distinguish its formal techniques from more scholarly prose. Such interdisciplinary collaboration should play a bigger part, I contend, in critical approaches to contemporary world literature.

"Worlding" may not be the same thing as "governing," but recent history makes it impossible to dissociate these terms, and scholars should be more alive to their relationship. I hope to persuade critics to interpret English-language fiction from around the globe as a resource for understanding what it takes to administer global affairs. Existing models for studying world literature are not dead set against this intervention. Some critics argue that world literature denotes a genre whose forms are designed for global travel and whose linguistic contents reveal cosmopolitan interactions. Such novels are "born translated," as Rebecca Walkowitz puts it; they are "actively present" beyond their culture of origin, feature hybrid vernaculars that embed migration, and formalize interconnection in narrative and verse ("Comparison" 569).[6] Other scholars define world literature

---

[6] This is the world literature for a reinvigorated, post-national, post-European comparative literature. Damrosch belongs in this camp, as perhaps does Dimock, who specifies African-American "street vernacular as a linguistic form bearing the imprint of many geographies, many chronologies" (Dimock and Buell "Introduction" 13).

less as genre than as ideology. For Aamir Mufti, "ongoing discussion about world literature, in the singular and plural, is both hugely encompassing and strangely timid," seemingly "unaware of the enormous role played by the institution of literature in the emergence of the hierarchies and identities that structure relations between societies in the modern world" ("Orientalism" 465–66). A third group of scholars studies world literature at the level of the market system rather than the academic institution or the novelistic text. When Franco Moretti asks questions like, "What does it mean, studying world literature? How do we do it?," his answers invariably turn on determining patterns of consumption ("Conjectures" 55).[7]

It is routine to accuse Moretti of sacrificing close reading in his attempts to render literature's worldly scale. This is not my complaint. Moretti can read closely when he wants to, and none of his number crunching prevents us from doing so. The blind spot of his data analysis, I contend, lies in its inability to model texts as elements of a process. Moretti shares this blind spot with many who see world literature as genre or as ideology. In these cases, world literature names a particular kind of object embedded in one institution or another, literature as a thing in the world, an "it" whose boundaries are to be defined, defended, or questioned. I argue that we might better see literature as practice or manner of producing the world.[8] To be sure, novels succeed or fail as commodities *in* the global market.

---

[7] See too Apter, who contends that the novel's generic properties get decided in a "state of Malthusian survivalism," in which "small languages succumb to big ones" and Amazon.com joins with an integrated network of university literature departments to reproduce an ever more homogeneous literary object ("Translation" 11–12). Centralization in the publishing industry ensures this outcome, argues Casanova, as Paris and New York and London promote world fiction "products based on tested aesthetic formulas and designed to appeal to the widest possible readership" (*Republic* 155).

[8] Hayot offers another response to this same issue, asking where in novels a property for shaping worlds emerges and answering with a series of textual variables from "amplitude" or "relative spread of narrative attention" to "metadiagetic density" or the relative intensity of certain passages that "call out … for interpretation" ("Literary" 143, 150).

But fiction has also long been a medium for commentary *on* the market. As such, it competes and collaborates with the other disciplines that tell us what the market is and does, as well as what it is not and should not do. If – as experts in many different disciplines now acknowledge – there is no "global market" apart from its representation, literature and literary criticism are surely part of the process that makes it. This is not an unfamiliar observation. If "Dickensian" has idiomatic meaning detached from any particular Dickens novel, this is at least in part because the term connotes a distinctive account of commercial ethics. To take a more recent example, William Gibson's speculations on the future of transnational markets and marketing in novels such as *Pattern Recognition* (2003) have seemed to many commentators as having a kind of diagnostic value. By formalizing stories of commercial actors and their state-of-the-art management styles, literature moves beyond the nation in networks of exchange and communication that it helps to theorize as such.

Similarly, literature serves as a meeting point for migrant vernaculars of all sorts, from scholarly idioms like sociology and philosophy to socio-cultural tongues like Cockney and Swahili. Following Mikhail Bakhtin, scholars expect novels to facilitate the combination of such vernaculars, and to thereby multiply and conjoin interpretations of events. At the same time, readers are used to fiction linking language to population, specifying how a way of speaking equates to a way of seeing the world. As much as any novel registers the centrifugal force of heteroglossia, in other words, fiction equally depicts the centripetal power of language community. Novels render global interconnection as a mash-up of various linguistic materials, while depicting global multiculture as the proliferation of groups and peoples.[9] The frame of

---

[9] Harootunian contends that literary studies learned how to understand such zoning of populations in part from area studies with its instrumental accounts of regional culture ("Desire" 141–42).

"the world" makes visible not only literature's worldly aspect, but also its worldly work, which entails collaboration and competition with other specialized forms of writing to organize global populations as they interact. The stakes of such literary innovation emerge with greater clarity the less we confine fiction in singular genres or schools (from modernism to realism, postmodernism to postcolonialism), the less we reduce novel writing and reading to ideologies and markets, and the more we treat literature as a means of governing.

I provide a conceptual and historical basis for specifying contemporary and twentieth-century novelistic governmentality in Chapter 1. My central contention is that fiction helps explain how governmental practice changed in the wake of eighteenth- and nineteenth-century political economic and literary theories of liberalism. Perhaps the most pronounced feature of this change is the presumption that, after liberalism, the value placed on individual freedom should concern us less than the techniques and practices for educating individuals, modulating their interactions, and cultivating their propensity to group. With this new emphasis, fiction helped to organize a century that began with doubt about the bourgeois individual's capacity to govern himself and ended with progressively larger economic bubbles that demonstrated the inability of the global market to govern itself. Fiction, like scholarship, presents these crises as clarifying the need for revised strategies of representation, and as generating opportunities to establish new authority for those experts deemed capable of helping individuals and regulating markets, among other professional forms of oversight.

Because novels seek to represent populations in literary form every bit as specialized as any academic article or monograph, fiction presents political and ethical problems similar to those posed by scholars including David Harvey, Partha Chatterjee, and other theorists of neoliberal administration. There is always a potential for bad faith involved in representing the interests of people who also are perfectly capable of representing themselves, even if they lack the authority to do so in an official capacity. This was the preoccupation of Barbara and John Ehrenreich in their 1977 essay on the professional-managerial class, which debated whether such a class was capable of democratizing expertise. When novels imagine ways in which laypeople might intervene in governance, I argue, they rework this old problem. When fiction discovers laypeople to replace administrative officials and expert observers, it enlarges the field of meritocratic politics. Instead of disavowing managerial authority, fiction asks what we can do with it.

In order to demonstrate how contemporary literature's contribution to debate about the status of liberal concepts finds precedent in earlier administrative experiments, each of the four case studies that follow is organized genealogically. Each chapter focuses on one key concept or analytic problem that reveals how literary and scholarly texts have altered governance. Chapter 2 explains how social science and fiction reconfigured the "state" after liberal developmental schemes yielded pride of place in policy circles to concerns about geopolitical stability. *Foreign Policy* magazine's annual "Failed States Index" employs a method that uses statistics to present the full range of instability that confronts political observers today. My argument in this chapter begins by considering such indices and by framing the political scientific problem of state failure as a contrast between legal and normative approaches. Starting with analysis of Chimamanda Ngozi Adichie's *Half of a Yellow Sun* (2006), I show what happens when literature evaluates crisis as a deviation from, but not exception to, the norm. Even as it recapitulates political science, I argue, literature alters the division of labor between political scientists and the populations they describe and manage. Adichie identifies authoritative actors within the distressed groups that foreign policy experts analyze. As I show,

Half of a Yellow Sun is far from alone in conducting such risky experiments. Other contemporary examples include Yvonne Vera's 2002 fiction, *The Stone Virgins*, memoir-style child-soldier novels ranging from Ken Saro-Wiwa's *Sozaboy* (1985/1994) to Chris Abani's *Song for Night* (2007), Timothy Mo's *The Redundancy of Courage* (1991), and James Kelman's *Translated Accounts* (2001). Through references to Saadat Hasan Manto's Indian partition stories from the late 1940s and early 1950s, I show how earlier writers pioneered the portrayal of noncredentialed experts common in more recent fiction. In Rebecca West's work of travel writing, *Black Lamb and Grey Falcon* (1941), I find a significant early precedent for later efforts to narrate the connection between self-governance and crisis management. The chapter ends with a brief consideration of how canonical postcolonial tomes such as Ngũgĩ wa Thiong'o's *Petals of Blood* (1977) and V. S. Naipaul's *A Bend in the River* (1979/1989) fit into this genealogy. I contend that by portraying the so-called "failure" of the postcolonial intellectual, such novels provide motivation to grant that figure a revised job description of the sort detailed in *Half of a Yellow Sun*.

Chapter 3 moves from state to social hierarchy and considers how professional administration takes the prospect of universal humanism off the table, proposing in its stead a meritocratic twist on the classic liberal problem of "inequality." I begin by arguing that fictions such as Michael Ondaatje's *Anil's Ghost* (2000) contemplate how to live with inequality when they infuse stories of teamwork with robust fellow feeling. Ondaatje's portrayal of experts and their adjutants leads me to a range of interdisciplinary efforts to reimagine such working relationships. For instance, I discuss Anna Tsing's *Friction* (2005), which describes her fieldwork on the various hierarchical arrangements among environmental activists working and living in Indonesia. I also attend to Michel Callon, Pierre Lascoumes, and

Yannick Barthes's provocative theory of "hybrid forums" for collaboration among researchers and their objects of study, which they spell out in a volume entitled *Acting in an Uncertain World: An Essay on Technical Democracy* (2001/2009). I track efforts to portray collaboration among unequals in sentimental terms back to a range of imperial strange bedfellows that include Rabindranath Tagore's *The Home and the World* (1915/1985), Krupabai Satthianadhan's *Kamala* (1894/1998), and E. M. Forster's *Howards End* (1910/1985). Collectively, the works in this chapter show that fiction has long been impelling readers to ask not whether literature can help rid the world of inequality, but how it facilitates expert management of social hierarchy in radically differing situations.

Chapter 4 turns to the domain of neoliberal and liberal governance known as civil society and to its privileged denizen, the "entrepreneur." This figure is not only the hero of recent economic policy and political commentary, I show, but also the protagonist in notable works of historical fiction. The first portion of the chapter focuses on Amitav Ghosh's influential novel, *The Glass Palace* (2000/2002), which identifies the networks and collectives that engender enterprising actors at the height of British Empire. I gesture towards the wide range of comparable recent historical novels by turning to Abdulrazak Gurnah's *Desertion* (2005), Ahdaf Soueif's *The Map of Love* (1999/2000), and M. G. Vassanji's *The Gunny Sack* (1989). I briefly note two mid-century texts that anticipate contemporary tendencies by referencing Attia Hosain's *Sunlight on a Broken Column* (1961) and Venu Chitale's *In Transit* (1950). In addition to sharing an interest in political and commercial diasporas, the genealogical structure of these novels reworks the usual chronology of epochal transformation in which precolonial social order yields to colonial domination only to be supplanted by postcolonial rule. There is precedent for contemporary accounts of imperial civil society,

I argue in the last section of this chapter, which focuses on a range of early twentieth-century works of historical fiction, including Joseph Conrad's *Nostromo* (1904/1985) and Sarath Kumar Ghosh's *Prince of Destiny* (1909). These fictions portray imperialism as inadvertently providing the tools for its own undoing. *Nostromo* in particular suggests that such undoing may well derive from the way empire extended the ability to take risks and forge transnational social networks to the most enterprising factions of colonized populations. Collectively, I maintain, these provide me with the means to update the classic formulation of historical fiction offered by Georg Lukács. Where Lukács describes a historical novel whose narrative testifies to the force of epochal change, Amitav Ghosh's *The Glass Palace*, for example, limns a history that records the migration of liberal civil society and its entrepreneurial actors.

Chapter 5 turns to the future and to the working women who herald global political economy's next phase. This chapter begins by locating gender in a history less focused on extending the franchise than on explaining what happens when women become a new majority in the workforce. In this history, suffrage is no longer a watershed moment that ends the Victorian era of separate spheres. It is, rather, part and parcel of classic liberalism's transformation over the course of the twentieth century. Fiction demonstrates how working women index that transformation, as I show by concentrating on William Gibson's *Pattern Recognition* (2003) and Monica Ali's *Brick Lane* (2003), and a trio of canonical works from earlier in the century, Jean Rhys's *Voyage in the Dark* (1934/1985), Virginia Woolf's *To the Lighthouse* (1927/1981), and Elizabeth Bowen's *The Heat of the Day* (1948/2001). By portraying women who learn to make choices in trying environments, these novels testify to the twentieth-century renovation of "calculative agency," one of classic liberalism's most vital concepts. They equally remind us that liberalism was never only a legal structure or a democratic philosophy, but was also an administrative protocol. Taken together, my four topical chapters offer pointed examples of what twentieth- and twenty-first-century novels contribute to our understanding of how the organization of society is changing. I conclude with a brief postscript that returns to the question broached in this introduction of how best to historicize the fears of, and aspirations for, social reorganization that fiction offers.

CHAPTER I

Fiction after liberalism

On or about December 1910, fiction circulating in Britain and its colonies began to abandon interest in self-governing citizens and the women who love them. From that moment or thereabouts, many writers of novels started to focus instead on how they might compete and collaborate with writers from across the disciplines to imagine societies managed by diverse teams of professionals. To this end, novelists retooled old literary forms such as the historical novel and *Bildungsroman*. They adapted tried-and-true ways of representing love and friendship in the workplace and in the home, thereby figuring new relations among administrators as well as between administrators and the populations they promised to make secure and productive. In the process, novelists contributed to the shift from imperial to postcolonial forms of governance.

When fiction discovered affective bonds among colleagues and collaborators, entrepreneurs and bureaucrats, it sentimentalized the notion of meritocracy. When fiction discovered laypeople with the experience and cunning to second-guess and occasionally supplant administrative officials and expert observers, it dramatized meritocratic politics. Through these innovations, fiction offered tales of social life not only after imperialism but also after liberalism – after, in other words, the fantasy of expert oversight had thoroughly reworked and subordinated the fantasy of an autonomous individual citizen dreamt of by liberal political economists from Adam Smith to John Stuart Mill.

That twentieth-century novels offered pointed critiques of liberalism is well established. That twentieth-century literature also formulated new strategies and tactics for governing is less well documented. This may be because there is no singular world literature of regulation nor neatly identifiable novelistic genre of global administration. Instead, novels shape a literary sort of governmental thought whenever they associate character with group, population with territory, and administration with defining what it means for a population to be secure, productive, or otherwise well-off. Literary governmentality contests and complements census data, research on migration, and bureaucratic decision-making. This supplementary activity exceeds literature's most expected critical modes of repudiation and defamiliarization. When literature serves as a vehicle for policy review and the formulation of best practices, it encourages us to revisit our understanding of "critique."

Judith Butler observes that critique need not be thought of solely as an act of negation, "not merely or only . . . an effort to take apart and demolish an existing structure" ("Critique" 787).[1] The critical question of "how not to be governed," she observes, "is always the question of how not to be governed *in this or that way*. But it is not a question of how not to be governed at all" (791). When literature is critical, it does more than rebuke administrations for failing to live up to political ideals. Instead, it contributes to governmentality by adding to the store of knowledge about various groups, their production and composition, their patterns of mobility and affiliation. Twentieth- and twenty-first-century fiction constitutes a record as well as analysis of myriad representations of social life. It furthermore contains a trove of arguments about how people organize their world and contributes to the ongoing debate about

---

[1] See also Latour, who argues that critique has "run out of steam" ("Critique" 248).

who should have governmental authority and what that authority should look like.

This way of reading English-language fiction from the 1900s to the present day requires a suspension of conventional periodization. The novel's broad investment in problems of governance cannot be grasped so long as critical attention remains divided by the breaks that organize many histories of twentieth- and twenty-first-century literature. These pages will not recapitulate a history in which modernist promise and disappointment gives way to postcolonial promise and disappointment, only to be followed by still-lingering disappointment with the promises of globalization. Instead, they relate how fiction and its interdisciplinary interlocutors discovered precedents for contemporary social organization in the political and economic arrangements of British imperialism and then developed them.

The story of how novels rework other forms of expression in order to represent imperial social relations begins at least as long ago as the turn of the nineteenth century, when Sir Walter Scott retooled the historical novel and thereby reimagined the formation of Great Britain. Novels are capable of performing this sort of revision regardless of where one locates them on an aesthetic spectrum running from realism to formalism. As Jacques Rancière tartly observes, even the most self-reflexive literature "always says something" (*Politics* 54). He contends that the intransitive quality of certain species of twentieth-century prose, the way such writing makes "subject matter ... a matter of indifference," is best contrasted neither with Victorian nor socialist nor any other realism but with a far earlier "system where the dignity of the subject matter dictated the dignity of genres of representation (tragedy for the nobles, comedy for the people of meager means ...)" (54, 32). Only once literature discovered "that it was not necessary to adopt a particular style to write about nobles, bourgeois, peasants, princes, or valets," he argues, could it then entertain "the possibility of abandoning all subject matter for abstraction" (54). Twentieth-century literary abstraction shares with twentieth-century realism a desire to pluralize the contents of fiction. Both take part in a shift of focus from illuminating "great names and events" to discovering "symptoms of an epoch, a society, or a civilization in the minute details of ordinary life" (33). Where late twentieth-century anthologies and introductory courses habitually find an epochal break between Victorian realism and modernist abstraction, Rancière locates the major change at the moment of Romanticism. This was when, he argues, the rules of form were overturned. Romanticism "plunged language into the materiality ... of the historical and social world" (36). It gave literature the goal of rendering every aspect of social life in aesthetic terms and sparked a desire to innovate a plurality of new relations between form and content.

Rancière's aesthetic history makes it possible to see what certain scholars and writers who are usually presumed to be enemies actually share. We would not be wrong to hear something of Fredric Jameson's "political unconscious" and F. R. Leavis's "minority culture" in Rancière's description of an approach to literature that "explains the surface by subterranean layers" and "reconstructs worlds from their vestiges" (*Politics* 33). Nor would we be wrong to detect in his description a resemblance to Victorian and postcolonial efforts at employing the novel as a technology for preserving lost communities – efforts that encompass fictions from *Waverley* to *Things Fall Apart*. Novels from the nineteenth century to the twenty-first century have considered it their writ to testify to what life should be like but is not. Thus, Rancière understands art after Romanticism as calling into question any existing "distribution of roles, territories, and languages," while also offering new and "polemical distribution of modes of being and 'occupations'" (40–42). This complementary pairing of interrogation and reconfiguration takes many forms. While historical novels recall social worlds that have been destroyed, novels of Charles Dickens imagine pockets of domestic warmth amidst the urban chill, tomes by Samuel Beckett portray societies so constitutively dysfunctional that readers must feel the need for an eviscerating critique, and Michael Ondaatje's works render small acts of collegiality that illuminate the full horror of civil strife. Whether or not novels actually represent social alternatives, they share a goal of imagining a more committed, smarter community of readers. That community may be conjured by the work of reading even when it is not represented on the page.

In any case, when literature asks "What subjects are included in the community?" and "Which subjects are able to see and voice what is common?," it does not pose such questions in a vacuum (Rancière "Aesthetic" 8). Rancière may reveal alliance among nineteenth- and twentieth-century aesthetic treatments of social transformation, but in the twentieth century the contexts for imagining and, more importantly, for administering social change altered considerably. Fiction circulated alongside an array of other disciplinarily specific forms of writing that were also increasingly influenced by the pedagogical techniques and curricular priorities of a growing university system. Given this development, it may be possible to conclude that what changed during the period now recognized as modernist was less the relationship between literary form and content, and was more the connection between fiction and the work of writing and reading understood as expert activities.[2]

When twentieth-century novelists imagine communities, they join writers in geography, anthropology, accounting, and political science

---

[2] I offer one case study of modernist professionalization in the first chapter of my first book, which focuses on the example of Conrad (*Modernist*).

who employ their own equally specialized techniques of representation to engage in comparable efforts to portray collective life. Bruno Latour describes disciplinary study as a twofold process of first identifying matters of concern and then representing them in a manner that designates ownership.[3] For the novel or any other specialized sort of writing to claim ownership of community, a certain amount of trial and error is necessarily involved as writers seek an effective match of form and content. For Latour, it is imperative to track those experiments, to follow the worlds, communities, and actors imagined by literature, geography, or sociology "back into the rooms where [they are] produced" ("Spheres" 142–43). The point is neither to condemn nor to celebrate the elitism of these rooms, especially if they happen to be located in departments and schools of higher education. It is rather to observe that what we think of as the twentieth- and twenty-first-century politics of literary, geographic, or sociological representation is inextricable from the disciplinary politics of specialized knowledge, expert authority, and professionalism.

Latour spells out what this means in his home discipline of sociology: "Group delineation is not only one of the occupations for social scientists," he observes, "but also the very constant task of the actors themselves. Actors do the sociology for the sociologists and sociologists learn from the actors what makes up their set of associations" (*Reassembling* 32). "Actors," in other words, are both objects of study – some social scientists call them data – and active collaborators whose behavior alters research outcomes. This collaboration rarely gets recognized as such. Nonetheless, it becomes obvious when active social scientific objects question a study's findings or protest governmental policies derived from

---

[3] In his words, a project of "*extending* the range of entities at work in the world and actively participating in *transforming* some of them into faithful and stable intermediaries" (Latour *Reassembling* 257).

research. According to Latour, this is what meritocratic politics looks like: an ongoing push and pull between experts and their active objects. Crucially, this dynamic sometimes leads those objects to behave as if they are the experts.

Novelistic "characters" bear a relationship to sociological "actors," but they are also obviously different. Actors, for instance, may well have the opportunity to read the texts produced about them. Even when fiction features "real-life" characters – such as Thibaw Min, the Burmese king who appears in Amitav Ghosh's *The Glass Palace* – the evidentiary standards attached to novels simply are not the same as those attached to social scientific analysis. Novels are expected to generate accounts of the world that readers can recognize, but to change the particulars in ways that allow readers to think about the world differently. Novels construct "fictions": "*material* rearrangements of signs and images," Rancière calls them, rearrangements of "what is seen and what is said ... what is done and what can be done" (*Politics* 39). The politics of literature inheres in its capacity to use such rearrangements to encourage readers to imagine a better life – with all the uncertainty that entails.

Novels do this, in part, by employing narrative exposition, figurative abstraction, and indeed all the devices of fiction to explore what can or should happen when patterns of professional interaction change. They imagine different ways of distributing authority among civilians and government bureaucrats, patients and doctors, students and teachers, and, not least, readers and novelists. In truth, the last pair in this series is not like the others, but rather redoubles the problem. Part of what distinguishes literary accounts of professional/layperson dynamics from accounts generated in other disciplines is that ordinary novel readers may be civilians and patients and students, but they may equally be bureaucrats and doctors and teachers. Literature reimagines professional hierarchy on the page as well as in the relationship between the page and its readers.

When it dwells on professional intervention in the collective life, fiction joins with social science to update the classic liberal problem of the individual's relationship to society. John Stuart Mill frames this matter in *On Liberty*, wherein he weighs "the nature and limits of the power which can be legitimately exercised by society over the individual" (1). To ensure the individual's sovereignty "over his own body and mind," Mill charges government with responsibility for making "fitting adjustment between individual independence and social control" (5). For government to do so, he explains, entails securing "as much of the advantages of centralized power and intelligence as can be had without turning into governmental channels too great a proportion of the general activities" (110–12). Mill's vision of good government involves an administration that achieves "the greatest dissemination of power" by balancing "the greatest centralization of information and diffusion of it from the center" (112). In this, *On Liberty* anticipates and shapes twentieth- and twenty-first-century debates about how to "balance" social safety with individual agency, rights, and abilities.

Those debates also reprise Adam Smith's project of explaining "how 'human nature' manifests itself in the market system," the better to demonstrate, as Mary Poovey puts it, "how legislators can come to know (and actualize) the system they cannot see" (Poovey *Fact* 217). Smith imagined a state whose primary purpose was securing subjects defined by a tendency to act in their own interest and to the benefit of others.[4] But he and his nineteenth-century

---

[4] "The game of freedom and security is at the very heart of this ... governmental reason," Foucault comments (*Birth* 65).

inheritors never took that tendency for granted.⁵ Mill in particular argued that people wanted schooling if they were to behave as rational actors, to reliably "distinguish the better from the worse" and "choose the former" (74).⁶ Mill does not stipulate apparatuses and disciplines for sorting and evaluating information about the state's populations, however. His keen appreciation for education only hints at the twentieth-century growth of universities, professional associations, and lobbying firms.

"[T]he seductive revolution of the professionals," as Harold Perkin calls the collective effect of expert authority's rise, caused nothing short of a "revolution in human organization" over the course of the nineteenth and twentieth centuries (*Third* 6). Revolutionary though professional social order might appear, Perkin contends that it in fact retains much of "Adam Smith's division of labour, raised to a higher power of applied intelligence and expertise" (xii). Timothy Mitchell agrees that professional oversight and liberal political economy are hardly opposed. He explains how specifying "the market" as both a domain and an abstract agent enabled colonial officers and policy wonks to generate "principles true in every country," and thereby to justify their involvement in the nitty-gritty of social life everywhere from

---

⁵ As Gordon observes, "It is the paradox of liberalism in all its forms (neo, advanced, post . . .) that much action is necessary before one can *laisser faire*" (Donzelot and Gordon "Liberal" 56). Dean notes that "in the interstices of Smith's felicitous liberal economy, we find Jeremy Bentham's pauper management scheme, the centralized national administration of poor relief in England and Wales after 1834 and the nineteenth-century workhouse" ("Liberal" 51). See Gallagher on the competing brands of "organicism" that guided policy ideas among political economists and Romanticists (*Body* 7–8).

⁶ J. R. McCulloch was among the earlier nineteenth-century commentators who "counted on public education to supplement the freedom he attributed to the market" (Poovey *Fact* 302). Nancy Armstrong shows how Victorian fiction furthered such education by providing narratives in which the development of a character's "individuality depends on how he or she chooses to displace what is a fundamentally asocial desire onto a socially appropriate object" (*Novels* 8).

Egypt to Bengal (Mitchell *Rule* 54). As more forms of work became professionalized and new sorts of specialists claimed administrative authority, internecine squabbling among multifarious expert clans tended to shape politics in general. Arguments about who has the right to govern gave way in the process, replaced by arguments about who is best qualified for the job and arguments about how responsibility should be distributed.[7] Professional society turns on contestation among teams and departments and networks of researchers and statisticians and consultants, all of whom jockey to represent populations they divide and subdivide into ever more finely detailed demographics.

Professional society alters the terms as well as the players involved in Mill's governmental challenge to find the "limit to the legitimate interference of collective opinion with individual independence" (*Liberty* 5). The twentieth- and twenty-first-century individual is better understood as the effect of various techniques of expert intervention than as a natural subject whom government administrators might threaten or develop.[8] Jacques Donzelot notes that it is no longer usual for government to claim its responsibility to protect innate liberty or, alternatively, to curb "a freedom which is the expression of man's inevitably evil nature" ("Foucault" 122). Individuality itself means "something very different from what it meant a hundred years ago," Zygmunt Bauman laments, for liberalism no longer promises the "'emancipation' of man from the tightly knit tissue of communal dependency, surveillance and enforcement" (*Modernity* 31). Instead,

---

[7] See, for instance, D. Walkowitz's description of how the emergence of "social work" in American hospitals, courts, and schools precipitated the struggles of a largely feminized professional workforce to establish its class status by specifying the value of its expert knowledge (*Working* 27–28).

[8] Miller and Rose sum up this turn of the screw: "Personal autonomy is not the antithesis of political power, but a key term in its exercise, the more so because most individuals are not merely the subjects of power but play a part in its operations" (*Governing* 54).

myriad administrative projects endeavor to generate "individual entrepreneurial subjects," as Wendy Brown calls them, while figuring the state as a "firm whose products are rational individual subjects, an expanding economy, national security, and global power" (*Edgework* 57). Peter Miller and Nikolas Rose describe political economy and administrative policy that promises a future of "constant experiment, invention, failure, critique and adjustment," as health, welfare, and education apparatuses come and go, each offering their own recipe for bolstering the self-government of an autonomous individual who increasingly appears anything but (*Governing* 39).

We may think of the transition from nurturing and taming naturalized subjects to constructing and experimenting on subjectivity as representing the end of liberalism — if what we mean by liberalism is an ideology that features rational actors wisely making their decisions in minimalist states. But we might equally understand debates about the effects of expert oversight as still conditioned by liberalism — if what we mean by liberalism is an array of techniques for guaranteeing the reproduction of self-governing subjects and their society. I am indebted to Michel Foucault's definition of liberalism as just such an array of techniques, "not as a theory or an ideology ... but as a practice, that is to say, 'a way of doing things'" (*Birth* 318). For Foucault, liberal government does not begin with the "acceptance of freedom" but rather "it proposes to manufacture [freedom] constantly, to arouse and produce it, with, of course, [the system] of constraints and the problems of cost raised by this production" (65). This form of government de-emphasizes techniques for disciplining "the fine grain of individual behaviors" and instead optimizes "systems of difference," tolerates "minority individuals and practices," and brings action "to bear on the rules of the game, rather than on the players" (259–60). Liberal political economic concepts continue to predominate in a remarkable range of commentary not *despite* the fact that they no longer conjure their historic opposites of nobility and, more recently, communism, but *because* of it.

A dead metaphor, or "zombie idea" as economist John Quiggin would have it, "the market" no longer refers first and foremost to a physical place where goods exchange owners.[9] Its first, perhaps even commonplace, definition is the more abstract sense legislated into being by banking regulations and economic reports. Capitalism, Richard Posner sagely reminds us, "is not a synonym for free markets. It is the name given to a complex economic system with many moving parts," including "regulations designed to align private incentives with the goal of achieving widespread prosperity" (*Crisis* 1–2). In the wake of the 2008 economic crisis, John Comaroff notes, it remains habitual to measure effective governance "with reference to asset management, to the attraction of enterprise, to the facilitation of the entrepreneurial activities of the citizen as *homo economicus*, and to the capacity to foster the accumulation (but *not* the redistribution) of wealth" ("Neoliberalism?" 48). Liberal staples including "the entrepreneur" and "the market" do appear under pressure, and in need of better, smarter supervision.[10] "The most distinctive feature of capitalism's next era," Anatole Kaletsky argues in *Capitalism 4.0*, "will be a recognition that governments and markets can both be wrong and that sometimes their errors can be near-fatal" (5). If John Maynard Keynes and his contemporaries recognized this in a previous iteration of capitalism, the lesson was clearly forgotten by the movement led by Milton Friedman.

---

[9] Quiggin lays out the notion of such zombie ideas in the opening pages of his *Zombie Economics*.
[10] Posner chides his fellow economists for being "asleep at the switch," overinvested in "free-market ideology," and, despite appearances to the contrary, "weak" and divisive: fractured by "warring schools of macroeconomic thought, such as the monetarist, the Keynesian, the neo-Keynsian, the new classical economic, and the Austrian" (*Failure* 259–65).

Friedman, Posner, Friedrich von Hayek, Alan Greenspan, Gary Becker, Hernando de Soto, and colleagues gave the world a politics David Harvey finds notable for its "frequently partial and lop-sided application from one state and social formation to another" (*Brief* 13). Harvey treats neoliberal political economy as less a cogent school of thought than a series of roughly allied experiments. These experiments may share the same givens – such as the preeminent need to contain cost and the seemingly antithetical principle that state power should protect financial institutions – but their implementation amounts to a profusion of administrative tactics and strategies.[11]

Their implementation also encourages a confusion of administrative subjects and objects. On the one hand, Foucault allows, contemporary governmentality dreams of a subject who can learn to administer himself, become "an entrepreneur of himself, being for himself his own capital, becoming for himself his own producer, being for himself the source of [his] earnings" (Foucault *Birth* 226). On the other hand, Miller and Rose explain, contemporary governmentality insists on finding its entrepreneurial subjects within "'the community' as a new territory for the administration of individual and collective existence" (*Governing* 88).[12]

---

[11] A number of commentators make this point. See in particular W. Brown (*Edgework* 42), Dean ("Liberal" 37), and Burchell ("Liberal" 274). Read argues, "[d]eregulation, the central term and political strategy of neo-liberalism, is not the absence of governing, or regulating, but a form of governing through isolation and dispersion" ("Genealogy" 32). Panitch and Konings note that recent "massive interventions by the Bush and Obama Administrations in the course of the current crisis are merely the culmination of the long series of interventions that marked the neoliberal era" ("Myths" 72–73).

[12] Dean elaborates, explaining the "now barely contestable proposal that a certain art of national government becomes available when society is regarded less as a source of needs that are individually distributed and collectively borne and more as a source of energies contained within individuals' exercise of freedom and self-responsibility. A key corollary of the exercise of that freedom is voluntary association or – as it is known in various forms of political discourse – 'community,'" a field for the generation and exchange of "social capital," a domain where one might measure "levels of trust and civic participation," and the ground for advocating "communitarianism" or "reaffirm shared values" (*Governmentality* 152).

This general application of "community" updates the terms of what Mitchell Dean describes as classic liberalism's stern discrimination between subjects deemed capable of autonomy, "including the practice of exercising 'ethical despotism' upon themselves where necessary," and those "who, having reached maturity of age, are for one reason or another not yet or no longer able to exercise their own autonomy or act in their own best interests" ("Liberal" 48). Within the British Isles in the nineteenth century, Edwin Chadwick, Henry Mayhew, and others defined communities of "the poor" who could not care for themselves, while overseas entire colonial populations were deemed incapable of self-rule.[13] It was no less than Mill who limned a liberal geopolitics by drawing a bright line between societies capable of being groomed for self-governance and those under the tyranny of custom (*Liberty* 69).[14] *On Liberty* effectively authorized a despotic paternalism as the paradoxical means to preserve the possibility of universalizing liberty. "Despotism is a legitimate mode of government in dealing with barbarians," Mill wrote, "provided the end be their improvement and the means justified by actually effecting that end" (10). Historians chronicle the working out of this project via data gathering, which substantiated the supposition that some demographics were composed of religious and ethnographic cultures rather than civil societies.[15]

---

[13] On Chadwick and Mayhew, see Poovey (*Making*) and Gallagher ("Body"). On the imperial side, see Guha (*Dominance* 68) as well as Prakash, who explains that "[c]olonial governmentality could not be a mere 'tropicalization' of the Western norm, but its fundamental dislocation" ("Civil" 31).

[14] Custom-plagued societies represent a warning to Britons to guard their personal freedom, Mill argued. For "unless individuality shall be able successfully to assert itself," he warned, "Europe, notwithstanding its noble antecedents and its professed Christianity, will tend to become another China" (*Liberty* 69).

[15] See Prakash ("Civil" 27) and Chakrabarty, who explains that in India at "every census, people were asked to state their religion and caste," so that by the twentieth century counting "Hindus, Muslims, Sikhs, and untouchables" had become "a critical political exercise ... as the British began to include Indian representatives in the country's legislative bodies in very measured doses" (*Habitations* 85).

Community became the authorizing term in all manner of governmental programs and projects. In Egypt it authorized the granting of contracts to kinship groups, in sub-Saharan Africa it legitimated favoritism towards some "tribes" over others, and just about everywhere it guided the policing of sexual activity among administrators, settlers, and "natives."[16] Despotism and liberalism worked hand in hand across the Home Counties and throughout the larger empire. The result was, Barry Hindess argues, that "only a minority were actually governed as free individuals" ("Liberal" 99).

In the twentieth century, governmental strategies increasingly dictated that everyone, no longer only ethnic and religious minorities, find their place in a community. In addition to various cultural groupings, urban squatter settlements and suburban housing associations are among the sundry models of community that help target every form of governmental interaction from development projects to policing strategies. Even "when it works upon pre-existing bonds of allegiance," Miller and Rose argue, contemporary governance "transforms them, invests them with new values, affiliates them to expertise and reconfigures relations of exclusion" (*Governing* 93). In South Asia and sub-Saharan Africa, Partha Chatterjee observes, "classificatory criteria used by colonial governmental regimes continued into the postcolonial era," and were joined by new and proliferating communal categories, which collectively shape "the forms of both political demands and developmental policy."[17] Dipesh Chakrabarty

---

[16] See Metcalf on the empire-wide diffusion of census-driven practices first implemented in India (*Imperial* 16). Mitchell describes the complex interaction between free-market reforms and familial business networks in colonial Egypt (*Rule* 292–93). See Mamdani (*Citizen*) on the use of "tribe" in British and French African colonies. And see Stoler on the intersection between governmentality and sexuality in the colonies (*Carnal* 151).

[17] "So much so," Chatterjee notes, "that a huge ethnographic survey, recently undertaken by a governmental agency in India and published in 43 volumes, has actually claimed to have identified and described a total of exactly 4,635 communities that are supposed to constitute the population of India" (*Politics* 37).

describes the present government in India as devoted to organizing a "collection of communities whose progress or backwardness could be measured" by the state (*Habitations* 90). Aihwa Ong explains that "communities" are not bound by states, however, for "disciplinary institutions of ethnic enclaves, factories, and families" have rendered "migrant workers governable in ethnicized ways" (*Neoliberalism* 124). Tania Murray Li notes that such tactics span nations, guiding international aid and economic development missions of all sorts.[18] Around the world, communities are not only contrasted to one another but also hold up mirrors to reflect on their resemblance. In a recapitulation of what Rey Chow calls coercive mimeticism, communities (subnational, transnational, and national) struggle to live up to their definitions (*Protestant* 122).

Educators, organizers, political campaigners, and social workers affirm and encourage community bonding, and those experts work on themselves as much as their target populations. Willingness to experiment with the complex and highly changeable dynamics of community organization has emboldened neoliberal commentators and freakonomists alike to achieve the topical range of fiction writers. They contribute to discussions about all manner of social behaviors (from procreation to drug addiction) and reinterpret all sorts of policies (from the promotion of public health to the provision for national security). Each "assertion of community refers itself to something that already exists and has a claim on us," Miller and Rose observe, "our common fate as gay men, as women of colour, as people with AIDS, as members of an ethnic group, as residents in a village or a suburb, as people with a disability" (*Governing* 92). Community brings together administrators and

---

[18] Li's study of a World Bank-funded social development project in the late 1990s yields what she calls the paradox of "community," which is "assumed to be natural, yet ... needs to be improved" (*Will* 232).

their subjects, binding them in affective professional relationships. Police officers, social workers, healthcare specialists, and political organizers work in and on the community. Although it is obviously possible to study and govern communities of which one is not a member, few experts can be said to belong to no community at all. Equally, communities can be fertile soil for developing new experts, representatives, and intellectuals whose authority is derived in some measure from experiential knowledge gleaned from being part of a particular demographic.

Literature's historical ambition to participate in this administrative process is as profound as that of social science and is at least as longstanding. Literary governmentality was institutionalized in part through the mission statements for English study composed by F. R. Leavis. Where Matthew Arnold endowed "culture" with the capacity to generate an "expansion of our humanity," Leavis provided it with administrative support in the form of a well-trained English faculty (Arnold *Culture* 13). Leavis openly acknowledged that English contributed to a swarm of disciplines that inculcated experts in the administration of social organization. It was against the backdrop of a university designed to massify the professional class that he dreamed of educating readers capable of safeguarding culture and thus pioneered the humanities' own widely popular management training program. First implemented by the English School and its postcolonial inheritors, that program still equips readers to learn from novels, first, whether a society is well organized or not and, second, how societies might be better run.

Critical misrecognition of literature and public policy's common investment in the administrative mechanisms of what Chow calls coercive mimeticism can be blamed, at least in part, on Leavis's success in institutionalizing English as a vehicle for categorizing communities and providing them with literary substance. When he tied literary scholarship to culture, Leavis tried to claim the problem of population for fiction, for English departments, and for his "English School" at Cambridge. He maintained that novels reveal the core interests of the communities they represent, but that it takes a caste of highly trained literary interpreters – like sociologists, but better – to appreciate such revelations. Although this twofold claim deserves to be called Leavisite, it has in truth become utterly conventional around the world to argue that populations are intimately tied to specific modes of literature, if not to specific fields of literary criticism.

In his 1943 speech at the London School of Economics, Leavis rehearsed his theme about the "inevitable way in which serious literary interest develops towards the sociological" ("Literature" 6). This theme led inexorably to its companion: "thinking about political and social matters ought to be done by minds of some real literary education" (11). For the "reader capable of intelligent and sensitive criticism," literature and especially "prose fiction" reveal "a social culture and an art of living," "a civilization or 'way of life'" (11, 6). Fiction makes no promise to restore "the old organic relations between literary culture and the sources of vitality in the general life," Leavis cautioned, nor could it make such a promise, for "the Industrial Revolution had done its work . . . the traditional culture of the people was no longer there, except vestigially," and literature now lived in the academy (10). This is the consistent trajectory of Leavis's criticism: literature transforms from a component of what he recognizes as "traditional culture" into what he calls "minority culture."[19] It becomes the property and responsibility of that well-read minority called English majors.

---

[19] "In any period," he writes in "Mass Civilization and Minority Culture," "it is upon a very small minority that the discerning appreciation of art and literature depends . . . In their keeping . . . is the language, the changing idiom, upon which fine living depends" (Leavis *Education* 143–45).

This speech was not a one-off, for Leavis amplifies his argument in the opening pages of 1948's *The Great Tradition*, contending that "the few really great ... novelists ... count in the same way as the major poets, in the sense that they not only change the possibilities of the art for practitioners and readers, but that they are significant in terms of the human awareness they promote; awareness of the possibilities of life" (*Great* 10). "Life," as Leavis uses it, is no "abstraction," suggests Francis Mulhern, but rather a way of thinking about "human totality" as immanent to "the minutiae of lived experience" (*Moment* 170). "Life" is not defined in relation to an ideal, but entails a normative range. The novelists who best represent this life, Leavis argues, are "peculiarly alive in their time, peculiarly alive *to* it" (*Great* 33). This capacity allows fiction writers to do more than simply *represent* existing social arrangements. Their real talent, as Leavis describes it, resides in posing problems that would challenge the best of administrators. To be particularly alive to one's time as well as alive in it means analyzing current trends and evaluating new issues, confirming which policies work and which do not, and posing logical solutions to emergent and persistent organizational difficulties.

That this is the shared project of sociologists, literary critics, and fiction writers is evident from Leavis's prototypical reading of Joseph Conrad's *Typhoon* (1902/1986), as well as from subsequent reinterpretation by more contemporary critics who, it turns out, provide a surprisingly loyal opposition to their progenitor. The story begins by localizing its action and setting the stage for a kind of managerial test. The tale's "significance ... resides in the particulars," Leavis contends, "the actors, the incidents, and the total action: we are given the ship, her cargo, and her crew of ordinary British seamen, and the impact on them of the storm" (*Great* 213). *Typhoon* draws on these particulars to present a captain's efforts to maintain control over a "cargo" composed of Chinese laborers. Leavis zeroes in on Captain

MacWhirr's accomplishment: the "crowning triumph of the spirit," he calls it, "in the guise of a matter-of-fact and practical sense of decency, is the redistribution – ship devastated, men dropping with fatigue – of the gathered-up and counted dollars among the assembled Chinese" (*Great* 214–15). The captain is guided, Conrad tells us, by a conviction that his Chinese charges may be treated as rational actors. Different though their appearance from English seamen, the "coolies" are sufficiently well-versed in the rituals of the market to understand its contractual notion of equality. "[A]ll the coolies having worked in the same place and for the same length of time," the captain reckons, "he would be doing the fair thing by them as near as possible if he shared all the cash" that had been scattered about the hold "equally among the lot" (Conrad *Typhoon* 101). As if to satisfy Leavis's rule that great novels produce order out of disorder, the captain generates a civil society out of a "struggling mass of Chinamen" who, moments before at the storm's height, had atavistically degenerated into a "mound of writhing bodies," a "multitude of clawing hands" "swarming" in "blind panic" (*Typhoon* 77, 62–63, 58). His approach salvages not only a bad situation but also the rectitude of a British administrative model reliant on the sanctity of contracts. Captain and tale conspire to assure Leavis and readers everywhere that even the most multifarious of populations can be managed and, further, that novels can show us how.

If this lesson helps explain why Leavis would believe that fiction has much "to offer the sociologist," not to mention the middle manager, the chief agent, or the diplomat, it also creates an opportunity to distinguish among ways of reading novelistic commentary on administration.[20]

---

[20] What Leavis offers managers, Mulhern glosses, is nothing short of "*control* – control of 'the enormous technical complexity of modern civilization' through the 'coordination' of 'knowledge and understanding,'" "witness to the moral community of the past and incarnation of the possibility, foreshadowed in the act of literary judgment itself, of a new 'centre of real consensus'" (Mulhern *Moment* 108, 18).

For readings to diverge on the question of whether literature enforces, resists, or recasts administrative hierarchy, they must first agree that fiction has something to say about what it means to govern, including potentially specific recommendations for exercising power in particular situations. With this in mind, I read Leavis with a keen awareness that critiques of his work often involve attempts to out-Leavis him. When Mulhern observes that Leavis turns Conrad's story into an apology for empire, he does not take issue with the contention that fiction can model social order.[21] Instead, he announces his support for the contrasting social order depicted by Raymond Williams, which illuminates "classes and populations, at home and on other continents, that [Leavis's English literature] marginalized or silenced" ("English" 263). Likewise, Linda Hutcheon's charge that Leavis occults "the Englishness of English ... in favor of the universal" is the point of departure for her campaign to make comparative literature better at capturing discrete social arrangements, while teaching students to "respect difference as well as encouraging cultural dialogue" ("Crypto-Ethnicity" 31). I take up this same project of besting Leavis through the professional criticism he modeled when (in Chapter 4) I explain how *Nostromo* (1904/1985) disrupts colonial authority by pointing out the similarity between Nostromo's commercial enterprise and the political brinksmanship of the American investor Holroyd and the British manager Gould. Even as we attack Leavis, we disseminate the Leavisite thesis that fiction tells readers how societies work, why they should be preserved, and what it

---

[21] Mulhern contends that Leavis's description of "ordinary men [who] impose sanity on a frantic mob" reveals an "ideological relationship to *Typhoon*," as well as a "strategy of reading" that requires Leavis to "rewrite" the story's ending and "*un*write the greater part of the narrative." "*Typhoon* works through a fearsome 'return of the repressed,'" Mulhern contends; "Leavis's reading functions to assist repression, indeed to perfect it" ("English" 256).

takes to mediate – or manage – relations among them in an ever more complicated world.²²

This disciplinary mission is by no means limited to English and comparative literature departments in Europe and North America. Simon Gikandi explains that Leavis's model "made it possible for his postcolonial successors to substitute for England the new nation that had emerged from decolonization" ("Globalization" 650). "[W]hen a group of African intellectuals called for the abolition of the English department at the University of Nairobi in 1968," Gikandi argues, they wanted to show how "African literature in English could make the same exclusive claims that F. R. Leavis had made for English literature in England" ("Globalization" 649). Ngũgĩ wa Thiong'o and his colleagues sought to abolish the English department in order to claim its authority. They wrote against the "assumed centrality of the English Department, into which other cultures can be admitted from time to time" and in favor of a department that would orient the University of Nairobi "towards placing Kenya, East Africa, and then Africa in the centre" ("Abolition" 146). Where Leavis imagined that "the various studies" of the university "are to find their centre" in the "literary-critical ... discipline of sensibility, judgment and thought," Ngũgĩ similarly envisioned "a multi-disciplinary outlook" coordinated around literature, which would shape and be shaped by the study of "music, linguistics, Sociology, Anthropology, History, Psychology, Religion, Philosophy" (Leavis *Education* 43; Ngũgĩ "Abolition" 148). To understand how local cultures were damaged by empire was to acquire permission to intervene in them: "The primary duty of any literature department," Ngũgĩ and his

---

²² I am, of course, not the only person to note this debt: Farred, Gikandi, and Claudia Johnson are among those testifying to the under-acknowledged flexibility and widespread appropriation of Leavis's contention that literature explains culture (Gikandi "Globalization" 653; Farred "Leavisite" 17; Johnson "F. R. Leavis" 227).

colleagues wrote, "is to illuminate the spirit animating a people, to show how it meets new challenges, and to investigate possible areas of development and involvement" ("Abolition" 146).

Comparison between Leavis's English School and Ngũgĩ's Department of African Literature and Languages encourages one to imagine a global network of university departments all geared to converting literature into the means for intervening in debates about local, national, and worldwide social organization.[23] Other exemplary nodes in that network include St. Stephen's College in Delhi, which during the 1970s saw the "Ghosh Generation" of future novelists, businessmen, and bureaucrats pass through its halls.[24] J. P. Clark reports that classes graduating from University College, Ibadan, in the early 1960s read the "metaphysicals and Augustan poets and Romantic poets," inadvertently discovered "a whole body of poetry here at home," and prepared to staff a bureaucracy: "we were all being trained for the civil service" (Wren *Magical* 112–13).[25] When professors at these and other universities and colleges teach students to understand fiction and poetry as providing insight into social organization around the world, their instruction contributes to the reproduction of a global version of Leavis's literate minority, even as the different readings of fiction that emerge out of these institutions introduce new variation into the discipline of literary study.

---

[23] Gikandi lists such schools as Elphinstone College in Bombay, University of Calcutta, University College, Ibadan, and Makerere University College, alongside Oxford and Cambridge. There is, it needs be said, a colonial precedent for this network: "The implicit claim here was that even students in colonial universities, such as Makerere and Ibadan in Africa, could be trained to read culture and morality in literary texts the same way that these tropes were read at University College, London, the 'mother' institution" (Gikandi "Globalization" 651).

[24] Advani describes a "college full of potentially creative and exceptionally intelligent people ... directing its population in one herdlike direction – towards the Bureaucratic Sublime" (Bhattacharjea and Chatterji *Fiction* 12).

[25] See Okunoye for a brief survey of other sub-Saharan college programs, their literary curricula, and the writers they produced ("Captives" 105).

Novelists and their novels are not passive vehicles for, but rather are active participants in, this pedagogical project. Writers as different as Chinua Achebe and Virginia Woolf agree that fiction should rework notions of individualism in light of historical change. In her 1924 essay "Character in Fiction" Woolf famously explains how novels should capture "human character" after its irrevocable change "on or about 1910" ("Character" 421). When she remarks that "human relations have shifted – those between masters and servants, husbands and wives, parents and children," Woolf imagines fiction as an active contributor to this shift (422). Where Woolf explains how the novel may refashion the world so that any Mrs. Brown can live a more exciting life, Achebe portrays a novelist who can epitomize the liberal subject while preserving the influence of community. In a formulation that reverberated through the postcolonial literary field, his essay "The Writer and His Community" identifies the fiction writer as the product of a hybrid "artistic and intellectual inheritance," which bestows upon him not only the moral rights of the author but also communal obligations.[26] In *Arrow of God* (1964), Achebe dramatized this dynamic through his portrayal of Ezeulu, a leader he describes as "in a very real sense subordinated to his community" ("Writer" 57). When Achebe makes what he calls the "daunting problems of identity that beset our contemporary society" into his question as a novelist, he joins Woolf in empowering the novel form to weigh in on matters of social organization (61).

More recent fiction follows suit. For example, Tsitsi Dangarembga's *Nervous Conditions* (1988) can justifiably be described in Leavisite terms

---

[26] Achebe begins his essay by specifying "the emergence of individual authorship" with its "will to ownership" ("Writer" 47–48). Community, in contrast, makes it "possible for artists to create objects of art which were solid enough and yet make no attempt to claim, and sometimes even go to great lengths to deny, personal ownership of what they have created" (48–49).

as the tale of a young woman "transcending" the "immemorial life" and "close intimacy" of the village, only to make the village her object of study when she becomes a writer. When Tambudzai worries that she has "been too eager to leave the homestead and embrace the 'Englishness'" of school, she rejects English novels but confirms fiction's preservative power by sitting down to write a story about the provincial world she has left behind (*Nervous* 203–04). This is akin to how Leavis describes *The Rainbow* (1915), which does not so much "exalt" in "the order presented by the immemorial life at the Marsh and the 'close intimacy of the farm kitchen'" but rather describes "the transcending of it" paradoxically combined with recognition that "the impulse to this development, as well as the vigour for it, comes from the life that is to be transcended" (Leavis *Lawrence* 123). As if to authorize the Leavis/Lawrence connection, Dangarembga's heroine reads "everything from Enid Blyton to the Brontë sisters," while her rebellious friend reads *Lady Chatterley's Lover* (*Nervous* 93). "Tss!" Babamukuru shakes his head on discovering the offending volume. "She has no sense of decency, none whatsoever" (81).

If *Nervous Conditions* presents the postcolonial novelist as caretaker of local culture, Upamanyu Chatterjee's *English, August* (1988/2006) offers critical commentary on the St. Stephen's model of literary education. The novel represents new graduate and Indian Administrative Service trainee Agastya Sen struggling to mediate between the "megalopolitan world of Delhi" and rural locations whose names are "strong with an idiosyncratic tang, still reeking of the tribals that had once been their only inhabitants" (*English* 311). "[T]oo many worlds," Agastya concludes. He decides that it is best to forego the dream of development, "banish all yearning, and learn to accept the drift" (311). Chatterjee is, as his critics cannot help but note, an administrator himself (Bhattacharjea and Chatterji *Fiction* viii, 171). As for the novel's portrait of school: "This place," a head of department tells the novel's protagonist, "is like a parody, a complete farce, they're trying to build another Cambridge here ... English in India is burlesque ... In my time I'd wanted to take this Civil Service exam too, I should have. Now I spend my time writing papers for obscure journals on L. H. Myers and Wyndham Lewis, and teaching Conrad to a bunch of half-wits" (U. Chatterjee *August* 32).

Ethiopia Unbound (1911/1969), J. E. Casely Hayford's novelistic experiment in designing a Pan-African university, presages the Leavisite goal of mediating the relationship between culture and administration. The novel's protagonist, Kwamankra, combines a conservationist approach with the desire to inculcate "an adaptability suggestive of the advanced state of society" (*Ethiopia* 17). Designed to cultivate an "unspoilt son of the tropics, nursed in a tropical atmosphere, favourable to the growth of national life," Kwamankra borrows from pedagogical experiments undertaken in Japan, Ceylon, Ireland, and elsewhere, while his program combines the teaching of Fanti, Hausa, and Yoruba in addition to English taught "as a subject and literature" and science taught in the vernacular (173, 95–97). "Not only must the Ethiopian acquire proficiency in the arts and sciences, in technical and industrial training," the narrator explains, "but he must pursue a course of scientific enquiry which would reveal to him the good things of the treasure house of his own nationality" (170). Hayford imagines, further, that "the West ought not to be adverse to taking hints from the East as regards the preservation of national institutions" (171).

Hayford's Gold Coast academy, Dangarembga's mission school, and Chatterjee's literary college offer fictional supplements to, and anticipations of, Leavis's English School, with its campaign on behalf of cultural "continuity" administered by expert readers and writers of novels (Leavis *Education* 56). Literature's ability to generate alternatives to existing governmentality is readily apparent in novels that authorize even more discrepant forms of administration. For example, I show in Chapter 2 how such figures as Chimamanda Ngozi Adichie and Timothy Mo identify authoritative actors within the kinds of distressed groups and dissidents that foreign policy study locates in "failed states." Novels like Adichie's *Half of a Yellow Sun* (2006) foreground the expertise of child soldiers and victims of atrocity, turning them into veritable administrative reformers of community rather than representatives of communal experiences. Such literature does not eradicate the professional hierarchy intrinsic to contemporary government so much as it broadens the potential answers to questions about who qualifies as an administrative expert. In this way, fiction imagines renovating the governmental arrangements that postcolonial states inherited from imperialism. To an extent literary critics have sometimes been reluctant to imagine, novels do this by addressing the very social scientific professionals with whom they compete – and with some success.

Twentieth-century literature helped formulate narrative means for specifying the symptoms of societies, the better to identify and administer to their needs. While academic protocols insist that we sort novels into separate fields and subfields, often employing the very categories of ethnic and other types of community propagated by state and non-governmental administrators, I follow Rancière in imagining that twentieth-century fiction in all its forms facilitates the arrangement and rearrangement of given social relations. It does so, I argue, in dialog with social scientific as well as fictional precedents. When Leavis made his pitch for the English School at the London School of Economics, he provided a way to understand how literature shapes cultures. His approach, though much revised and updated by subsequent scholars, still resonates today. Where Mill's liberalism tended to legislate a distinction between autonomous actors and communal populations, twentieth-century writing blurs that division. It recognizes discrepant specialists within the very populations government purports to oversee. Late twentieth- and early twenty-first-century fiction finds itself thoroughly embroiled in the process of managing the unstable hierarchical arrangements that challenge postcolonial governments. It discovers how to think about governance in part by recollecting early twentieth-century novelistic efforts to imagine a world after empire. Novels now and then offer more than critique and more than a record of existing administrative protocols. They also conduct literary experiments. Fiction models solutions to the administrative dilemmas posed by a world far more thoroughly professionalized and bureaucratized than Mill's liberalism could have imagined. Different though this world is, fiction makes sense of it by recycling durable figures like the entrepreneur and the paternalistic state. Like governance, fiction after liberalism remains tempered by its terms.

CHAPTER 2

How literature administers "failed" states

Fiction has an investment in the state's future, which it demonstrates by treating war as a setting for literary experimentation. Recent novelistic experiments revise fictional forms and rework genres in a manner that accommodates them to civil war and state instability. As a result, instability appears less an exception in recent fiction than an expected part of the life of the state as the novel sees it. A comparable expectation figures in recent political scientific research, which defines the "failed state" as a more or less normative condition in much of the world. By treating failure as normal, writing in both disciplines subordinates the notion of the state as a setting for national development to that of the state as a context for professional intervention. The ideal of citizenship cedes center stage, as scholarship and literary prose present competent management as an aspiration every bit as compelling as the goal of national liberation. Fiction diverges from its interdisciplinary collaborator, however, on the matter of who qualifies as a manager. Novels including Chimamanda Ngozi Adichie's *Half of a Yellow Sun* (2006) present a problem for political science, as well as for conventional wisdom, when they identify child soldiers and refugees as participants in state organization rather than mere symptoms of state failure.

If national literature presupposed a world composed of nations, novels about states have a more than local scope as well. When a fiction such as *Half of a Yellow Sun* portrays life during wartime as both intensely violent and remarkably ordinary, it suggests that what goes on in the most unstable of states is never so extreme that it cannot be related to life in more secure environments. In Adichie's novel, the most conventional novelistic content of household intrigue and personal growth appears alongside description of coups and mass killings that would otherwise define a "state of exception." In *Half of a Yellow Sun*'s account of the Nigerian crisis that culminated in the Biafran War, couples fall in and out of love, families mourn, and children grow up in communities displaced and devastated by conflict. People starve and die in the refugee camp where the novel's final chapters are set, but they also write poetry, have sex, and engage in intellectual debate about, for instance, "racism ... as a basis of conquest" (*Half* 402).

Influential work in the social sciences shares the conviction that pragmatic questions of governmentality predominate precisely where one might anticipate crises of legitimacy and bare life. Where social science privileges quantitative data in its study of conduct during state crises, however, literature counters with the quality of local color. Adichie's *Half of a Yellow Sun* supplements think-tank statistics with a narrative of the Biafran War written from the standpoint of its survivors. In so doing, the novel operates as if it might contribute meaningfully to the body of knowledge concerned with how states work, especially when they do not appear to be working very well.

Social scientists who acknowledge literary efforts tend to think of fiction as giving crisis a human face. "[D]evelopment studies generally conceives of the Third World as a problematic of progress that can be arrayed well in statistical terms," notes scholar of international relations Christine Sylvester, whereas "[e]veryday lives feature in ... novels" ("Life" 66). Stephen Chan goes even farther, characterizing fiction as "a medium that does not claim it is *knowledge*, as much as it claims to represent an *unknowable* interior of disproportion, dislocation and terror, that is simply *felt*" ("Memory" 372). For the sociologist Patricia Ticineto Clough, such affective emphasis makes fiction "resonant with," and capable of providing, insights on governmental discipline, especially as it "shifts to the modulation of preconscious affect, changing the way we read (or should I say compute) as well as the way the legal, the normal, and the real are authorized and their measure and value determined" ("Sociology" 640). Literature reveals anomalies that do not register on statistical curves – "inconsistent objects," Sylvester calls them, "that beckon our attention" ("Life" 70). With stories that "stick to the gut and the brain," she finds, postcolonial fiction makes it difficult for social scientists to turn away from "biopolitical horrors [that] stand side-by-side, incongruously, with clear markers of development" (75, 70). If fiction forces "the coolly distant development expert to the inside of a maelstrom" (75), political science entices fiction to perceive the state less as art's habitual antagonist – the sovereign power that censors and bans, imprisons and exiles – than as an object that art may help to reform. We can imagine this relationship as a collaborative model in which fiction brings anomalies to the attention of researchers, who then tweak their statistical analyses and policy recommendations to account for this new data.

But fiction does not always collaborate on these terms. It does not necessarily see its role as fleshing out social scientific practice. Instead, novels such as *Half of a Yellow Sun* shape a counterdiscourse. They may offer a humanizing counterpoint to the cold facts of statistical calculation, but they also portray life in the failed state as an education – the sort of education, in fact, that might make one more expert than the experts. Just so, Adichie delegates the authority to compose the definitive book on Biafra to a home-schooled refugee. *Half of a Yellow Sun* goes even further when it stipulates that serving time in the army helps prepare one to do the work of writing. The singular importance of this gesture lies in its effort to democratize expertise. The heroes of Adichie's novel are not political scientists making charts in the London School of Economics or pulling strings at the World Bank. They are the sorts of people whom empire builders have historically treated as native informants. As much as fiction privileges expertise, therefore, it also reimagines the hierarchy of global administration. It envisions a redistribution of the authority to describe atrocities and to show how such events relate to the state's more stable aspect. In this effort, Adichie's novel is not without precedent, and considering its precedents allows us to see the novel's relationship to the state anew. The issue of how the literary present revises its past must wait, however, until I have specified the meaning of the "failed state" in twenty-first-century political and academic commentary.

FAILURE IS NORMAL

There are marked differences between the normative model of state failure and the competing legalistic definition of political crisis. The distinction is perhaps most readily apparent in discussions about intervention. Commentators who consider state failure in statistical terms tend to speak less about humanitarian emergencies and more about relative degrees of effective (and ineffective) governance. They proceed as if state and civil society were alive, if not well, in war zones and refugee camps, and they encourage intervention that fortifies both the semblance and substance of political stability. "It is frequently assumed that the collapse of state structures, whether through defeat by an external power or as a result of internal chaos, leads to a vacuum of political power," write the editors of the volume *Making*

States Work (Chesterman, Ignatieff, and Thakur "Introduction" 1). "This is rarely the case," they argue, for "[e]ven where non-state actors exist as parasites on local populations, political life goes on" (1). "Even in a failed state," echo scholars at the London School of Economics Crisis States Research Centre, "some elements of the state, such as local state organisations, might continue to exist" (CSRC "Fragile"). In addition to discovering order in disarray, normative study locates pockets of failure in otherwise stable states. Oft-cited instances include Kashmir, the United States Gulf Coast after Hurricane Katrina, and the *banlieues* of Paris in 2005; one might also adduce the Swat Valley, the Xinjiang Uyghur Autonomous Region, and, in the recent past, Northern Ireland. The normative approach treats such differing examples not as exceptions but as data to be assimilated to a statistical model. To be clear, the "norm" in writing about state failure is a statistical measure rather than the sort of norm spoken of as a philosophical ideal or the norm conceived of as a socially expected (and enforced) pattern of behavior. The norm for scholars of state failure is a statistical average tabulated, in the most evocative example of this style of thinking, on a "Failed States Index" that encompasses 177 of the world's states. Because averages change, state failure is re-normed each year, when the new edition of the "Failed States Index" appears in the pages of *Foreign Policy* magazine and on the web site of The Fund for Peace.

Foreign Policy began codifying this notion of state failure in 1992, when in its pages Gerald Helman and Steven Ratner argued, "a disturbing new phenomenon is emerging: the failed nation-state, utterly incapable of sustaining itself as a member of the international community" ("Saving" 3). By the late 1990s, the journal had ceased trumpeting the novelty of such crises and started presenting them as usual enough to deserve an annual update. The "Failed States Index" tabulates data culled from open-source articles and reports using a proprietary methodology called CAST (conflict assessment system tool). That data yields country-specific case studies, a world map, and the Failed States scores. The score chart is color-coded: on the Fund for Peace web site, a critically unstable red shades into a broad swath of borderline orange, stable yellow, and most stable green.[1] Red in 2011 featured Somalia, Zimbabwe, Burma, and Pakistan.[2] Green in 2011 identified the most stable polities as Sweden, Finland, and Norway. In years past, much is the same: Scandinavia is consistently the most stable region in the world; Sudan and Iraq are among the least stable states. Lest readers mistake such predictability as a statistical constant, the editors of *Foreign Policy* are careful to note significant changes year to year. In 2011 Niger "leapt four spots amid a devastating famine," Ivory Coast "rejoined the top 10, grimly foreshadowing its devastating election crisis," while "the global fallout of the Arab revolutions" appeared likely to have "consequences ... far beyond the Middle East" ("Index 2011" 48). In 2010 they put Nigeria on a "watch list" when the shake-up after President Umaru Yar'Adua's death "exposed gaping social rifts in what was already one of Africa's most troubled countries" (Dickinson "List" 84–85). Guatemala demanded watching for "its utter inability to combat organized crime," and in neighboring Honduras "drug traffickers had a field day while the country was distracted by last year's coup" (84–85). In 2009 the editors warned that a "perfect storm of state failure [was] now brewing" in Yemen, "Guinea-Bissau [was] fast becoming Africa's first narcostate," and Georgia "jumped 23 places ... due

---

[1] The color coding on the truncated rankings available via *Foreign Policy* are slightly different, and represent only the sixty least stable countries.
[2] Although its methodology differs substantially, the *2011 Ibrahim Index of African Governance* places Somalia at the bottom of its rankings as well (Mo Ibrahim Foundation *Index*).

to a substantial spike in that elusive indicator, 'Invaded by Russia'" ("Index 2009" 82, 84). In 2008 they identified "the implosion of the U.S. subprime market" and its worldwide ripple effects as primary among the "year's shocks" while also remarking that Israel's ongoing "inability to fully integrate its Arab minority" and "the increased factionalization of its political leaders" had resulted in the country's "first appearance in the top 60" of most unstable states ("Index 2008" 66, 68). That said, they also noted in 2010, "[a]ltogether, the top 10 slots have rotated among just 15 unhappy countries in the index's six years" ("Index 2010" 74). The risk of mistaking consistency for constancy arises with what James Ferguson describes as a vogue for geopolitical comparison that abjures the teleology of development. "Once modernity ceases to be understood as *telos*," he writes, "the question of rank is de-developmentalized, and the stark status differentiations of the global social system sit raw and naked, no longer softened by the promises of the 'not yet'" (*Global* 186).

As these combinations of states suggest, the "Failed States Index" is a comparative environment all its own. Strange bedfellows Syria and Burkina Faso sat side by side in the imaginary space of the 2007 rankings. When Syria moved across the line into the orange of greater stability by 2010, one could imagine the two states crossing paths as Burkina Faso lurched into the most unstable red. In 2011 Burkina Faso moved back into the orange while events late in the year in Syria appear likely to return it to the extremity of the red.[3]

---

[3] In 2008 Burkina Faso ranked thirty-six in the orange, while adjacent Syria ranked thirty-five in the red (Fund for Peace "Index 2008"). By 2009 their situations were reversed, with Syria in the orange at thirty-nine in 2009 and forty-eight in 2010, while Burkina Faso moved several slots up the list in the red at thirty-five (Fund for Peace "Index 2009," "Index 2010"). The 2011 index listed Burkina Faso at thirty-seven, just barely in the orange and Syria at forty-eight; these scores do not appear to have accounted for the events of the Syrian uprising (Fund for Peace "Index 2011").

In any given year states shift positions for all manner of reasons: Liberia makes gains "due to a renewed anticorruption effort and the resettlement of nearly 100,000 refugees," while Bangladesh takes a fall after a "devastating cyclone ... left 1.5 million people homeless" and "the imposition of emergency rule ... dragged on" ("Index 2008" 68). As the analysts behind the index sum up, "[f]ailing states are a diverse lot" ("Index 2007" 56). "After all," they say, "as Tolstoy might have put it, every failing state is failing in its own way" ("Index 2009" 82). With this assertion, the "Failed States Index" attempts not only to sidestep political scientific jostling to stabilize the definition of state failure but also to avoid becoming mired in the discipline's more general and fundamental disagreement about what a "state" is, about whether it is best defined in Lockean, Weberian, or more broadly juridical terms.[4] Instead of legalistic definition, the "Failed States Index" encourages statistical comparison among demonstrably different combinations of civil war and natural disaster, bureaucratic corruption, and economic malaise.[5]

The philosophical shorthand of Michel Foucault versus Giorgio Agamben goes a long way in capturing the difference between efforts to norm state failure and to define crisis in legal terms.[6] Foucault theorizes the eighteenth-century rise and subsequent

---

[4] A not entirely successful maneuver, it turns out, since any number of political scientists have questioned the FSI methodology and its findings. *Foreign Policy* published the comments of one such critic, Robert Rotberg of the Kennedy School of Government, who craves a more "objective system of rankings" to "better help policymakers analyze the options available and choose the prescriptions that best fit the country in peril" ("Index 2009"). Sebastian von Einsiedel rehearses these definitional debates ("Policy" 14–15). He attributes the most cited definition of state failure in Zartman, for whom "[c]ollapse means that the basic functions of the state are no longer performed" (*Collapsed* 5).

[5] See the explanation of CAST methodology for a complete description of how such events appear as statistical "indicators" (Fund for Peace "Methodology").

[6] Distinguishing the work of these two thinkers is a cottage industry. See, for instance, Bull ("Vectors"), Fassin ("Humanitarianism"), and Medovoi ("Global").

transformation of a state devoted to "normalization," the "government of men" guided by the collection of statistical information about the health and welfare of subject populations (*Abnormal* 49).[7] In contrast, Agamben's state is defined by its reliance on legal exception, "fictitious lacuna in the order for the purpose of safeguarding the existence of the norm and its applicability to the normal situation" (*State* 31). For Foucault, the "suspension of, or temporary departure from, laws and legality" is less an exception than one in a range of periodic eruptions: coups d'état, acts of sedition, or civil war, all appear "normal, natural phenomenon, immanent as it were to the life of the *res publica* ... [L]ike tempests, they arise periodically when they are least expected, in the greatest calm, in periods of stability" (*Security* 267).[8] "[R]aison d'État," as Foucault discovers it in the likes of Francis Bacon and B. P. von Chemnitz, "must command, not by 'sticking to the laws,'" but by controlling "the laws themselves, which must adapt to the present state of the republic" (261). The latter-day revision, "*l'État de droit*," which he finds in the work of Friedrich A. Hayek, "must define a framework," the rules of the game, so that "agents can freely make their decisions" (*Birth* 173–74). As the eighteenth-century state evolves into its twentieth- and twenty-first-century forms, standardization gives way to flexibility, "hierarchical individualization" of normal and deviant subjects warps into "an environmentalism open to unknowns and transversal phenomena" (261).

Where Agamben imagines sovereignty that survives by creating exceptions to laws it professes to uphold, Foucault better describes the

---

[7] Ewald defines normalization as "the production of norms, standards for measurement and comparison, and rules of judgment" ("Norms" 148).
[8] Where Agamben's law masks the sovereign right to judge what counts as an exception, Foucault understands exceptions as "extensions of the norm," as opportunities to bring new objects of study within a disciplinary purview (Ojakangas "Impossible" 16). See too Hussain, who explains the "limitations of the concept of the exception in understanding contemporary governance" ("Beyond" 735).

administration envisioned by the "Failed States Index" when he depicts an art of government that conceives of "no prior, external purpose," "no problem of origin, of foundation, or of legitimacy" (*Security* 259). "Political economy," he calls this, that does not question governmental practices "to determine whether they are legitimate in terms of right" but rather "considers them in terms of their effects" (*Birth* 15). Foucault presents a tactical, reflexive approach to administration that is constantly questioning and measuring the impact of its policies and programs. Its "theoretical horizon" is not "the edifice of law" but rather the expertise of administrators and the "jurisprudence" of "clinical knowledge" employed to weigh the costs and benefits of government on the activities of subject populations (*Society* 38).[9]

From the perspective of what Foucault calls "a government which nothing escapes," and Gilles Deleuze calls a mode of governing in which "nothing is left alone for long," it is possible to imagine that every social condition might be catalogued, every population segment recognized and understood, and every location mapped (Foucault *Birth* 296; G. Deleuze with Antonio Negri "Control"). The research program of contemporary political science expresses ambition on this scale. In his working paper outlining the 2001–10 phase of study for the Crisis States Research Centre, James Putzel offers two "over-arching questions": "A) Why and how, under the conditions of late development, are some fragile states able to respond effectively to contestation while others collapse and/or experience large-scale violence? B) What are the factors that contribute to and impede state reconstruction in post-war periods?" ("War" 3). The answers would amount to nothing less than a total historical accounting of geopolitical variation.

[9] See Bhuwania on how "the techniques of discipline have invaded and found places in law" ("'Law'" 141). And see Foucault on the redefinition of "politics" as the struggle among arts of government associated with sovereignty and discipline (*Birth* 313).

In studies published by the Crisis States Research Centre and elsewhere, governance takes myriad forms, from the all-enveloping "societies of control" described by Deleuze ("Postscript" 4), to the attenuated states described by Anna Simons and David Tucker in *Third World Quarterly*:

> [C]onsider Lebanon in the 1980s, Yugoslavia in the 1990s, Afghanistan both before the rise of the Taliban and immediately thereafter, and Somalia still ... To anyone on the outside life [in such places] may have appeared chaotic, but the fact that local residents in Beirut, Mogadishu, Sarajevo, and Kabul knew exactly where they could safely venture, whose militia would protect them, and who would gun them down points to latent order within the chaos. ("Misleading" 391)[10]

In these examples, governance is patchy. It is in flux. Its agents are subject to change. It may prove fully intelligible only to insiders with experience and outsiders expert in their observation. If what Simons and Tucker notice qualifies as state administration, however perverse, then the problem facing scholars and policymakers is not only discerning how states fail but also learning how to differentiate among states in crisis. "All states consistently fail some portions of their population," Simons and Tucker argue, which means that understanding the variety of failure must entail an overhaul of the distinction between functioning and dysfunctional (400). This is not a merely academic distinction for Simons and Tucker, whose interest in "the kinds of failure that matter most" stems from concern about the relationship between instability and terrorism (400). Even if, they argue, all states fail to some extent, not every state fails in a manner that leads to what gets called terrorist violence. Thus, U.S. Secretary of State Condoleezza Rice was wrong to maintain that "weak and failing states ... serve as global pathways

---

[10] See also Englebert, who asks provocatively "why Congo persists" even though it seems as if it "should have collapsed some time ago" (119).

that facilitate ... the movement of criminals and terrorists" (387).[11] Some do and some do not, and if commentators wish to discover which ones do, they must learn to differentiate among failure's permutations, including its appearance in states that the United States enlists as allies, like Pakistan or Israel.[12]

The old rules no longer apply: states must no longer be thought of as defined by their ability to monopolize violence within their borders. A far more partial enactment of the aspiration to control may indicate administration that is statelike. Or, perhaps, state lite. Not only war-torn cities but also refugee camps can be seen as evincing this kind of aspirational administration. Where Agamben describes "the refugee" as "nothing less than a limit-concept" and "the camp" as "the pure space of exception," normative political science detects sundry activities of state formation (*Means* 21–22; *Homo* 134).[13] Jacob Mundy argues in the *Journal of Modern African Studies* that even the stark Western Saharan camps in southwest Algeria represent an "experiment in prefigurative national pedagogy and socio-political organisation. The camps' institutions derive from a nationalist project and mirror them in all their aspects" ("Performing" 284–85). For Jacob Stevens, that evolution of camp into proto-state creates new administrative challenges, as "camps become a parallel economy that draws money and skills away from the locality" that hosts them, generating a hybrid form with its own distinctive social dynamics ("Prisons" 66). As Jonathan

---

[11] The editors of the "Failed States Index" note that a "recent report by West Point's Combating Terrorism Center ... revealed that Osama bin Laden's outfit had an awful experience trying to operate out of Somalia, for all the same reasons that international peacekeepers found Somalia unmanageable ... terrible infrastructure, excessive violence ... and few basic services" ("Index 2009" 82).

[12] On Pakistan as a failed state see Zaidi ("Failed" 10–11). On Israel see the 2008 "Failed States Index" ("Index 2008" 68) and the bracing polemical account by Retort (*Afflicted* 108–09).

[13] As many have noted, Agamben is following Arendt, who described "an ever-growing new people comprised of stateless persons, the most symptomatic group in contemporary politics" (*Origins* 277). For an attempt to reckon with this appropriation of Arendt, see Butler and Spivak (*Who Sings* 36).

Joseph observes, "[w]ith multiple actors involved, the provision of security becomes a competitive game governed by market rules" ("Governmentality" 418). He deems such administrative contexts to be thin governmentality, in which entrepreneurial actors bump up against myriad local authorities that include religious and other institutions devoted to the disciplining and recruiting of new members.

This more diverse sense of what goes on in states suggests a more flexible notion of state power than that associated with sovereignty. Agamben considers "the Rwandan child ... the most telling contemporary cipher of the bare life that humanitarian organizations, in perfect symmetry with state power, need" (*Homo* 133).[14] But this is what state power needs only if state power is thought of as the capacity to say who lives and who dies. For Foucault, such was the right of the medieval sovereign. But liberal governmentality, he famously argues, replaced the "ancient right to *take* life or *let* live" with the "power to *foster* life" (*History* 138).[15] This is a power that, unlike sovereign rule, presumes multiple agents and a good deal of political competition.[16]

---

[14] This passage reads in full, "It takes only a glance at the recent publicity campaigns to gather funds for refugees from Rwanda to realize that here human life is exclusively considered (and there are certainly good reasons for this) as sacred life – which is to say, as life that can be killed but not sacrificed – and that only as such is it made into the object of aid and protection. The 'imploring eyes' of the Rwandan child, whose photograph is shown to obtain money but who 'is now becoming more and more difficult to find alive,' may well be the most telling contemporary cipher of the bare life that humanitarian organizations, in perfect symmetry with state power, need" (Agamben *Homo* 133).

[15] Medovoi observes, "Neither Hardt and Negri nor Agamben seriously entertains Foucault's underlying proposition about liberal modernity: within the general economy of power, sovereignty (despite its continued visibility) has steadily retreated, giving way to less dramatic but far more effective disciplinary and regulatory regimes of power that can administer life from the individual level of the body all the way up to the statistical amalgam of the population" ("Global" 56).

[16] On this topic, see Žižek, who argues that Agamben "precludes the very possibility of the emergence of political subjectivity" (*Parallax* 341–42), and Butler, who contends that "if the language by which we describe destitution presumes, time and again, that the key terms are sovereignty and bare life ... [it] seems to me that we've actually subscribed to a heuristic that only lets us make the same description time and again, which ends up taking on the perspective of sovereignty and reiterating its terms" (Butler and Spivak *Who Sings* 42).

Mahmood Mamdani's commentary on Darfur makes the practical implications of foreclosing such competition abundantly clear.[17] He describes the United Nations and non-governmental organization (NGO) view of "the people of Darfur" as employing terms that Agamben would have us see as defining contemporary governance in general. Mamdani regards this treatment of "the people" as far more narrowly instrumental. They are "as wards in an international rescue operation with no end in sight" (*Saviors* 297).[18] By characterizing local populations as "minority victims of ongoing barbarities," Mamdani contends, aid organizations justify their presence ("Politics" 8). The need to reproduce a dynamic of victim and savior keeps the NGOs from recognizing, much less supporting, indications of social order in Darfur. Bringing together "political figures and representatives of civil society for an open discussion" is discouraged, Mamdani explains, for to do so "risks conveying a feeling that normality is returning to Darfur, when it is actually the depth of the crisis that should be emphasized" (*Saviors* 297).[19]

If Mamdani's NGOs strive to disempower those they help by talking like Agamben, Mamdani himself strives to recontextualize Darfur's violence as part of an "internal political process" ("Blue-Hatting" 20). What may look exceptional – the particularly brutal activities of the Janjawiid, for instance – reappears as a devastating but recognizable problem of state administration. "They are

---

[17] Mamdani first published the argument I refer to here in a pair of articles appearing in the *London Review of Books* in 2007, "The Politics of Naming" and "Blue-Hatting Darfur." An expanded and more thoroughly historicized version appeared in the 2009 book *Saviors and Survivors*. My quotations come from both sources.

[18] Fassin argues that this "process essentializes the victims: against the thickness of biographies and the complexity of history, it draws a figure to which humanitarian aid is directed" ("Humanitarianism" 512).

[19] De Waal, who has written extensively about Sudan as well both in print and on his blog "Making Sense of Sudan," offers the more general comment that "[s]tate-builders ignore vernacular politics, to the detriment of the countries they leave at the end of their contracts" ("Dollarised" 38).

nomadic forces on horseback," Mamdani quotes General Henry Anyidoho of Ghana and the African Union as saying; the Janjawiid "are spread across Sahelian Africa: Niger, Sudan, Chad, the Central African Republic. The problem is that the AK-47 has replaced the bow and arrow. The Janjawiid should be disarmed before the rebels turn in their arms" (*Saviors* 298).[20] The point of normalizing violence in Darfur is not to affirm it, but to think of intervention as facilitating conciliation among parties designated as players in a political process. In this way, Mamdani envisions shifting the international mission from one of keeping people alive (which requires that they be always on the brink of extermination) to one of fostering the governance of intelligible political, cultural, or other sorts of social differences. This would require us to contemplate the possibility that the real news about life in Sudan is not its abject lawlessness but rather its continuity with dynamics facing states everywhere. Not every administration has Janjawiid to deal with, it is clear, but every population contains destabilizing dangers of some sort or another, potentially destructive agents that in challenging state stability also provide the occasion for state power to extend its reach.

This politics of conciliation conceives of population as not simply ordered but produced by the state. We will mistake Mamdani's proposal if we understand the state as generating unity out of a civil society composed of seemingly preexisting groups and interests. Instead, government strives to reproduce, adapt, and revise social order comprising group dynamics that it defines as relevant. Mamdani summarizes one familiar version of this process when he notes that administrations "in colonial and post-colonial

---

[20] A former governor of South Darfur disagrees, Mamdani recounts, arguing that "[t]he Mahamied [from whom many of the Janjawiid are recruited] have their problem: where to go. It is not necessary to disarm them; it is necessary to give them a solution" (*Saviors* 298).

Uganda, as in other parts of Africa colonized by Western powers in the twentieth century, defined every individual as belonging to a race or an ethnic group" ("African" 494).[21] Ethnicity and culture are not the only divisions that states produce, of course, nor does their production necessarily lead to violent conflict.[22] Instead, it is through such divisions, of whatever sort, that both the colonial state and the postcolonial state give shape to politics, that "civil peace," as Foucault calls it, that continues war by other means (*Society* 16). "Civil society is ... a concept of governmental technology," he argues, through which states designate both their limits – the domains they consider private as opposed to public – and "field of reference" – the population and economy that the state promises to administer (*Birth* 295–96).

If we read Mamdani's argument in light of Foucault's, it is possible to say that the Janjawiid are not a given part of civil society, but that government technologies might extend civil society to include them. Precisely because it is codified in legislation and law, the state's public is as mutable as the state itself, as capable of as much change as the arts of governmental policy and rule-making allow. Its groups and relations, hierarchies and castes are as modifiable as state administration can make them, and as particular as the rights and privileges,

---

[21] Mamdani elaborates, "From Sudan to Ethiopia, Uganda to Mozambique and Angola, and Ivory Coast to Liberia, most political violence in post-colonial Africa seems to be organised along ethnic lines. Why is that? Some have suggested that it has to do with the importance of ethnicity in African culture. I argue instead that it has to do with the politicisation of culture in the African colonies. When colonial reform replaced 'direct' with 'indirect' rule through compliant local authorities the effect was to make cultural difference the basis for administrative, legal and political organisation, thereby politicising ethnic difference and making ethnic identity the basis for political discrimination" ("Letters" 4).

[22] "Nor should policy makers or academics infer that ethnic diversity is the root cause of civil conflict," argue James Fearon and David Laitin. Rather they should attend to the ways that states in crisis produce and redefine group dynamics. "We find little evidence that civil war is predicted by large cultural divisions," they argue. "But it seems quite clear that intense grievances *are produced by* civil war" ("Ethnicity" 88).

grievances and petitions the state is able to recognize. The successful state would know how to incorporate even such potentially destabilizing parties as the Janjawiid and their ilk.[23] If it cannot do this, for whatever reason, then the state fails a little bit. State failure, in this way of thinking, is the inverse of state flexibility.[24] The most stable state is the one most capable of adapting its demographic criteria, designating new and changing populations, and increasing the detail of its census.[25] From its philosophical inception in the eighteenth century, the liberal state manifests increasing flexibility in conceiving the divisions that run through its public, and it does so in the name of extending dominion. Nothing could be farther from the Hegelian ideal of statecraft, in which a civil society learns to set aside its differences and to found a democracy.[26]

---

[23] Thus Mamdani's policy recommendation: "What I counsel in lieu of a military intervention is a political process with two objectives in mind: a reform of the state that will build on the peace settlements in the south and east by extending power-sharing to insurgent elites in the west; and a resource-building initiative (the conflict in Darfur is driven in part by a lack of resources that the international community is best equipped to address but has yet to show serious interest in). The example to emulate is not Nato's intervention in the former Yugoslavia, but the political settlement in the south of Sudan, which the Bush administration can count as its solitary foreign policy success" ("Letters" 4).

[24] On the latter, see Nugent ("States") on the rebuilding of state institutions across Africa.

[25] "[F]or those who govern," Foucault contends, "it is not only a matter of taking into account and taking charge of the activity of groups and orders ... [T]here is no limit to the objectives of government when it is a question of managing a public power that has to regulate the behavior of subjects" (*Birth* 7).

[26] Hegel's formulation is in paragraph 182 of *The Philosophy of Right*: "If the state is represented as a unity of different persons, as a unity which is only a partnership, then what is really meant is only civil society ... [T]he whole sphere of civil Society is the territory of mediation where there is free play for every idiosyncrasy, every talent, every accident of birth and fortune, and where waves of every passion gush forth, regulated only by reason glinting through them" (266–67). In Hardt's gloss, "civil society takes the natural human systems of needs and particular self-interests, puts them in relation with each other through the capitalist social institutions of production and exchange and, thus, on the basis of the mediation and subsumption of the particular, poses a terrain on which the State can realize the universal interest of society in 'the actuality of the ethical Idea'" ("Withering" 25).

Accordingly, it should come as no surprise that parenting provides the framework for prevailing discussions of how to reform statecraft. In their 1992 outline "Saving Failed States," Gerald Helman and Steven Ratner maintain, "[t]he conceptual basis for the effort should lie in the idea of conservatorship" (12). "Figuring out which faltering states to help depends in large part on what they need," wrote the editors of the "Failed States Index" in 2009 ("Index 2009" 82). Domestic discipline is the model for this process of assessing international order: "In domestic systems when the polity confronts persons who are utterly incapable of functioning on their own," Helman and Ratner explain, "the law often provides some regime whereby the community itself manages the affairs of the victim. Forms of guardianship or trusteeship are a common response to broken families ... It is time that the United Nations consider such a response to the plight of failed states" ("Saving" 12). As it turns out, the editors of the "Failed States Index" found that a "common thread link[ed]" the "most improved players" on the 2008 chart: "All three host U.N. peacekeeping operations" ("Index 2008" 68).

"[T]here are many problems with the trusteeship model," cautions Oxford international relations professor Richard Caplan, and "these include its neocolonial overtones" ("Collapsing" 242).[27] Not to mention explicitly and unapologetically colonial ones: it can be challenging to distinguish the parental logic of trusteeship from the paternal despotism endorsed by Victorian liberals like John Stuart Mill.[28] Mill's means-ends thinking is echoed in the words of Simon Chesterman, the executive director of the Institute for International Law and Justice at New York University. Chesterman is among those

---

[27] "[I]t is possible to identify remedies that can soften the rough edges of international control," Caplan allows, but the tendency of international actors to "give insufficient weight to capacity building" and to "accountability" is "difficult to overcome" (242).

[28] Mill justifies despotism "provided the end be ... improvement" (*Liberty* 10).

to defend trusteeship, contending that "local ownership ... must be the end of a transitional administration, but it is not the means" ("Transitional" 344).[29]

Literature intervenes in this discussion, often by questioning whether the normative study of state crisis must yield a stringently hierarchical approach to policy implementation and by wondering whether it always makes sense to imagine that global experts can solve problems caused by local agents simply by offering their services as mentors. Through stories about civil war and collapsing government, novels give voice to multiple positions and leave room for multiple interpretations of what caused and what might resolve a given crisis. When fiction imagines competing authorities and authorizes competing readings of state failure, it suggests the mentors and trustees endorsed by the United Nations and by international relations scholars may not always know best.

FAILURE IN FICTION

Although contemporary fiction reproduces certain aspects of political scientific treatment of state failure, it does not reproduce that discipline's international division of labor. Instead, it retools an identifiably novelistic approach to representing subjectivity as the means for introducing new sorts of local, and often unaccredited, expert participants in the project of administration. Adichie's *Half of a Yellow Sun* presents the Biafran War as an instance of state failure twice over – first, a Nigerian failure so severe that it led to civil war and a breakaway republic and, second, the Biafran state's own

---

[29] It only makes sense that outsiders are the best guides to stabilization, Chesterman claims. "Since the malevolence or collapse" of local political dynamics "is precisely the reason that power is arrogated to an international presence," he reasons, "the light footprint is unsustainable as a model for general application" (344).

collapse under attack from Nigeria and its international allies.[30] This presentation appropriates the terms of political science in the service of a counterdiscourse: in *Half of a Yellow Sun*, the question of who is best qualified to analyze and to manage the failed state is up for grabs.

In addition to revising political scientific hierarchy, *Half of a Yellow Sun* supplements the most habitual literary approach to portraying political subjectivity. The novel performs a makeover on the home, which appears less as a private venue for the generation of public individuals than it does as the setting for a kind of ad hoc professional training. By simultaneously politicizing and professionalizing the household, *Half of a Yellow Sun* performs a kind of gesture familiar to readers of postcolonial novels. Fredric Jameson's argument about the "necessarily ... political dimension" of postcolonial literature brought swift condemnation for what critics charged was a rhetoric of otherness.[31] The response to Jameson's assertion that postcolonial plots are "necessarily" political served as a reminder of the remarkably various ways in which contemporary fictions reconfigure the private/public distinction we have been taught to think of as traditionally European and bourgeois. In the case of *Half of a Yellow Sun*, the domain once called "private life" is hardly separated from politics, not because the home is thought of as figuring national aspirations but because it is so thoroughly assimilated as part of a story about professional self-determination.

---

[30] Scholars have identified interest in Biafra as a key theme of "third generation" Nigerian fiction (Hawley "Heritage"; Krishnan "Aesthetics").

[31] Jameson's thesis drew fire as much for stipulating the allegorical form of postcolonial politics as for asserting that every postcolonial plot must be read in strictly political terms: "Third-world texts, even those which are seemingly private ... necessarily project a political dimension in the form of national allegory" ("Third-World" 69).

This tendency is demonstrated by the story of Odenigbo and Olanna, husband and wife as well as educators in the fields of mathematics and sociology, respectively. The air raid interrupting their wedding reception exemplifies a motif: throughout the novel, the couple's romantic turmoil directly parallels Nigeria's defining postcolonial crisis as well as being punctuated by it (*Half* 202–03).[32] In and of itself, this is not a radical innovation. *Half of a Yellow Sun* has a lowbrow cousin who can be found in the "historicals" section of the romance-novel shelf. But such a combination is still significant in suggesting, first, that problems which more than two centuries of novel writing have taught readers to understand as normal still organize lives during political strife and, second, that the form of domestic romance is perfectly capable of stretching to accommodate the setting of civil war. That said, these refugees are not helpless victims or ciphers of bare life. Neither does their home provide a setting for the formation of reflective persons whose self-discipline equips them to be national citizens. Odenigbo and Olanna are such persons, but *Half of a Yellow Sun* establishes no such relation between private and public.

Instead, the novel transforms the function of the household by centering Olanna and Odenigbo's domestic life on their intellectual salon, a group whose membership includes key figures in the secession – among them Okeoma, the novel's incarnation of the poet and

---

[32] They court one another by arguing about dictatorship and African nationalism, while Olanna fears that marriage "would flatten" their relationship "to a prosaic partnership" (52). Later, as Nigerian politics become increasingly fractious their domestic life changes too when Odenigbo sleeps with a "village girl" his mother wants him to marry, fathering a child whom Olanna agrees to adopt (216). Later still, with the war entering its last punishing phase, Odenigbo sinks into depression, spends his days drinking at the Tanzania Bar, and rebuffs Olanna's advances at night with a blank, "I'm tired, *nkem*" (251). Finally, when news comes that one of their best friends has been killed, they fall into each other's arms, have loud therapeutic sex, and sink into a "sad and unsettling peace" (391).

war hero Christopher Okigbo – as well as a cast that combines demographic diversity with academic authority. Participants include Professor Ezeka, whom Adichie reports she "modeled on the Biafran leader Chukwuemeka Odumegwu Ojukwu"; Dr. Patel, "the Indian man who drank Golden Guinea beer mixed with Coke"; Miss Adebayo, loud, Yoruba, and flirtatious, nothing like what one expects "a university woman to be"; and Richard Churchill, an Englishman researching Igbo-Ukwu art who also publishes eyewitness journalism from inside Biafra (Adichie with Bolonik "Memory"; Adichie *Half* 18–19). The salon does not encompass a civil society so much as provide a university setting for demographic categories privileged by Nigerian politics in the 1960s. It focuses attention, in other words, on the very group distinctions highlighted by the plotting of politicians and army officers in the years immediately following independence, distinctions that were only reinforced when the young state of Nigeria was rocked by massacres, secession, and the Biafran War. No less a figure than Chinua Achebe observed regretfully in 1983 that in postcolonial Nigeria, a "self-conscious wish to banish *tribe* has proved largely futile because a word will stay around as long as there is work for it to do. In Nigeria, in spite of our protestations, there *is* plenty of work for *tribe*" (*Trouble* 6).[33]

Odenigbo and Olanna's salon does not present dispute among its participants as solely or even primarily a discussion about self-interest among citizens. By doubly marking discussants as expert and ethnic,

---

[33] Ekwe-Ekwe notes the persistence of colonial regionalization of Nigerian politics (*Biafra Revisited* 35). Badru argues that the January coup of 1966 "brought ethnicity to the fore of Nigerian politics" (*Imperialism* 75). And Forsyth's popular account of the Biafran War argues that the label "Igbo coup" provided rhetorical cover for ethnic cleansing executed by political and military functionaries in the North in response to what was, in fact, an "all-party coup in January" (*Biafra Story* 56). See Zeleza on the variety of postcolonial African state responses to colonial treatment of ethnicity (*Manufacturing* 421). See Bayart for a wide-angle approach to the "assumption that a so-called 'cultural identity' necessarily corresponds to a 'political identity'" (*Illusion* ix).

it distances them from the citizenry they might otherwise represent. They argue as scholars, even when they argue about what it means to be Nigerian or, later, Biafran. When his fellows accuse Odenigbo of being a "hopeless tribalist," they are not cajoling him into setting differences aside in the name of national unity so much as they are making a conceptual point about the historical derivation of such notions as "pan-Igbo" identity (Adichie *Half* 20–21). "Professor Ezeka snorted and shook his head," the narrator recounts, before beginning a pocket lecture: "The pan-Igbo idea itself came only in the face of white domination. You must see that tribe as it is today is as colonial a product as nation and race" (20). Scholarly independence, rather than critical publicity, explains why these specialists do not consistently or narrowly represent the interests of their respective ethnic groups.

In sum, when it domesticates coffeehouse congregation, Odenigbo and Olanna's salon does more than simply reverse Jürgen Habermas's formula of private people coming together as a public to debate the common concern. Adichie's emphasis on the scholarly aspect of political dialogue confirms what Habermas himself avers – namely, that the era of "bourgeois representation" is over (*Structural* 37). Instead of salvaging the public sphere, *Half of a Yellow Sun* offers a model for reproducing the feel of the seminar or colloquium when the universities are all closed down. And indeed, though the war forces them to relocate more than once, and to less welcoming abodes each time, Odenigbo and Olanna continue to preserve a space for political argument among experts. They welcome new interlocutors and encourage old ones to stop by as they are able. When Okeoma visits from the front, Olanna recaptures the salon's civility by inviting him to read one of his poems and asking, "Please remove your grenade while we eat" (*Half* 324).

THE AUTHOR-FUNCTION OF STATE

Half of a Yellow Sun confirms the social scientific hypothesis that life during civil war is not entirely abnormal – which is to say, life during civil war is not life as it should be, but something enough like the ideal to appear a significant deviation from it, rather than an exception to it. In a Harvard University lecture she gave in 2007, Adichie echoed Wole Soyinka's description of the war as "shabby, painfully shabby," but added that "it was also a time when my brother was born, when people discovered strength and talent and courage, when people came together in different ways" ("African" 53). Even though Adichie's writing appears to accept the hypothesis that state failure can be normalized, it does not cede authority to describe such "painfully shabby" versions of normality to think-tanks and resource centers run out of Geneva, London, or Washington. Instead, it describes the salon managed by its two Nigerian educators as the perfect setting for a young man to become an indigenous expert on failed states. *Half of a Yellow Sun* marshals the usual diachronic logic of *Bildung* for this effort, but, in its revised domestic setting, what might otherwise appear as personal experiences of growing up seem more like aspects of professional training.

Ugwu is the houseboy whom Odenigbo and Olanna raise as a son and invigilate like a promising graduate student. After a time of intense preparation, he demonstrates his membership in the class of people who "know Book" by writing a volume of his own (Adichie *Half* 129). His labor is a secret until the novel's final lines, however. Only then does it become clear that Ugwu, the boy readers have watched develop over the course of some four hundred pages, is the author of the book within a book whose composition appears in sections at the end of several chapters of *Half of a Yellow Sun*, in a different typeface from the main narrative, under the heading, "The Book: The World Was Silent When We Died." Ugwu is the answer, in other words, to a good old-fashioned question: "What matter who's speaking?" (Foucault *Language* 138).

This author-function is complicated by the various disciplines and styles of writing employed in "The Book." One chapter speaks in the manner of colonial history when it chronicles the disastrous implementation of indirect rule among the "non-docile and worryingly ambitious" Igbo (Adichie *Half* 115).[34] Another approaches civil war from the standpoint of international politics in considering what it meant that "Biafra was 'under Britain's sphere of interest'" (258).[35] A third foregrounds the economics of state failure, emphasizing what commentators call the resource curse, and regretting the foibles of neocolonial planners "too interested in aping the British" (205).[36] Even greater stylistic range appears in an initial section that recalls the memoir of witnessing – it describes a woman fleeing massacre in northern Nigeria, holding a calabash with a "child's head inside: scruffy braids falling across the dark-brown face, eyes completely white, eerily open, a mouth in a small surprised O" (82). Finally, a late section takes the form of poetic apostrophe:

> Did you see photos in sixty-eight
> Of children with their hair becoming rust:
> Sickly patches nestled on those small heads,
> Then falling off, like rotten leaves on dust? (375)

---

[34] The scholarly literature on this episode is, needless to say, substantial. See, for instance, Afigbo (*Warrant*), Isichei (*History*), and Ekechi (*Tradition*).

[35] Stremlau (*International*) remains a key reference point for the international politics approach to Biafra.

[36] On the resource curse, a 2003 World Bank study observes that "the presence of abundant primary commodities, especially in low-income countries, exacerbates the risks of conflict" (Bannon and Collier *Natural* ix). In a survey of state failure for Harvard's Center for International Development, Bates labels this paradoxical curse one of the primary themes of scholarship on political disorder ("Insecurity" 20). In *Half of a Yellow Sun*, Olanna's sister Kainene is among the characters to give voice to this argument: "It's the oil" that ensures Nigeria will wage war against the breakaway Biafran state. "They can't let us go easily with all that oil" (*Half* 180).

The puzzle of who might be capable of doing the failed state in such different voices is hardly restricted to the novel's plot. It also shapes expectations about the author whose name is on *Half of a Yellow Sun*'s cover. A bibliography and Author's Note only encourage such conjecture by referencing materials from an array of disciplines and citing survivors and relations whose interviews facilitated the novel's composition (434–36). In assigning the fictional author-function to the unlikely Ugwu, *Half of a Yellow Sun* satisfies a craving for unity invoked by that range of sources in Adichie's Note.

More significant still than the author-function that readers attach to Ugwu or Adichie is the authority that *Half of a Yellow Sun* claims for the novel as a genre. Fiction appears herein as an assemblage of humanities and social scientific forms that combine to provide a fuller picture of political crisis. Odenigbo and Olanna's professorial salon, like Ugwu's precocious authorial talents, reference the novel's heteroglossia. Ugwu's *Bildung* puts the experience of warfare on the novel's interdisciplinary curriculum. More than a participant observer, he is an expert whose authority derives from an intimate relation to his object of study, a relation that social science must disavow to preserve objectivity and analytic distance. Ugwu's education is not only thoroughly sentimentalized but also rooted in a mentoring model that looks downright populist when compared to the university program for generating accredited experts.

His mentorship begins in the novel's first chapter and in the *locus classicus* of postcolonial fiction – a library filled with tomes acquired in the course of a colonial education.[37] This archive appears as the

---

[37] Among the contrasting precedents for this setting is the library in Tayeb Salih's *Season of Migration to the North*, with its "four walls from floor to ceiling ... filled, shelf upon shelf, with books and more books," from Gibbon to Woolf, "[n]ot a single Arabic book" but instead "[a] graveyard. A mausoleum" of colonial materials (136–38). From these volumes, Salih's leading man Mustafa Sa'eed acquires an insider's knowledge of English writing, which he transforms into an insurgent weapon.

very definition of the quiet, well-lit place: "Sunlight streamed in through the windows, and from time to time a gentle breeze lifted the curtains" (Adichie *Half* 5). As is typical in such settings, the holdings on display in Odenigbo's library range widely, encompassing everything from statistics to history, from *Non-Parametric Methods* to *An African Survey*, from *The Great Chain of Being* to *The Norman Impact upon England* (6). As if to demonstrate the extent to which the library dominates the house in which Ugwu works and grows up, Adichie lingers over books that spill out into bedrooms and hallways, piled high on "shelves and tables ... on the sink and cabinets," and "stacked from floor to ceiling in the study" (6). The eclectic holdings of this home-cum-library encourage omnivorous reading habits: Ugwu avidly studies everything from *The Mayor of Casterbridge* to the *Socialist Review*, from books Odenigbo recommends to magazines scrounged as the household flees east to escape the Nigerian army. As the country lurches into war, Ugwu reads *The Pickwick Papers* in an attempt to make the change "hurtling toward him ... slow down" (175). After the war has been lost, he salvages what he can from Odenigbo's library, its books having been "heaped together before being set on fire" and laments the books burned in Nsukka's main square (418–22).

Odenigbo shows Ugwu how the library can be used to "decolonize our education" by explaining how to read against the grain (Adichie *Half* 75). "How can we resist exploitation," he catechizes his pupil, "if we don't have the tools to understand exploitation?" (11). Ugwu internalizes what he is told: although he may not understand Odenigbo's argument that "America was to blame for other countries not recognizing Biafra," Ugwu reproduces "Master's words ... with authority, as though they were his" (295). He persists in this mode when composing his book: the last chapters of the novel find Ugwu listening attentively "to the conversations in the evenings, writing in his mind what he would later transfer to paper" (399). Ugwu's dedication for "The Book" affirms the mentoring model by recycling one of Odenigbo's favored phrases: "For Master, my good man" (433).

Like any student, Ugwu comes into his own by submitting to a power relationship. To the habitual dynamic of mentor and pupil, however, *Half of a Yellow Sun* adds a sentimental supplement: Ugwu's motivating sense of guilt for his actions as a conscript in the Biafran army. When he is first pressed into action, being a teenage soldier perversely echoes life in the academic home. Ugwu's battalion has its headquarters in a former primary school where, in one of the classrooms, he finds a copy of the *Narrative of the Life of Frederick Douglass*. He handles this volume just like those from Odenigbo's library. He reads with care, sometimes out loud, and commits key sentences to memory, such as, "Even if it cost me my life, I was determined to read. Keep the black man away from the books, keep us ignorant, and we would always be his slaves" (Adichie *Half* 360). That Douglass's volume is itself a story of education provides a sharp contrast: where readers find in the *Narrative* an account of the triumph of mind over body, liberal subjectivity over corporeal definition and suffering, *Half of a Yellow Sun* features an expert whose authority derives at least in part from violence in which his body seems to act on its own accord.

The platoon treats Ugwu as the class nerd: his teenage comrades mock his bookish habits and tear out pages from Douglass's *Narrative* to use as rolling paper. Orders to kill and maim interrupt this middle-school dynamic soon enough, however, and the novel enlists Ugwu in wartime atrocity when he and his comrades cram into a saloon, drink steadily, and gang rape the "bar girl." Ugwu is goaded into participating: "[A]ren't you a man?" his comrades taunt. Much to his dismay, he achieves "a self-loathing release" (Adichie *Half* 365). This display of force confirms that Ugwu is not in charge of his own development: "He was not living his life; life was living him" (364).

Rather than undermining his authority, the memory of the rape helps turn Ugwu into a writer.[38] After escaping the battlefield, he writes in order to repress: "[T]he more he wrote the less he dreamed" (Adichie *Half* 398). Precisely because reminders of what he has done are ever present – he even learns that his sister has been raped and beaten to death by soldiers (421) – this process of sublimation proves reproducible. The internalized voices of his mentors are cops in Ugwu's head: he knows only too well what Odenigbo, Olanna, and her sister Kainene "would say, what [they] would do to him, feel about him, if [they] ever knew about the girl in the bar" (399). What they cannot know, he must remember – an act of atrocity that produces guilt that yields writing. The very title of his book confirms the productivity of this formula: "*The World Was Silent When We Died*. It haunted him, filled him with shame. It made him think about that girl in the bar," which makes him continue working (396).

If the remembrance of rape reinforces the dynamic of mentoring, and with it the authority such discipline bestows upon Ugwu, there is no character in *Half of a Yellow Sun* capable of describing how this process works or what it means. For that we must rely on the novel's narrator, a figure who represents the pedagogy of mentoring and the violence of war, and who explains that the two converge to generate Ugwu's unaccredited expertise. Such an author-function has been widely disseminated in recent years. It is associated with names as divergent as those of Aminatta Forna and Dave Eggers. Forna's

---

[38] Adichie acknowledges the precedent of Chukwuemeka Ike's 1976 Biafran novel *Sunset at Dawn*, but where that earlier novel narrates the transformation of its Dr. Amilo Kanu from medical researcher into field commander, and thus labors to explain how professionals under duress might evolve into battlefield heroes, *Half of a Yellow Sun* reverses that story when it turns Ugwu's time spent as a soldier into part of his training to become an author (Ike *Sunset* 71–72, 210–17).

name is on the byline of journalistic commentary about international justice and on the cover of both a memoir of political turmoil in Sierra Leone and the 2006 novel "of how it was to live as a woman in our country's past" called *Ancestor Stones*. The acknowledgments at the close of Forna's novel present the novelist as interviewer and researcher as well as writer of a book that, like Adichie's, does more than represent the disempowered. Both authors, and both novels, are in the business of representing the victims of state crisis as the authors of their own stories (Forna *Ancestor* 318). *What Is the What* (2006) is in this business too: its preface describes Eggers responding to Sudanese Lost Boy Valentino Achak Deng's appeal for "an author to help [him] write [his] biography." *What Is the What* proclaims itself both autobiography and novel, and indeed the book ratifies the sort of author-function activated by both genres, as the preface suggests when it explains how Deng and Eggers came to work together. "[I]n spite of the public-speaking opportunities available, I wanted to reach out to a wider audience by telling the story of my life in book form," Deng says in the preface. "Because I was not a writer, I asked Mary [Williams, of the Lost Boys Foundation] to put me in touch with an author" (Eggers *What* xiii). Though such examples indicate the current ubiquity of an author-function defined by its eagerness to give voice to unaccredited experts akin to Ugwu, in truth, fiction has been generating something like this authority for a while. A necessarily truncated genealogy will suggest something of the twentieth-century precedence for a recent novel such as *Half of a Yellow Sun*.

EXPERTS IN ATROCITY

Where social science displaces emotional investment onto fiction in order to claim scholarly distance, *Half of a Yellow Sun* uses Ugwu's guilt to sentimentalize education. This recipe for generating expertise is echoed by what amounts to the novel's guiding philosophy, put into words by Olanna's grandfather, who "used to say, about difficulties he had gone through, 'It did not kill me, it made me knowledgeable'" (Adichie *Half* 347). By disavowing such a sentimental supplement, political science makes it appear as though knowledge and credentials are the same thing. *Half of a Yellow Sun* is not the only novel to pull those concepts apart and to propagate the idea of an uncredentialed expert of the war zone.

Yvonne Vera's 2002 fiction *The Stone Virgins* identifies a kind of knowing-by-suffering that it compares to a more conventional archival mode of "replicating histories" (184).[39] The novel concludes with an extended reflection on the contrasting knowledge and skill possessed by Nonceba, a victim of atrocity, and Cephas, a researcher for the National Museums and Monuments agency in Zimbabwe who welcomes Nonceba into his home. While Cephas clips newspapers and annotates documents, Nonceba shuffles through fragmented memories of her assault. She considers that Cephas may imagine "he knows exactly what happened" to her based on his rescarches. "He knows nothing about the here of it," she demurs, and presents the secret she carries as a more multifaceted, more highly specialized form of understanding than an accredited expert could ever possess: "The feel of that here. The sight of it. The moment so full of here" (156). Meanwhile, Cephas wonders if his expertise can actually prepare him to help Nonceba. He contemplates retreating to the museum and his "restorations of ancient kingdoms" (184). "A new nation needs to restore the past," the narrator announces on the last page of *The Stone Virgins*, identifying a link that the novel's characters struggle to forge between

---

[39] I have borrowed this term "knowing by suffering" from Das's study of Indian partition violence (*Life* 75–78).

the specialized knowledge involved in archival reconstruction and the equally particular understanding connoted by the memory of atrocity (184). Like Adichie's *Half of a Yellow Sun*, Vera's novel offers the home as the setting for expert education, Cephas and Nonceba slowly figuring out how to work together in a relationship that is "undefined ... pleasurable ... supportive" (171). "She finds strength through each of his unexpected gestures," the narrator sums up, and they are "embraced by an innocence born of the tragic circumstances of their unity" (171).

Memoir-style child-soldier novels ranging from Ken Saro-Wiwa's 1985 *Sozaboy* to Chris Abani's 2007 *Song for Night* offer equally risky experiments in relating discrepant forms of knowledge. They represent thoughtful, self-reflexive killers as graduates of unnervingly specialized modes of education. *Sozaboy*'s Mene takes part in a catechistic exercise that Saro-Wiwa renders as a kind of linguistic discipline: "Just I will repeat what Bullet or the soza captain have said. And I will say it carefully with my mouth and with style so that if you hear me talking by that time, you will even think that I am oyibo man" (93). Time spent soldiering – such as it is, "sitting in this pit for a month" – leads Mene to feel he is "beginning to know one or two things" (93). He renders – not to say archly parodies – professionalization in what Saro-Wiwa calls the novel's famously "rotten English": "Even the big big grammar that used to confuse me proper proper before no dey confuse me too much again. Even, I can speak some big grammar sometimes myself" (93). Abani's child soldier My Luck is a mine sweeper whose training involves complete self-mastery: "[F]irst our eyes were made keen so we could notice any change in the terrain no matter how subtle ... Having trained our eyes, they began to train our legs, feet, and toes" (*Song* 32–33). Finally, "a week before graduation," My Luck and his colleagues are "led into surgery" where their vocal chords are severed so that if one of them gets blown up by a mine they neither alert the enemy to their presence nor "scare each other with ... death screams" (35). Mute but articulate, My Luck masters a sophisticated sign language and narrates his own tale: "I am not a genius," he notes, "I am just better versed at the interior monologue" than most (21).[40]

Timothy Mo's 1991 *The Redundancy of Courage* establishes the basis for including battlefield know-how in multivariate analyses of crisis. This novel narrates the invasion of East Timor as, first, a war about American influence; second, a demonstration of revolutionary nationalism; and, third, a conflict whose causality is of less importance than its effective revision of local social organization. Although the novel's final pages offer an account of the war that features U.S. submarines and deep water channels, the bulk of Mo's tale is devoted to showing how group hierarchy changes during battle. The ground-level plot centers on the participant observation of a marginally successful hotelier named Adolph Ng. When he joins the conflict, Mo's hero turns a "Chinese" affinity for "the make-shift, the third-hand, the modified, the refurbished" into the basis of mastery over the jungle booby trap, the guerrilla bomb, the cobbled-together mine, the "Adolf Ng special" (169, 311). With this skill, he not only earns a place among the rebels but also effectively goes native: he acquires "tribal eyes," a way of seeing that Mo associates with political conviction as well as tactical acuity (275). Whatever geopolitical calculations prompted fighting in East Timor, Mo's tale suggests, they cannot explain the reworking of ethnic stereotype and expert knowledge that allows rebels to know whose orders to follow and who is best equipped to carry out

---

[40] There are social scientists who think about child soldiers in this way as well. See Meagher's consideration of the "Bakassi Boys" and "property rights" in Nigeria's Abia state, as well as Peters and Richards's interviews with Sierra Leone "youth combatants" (Meagher "Hijacking" 96; Peters and Richards "Why" 183).

those orders. It stands to reason that any attempt to intervene in East Timor ought to be informed by a sense of how war has modified East Timorese populations. Mo's novel provides just a glimpse of what such insight would entail.

James Kelman's 2001 *Translated Accounts* suggests that garnering such information from unstable locales contributes to an ever-more comprehensive set of generic characters and plots, stereotypes of crisis that emerge with awful predictability when states collapse. By providing a veritable catalog of the characters, settings, and scenarios habitually appearing in literary and political scientific treatments of instability, Kelman turns his novel into a kind of laboratory for the comparison of what different players in failed states know. "Securitys" contrast their expertise with that of football players and "logicians, we killers"; foreign VIPS, lawyers, and journalists teach the locals to "respect humanity"; a witness treats memories of those killed and tortured as most valuable knowledge and is bereft when it "slips from [his] mind" (319, 284, 315). Familiar scenes of killing and rape, tenderness and domestic routine fill out fifty-four fragmented chapters, all set in an unnamed "occupied territory or land where a form of martial law appears in operation" (ix). Kelman's novel does not vest absolute authority with its putative translator and collator of eyewitness statements. Instead, *Translated Accounts* represents fractious engagement among various narrative agents, many of whom refer to one another quasi-professionally as "colleagues" rather than as citizens or neighbors, and who knowingly "irritate international experts," acknowledge that "[they] take part in [their] own subjection," and observe "'Official politics' is 'you must listen politics'" (87, 306, 170). "I could be anywhere," says one character, underscoring that state failure is no more a uniquely third-world phenomenon than failed-state fiction is a third-world genre, and succinctly capturing the scale and scope of a political scientific project like the "Failed States Index" (307).

Similar knowledge about state crisis can be construed very differently, as these examples show. What these works share, however, is an impetus to help readers recognize the secrets that characters possess as the bases for discrepant forms of expertise. In this, they collaborate with *Half of a Yellow Sun* in shaping an alternative to the habit of attributing specialized knowledge to those with university degrees. This is a paradoxical democratization of expert hierarchy, no doubt, which draws attention to the insights of unaccredited characters but still maintains that their understanding has value because it is specialized. Expertise against expertise, we might call it, a counterdiscourse that widens the circle but never extends to include the social totality. When fiction grants a range of types – the child soldier, the witness to atrocity – authority to contest the accounts of credentialed professionals, it supplements the players but does not alter the meritocratic game. One can certainly imagine how the inclusion of experts from below (as it were) would put pressure on the paternal model of international trusteeship (from above). So long as those new participants are regarded as some sort of expert, however, and not as representatives of some undifferentiated "people," the notion that specialized knowledge and governmental authority go hand in hand remains unchanged.

The creation of noncredentialed experts was pioneered by earlier writers. Saadat Hasan Manto's Indian partition stories from the late 1940s and early 1950s forecast an intimacy with atrocity taken more or less for granted in later fiction.[41] They thereby helped establish

---

[41] Zaman observes that the subgenre "literature of partition" lacks the biggest names of South Asian writing in English from the period. Bhattacharya suggests that the likes of Raja Rao, R. K. Nayaran, and Mulk Raj Anand were "too dazed by recent history to make it their material" and, as a result, they hardly deviated from their usual theme of transition from colonialism to independence (cited in Zaman *Divided* 19–21).

a connection between personal life and expert understanding of crises in subsequent novels. His tales establish bloody parallels between the loss of domestic household order and the failure of incipient state organization. In "Colder than Ice," for example, a woman accuses her lover of cheating and he confesses, explaining that he spent the night rioting, that he killed every member of another family but one, an attractive young woman whom he dragged off to rape in private. After some time, however, he realized that she too was dead and that he had been carrying around a corpse (*Mottled* 29).[42] Though small in scope and crisply short in length – sometimes as brief as a page – Manto's tales accumulate to give the sense of massive governmental failure. That there is no official presence in many of these stories does not mean that chaos rules. Instead, social structure emerges through the repetition of similar incidents, habitual personae, and chronic tropes. "Bitter Harvest" induces a pattern from the story of a father who comes home to find "the blood-soaked body of his wife" and "the nearly naked body" of his daughter (143). Enraged, he runs into the street, killing three men with his axe before breaking into a house and pouncing "like a wild beast" on a girl hiding inside (145). Where his daughter's killer was, he now is. The story ends with his victim's own father running into the house, recognizing what is going on (and recognizing his daughter's assailant as well), and rushing back outside, ready to perpetuate a daisy chain of slaughter.[43]

---

[42] Mufti places the "female victim of 'communal' sexual violence" in the context of Manto's fiction as a whole (*Enlightenment* 203).

[43] Das and Nandy gloss Manto's use of female characters in a manner suggestive of Vera's much later plot in *The Stone Virgins*: "Women ... are the media through which men concretise the pact of violence but, because they are not simply things to be looted and plundered but also subjects, they retain the memory of this loot, rape and plunder. The definition of the victim emerges in new relief since the victim is now defined as the object of, as well as the witness to, violence" ("Violence" 193).

By making the regularity of atrocity visible, Manto renders it difficult to bracket as outside the norm. He teaches a pragmatic lesson, one that runs contrary to the habit Gyanendra Pandey discerns among "journalists and other investigators" fond of identifying "exceptional circumstances ... behind such acts of collective violence" (*Routine* 30). Even "riots on the scale and with the frequency that we have seen since the 1980s" have not shaken faith in "the cherished national traditions of nonviolence and peaceful coexistence," Pandey contends (33). "The message of much of the writing on riots in the country since 1947 is the same as that found in the nationalist histories of the pre-Independence period," in contrast to which Pandey would offer a sense of collective violence in India as a "social fact" (32). Manto's fiction suggests that if partition's massacres are no exception, there ought to be continuity between the sorts of administrative practices required to curtail what tends to get called "communal" violence and those more generally responsible for reproducing a stable India. His writing inscribes the possibility, even the probability, of state failure at the very inception of independent Indian administration.

In her journalistic narrative of postcolonial Yugoslavia, Rebecca West's 1941 *Black Lamb and Grey Falcon* provides a significant early precedent for such challenges of self-governance: "The chief problems of Yugoslavia were its poverty and the antagonisms felt by sections of the populations which had different cultures" (603). "Such politics we know very well in Ireland. They grow on a basis of past injustice," West argues. "A proud people acquire a habit of resistance to foreign oppression, and by the time they have driven out their oppressors they have forgotten that agreement is a pleasure and that a society which has attained tranquility will be able to pursue many delightful ends" (82). Formerly colonized populations "continue to wrangle" out of habit, she alleges, "finding abundant material in the odds and ends of injustices that are left over from the period of tyranny and need to be tidied up in one way or another" (82).

West does not offer a recipe for such administrative tidying up, but in her travelogue she does present her readers with a narrative theory for making a link that would become habitual in later fiction between the care of the self and the order of the postcolonial state. To sort out the "bad book" of Yugoslav history, West proposes the "analogy [of] the sexual affairs of individuals" (*Black* 55). Bosnia's colonization by Turkey finds analogy in "a kind of human being, terrifying above all others, who resists by yielding" (301). West works this analogy by parsing her guide's marriage. He is Constantine, a.k.a. Stanislav Vinaver, aide to the Serbian leader Stojadinovic.[44] He fought in World War I ("very gallantly"), is Jewish and is the son of a Russian émigré, and, thus, embodies Yugoslavian multiculture as well as helping to administer it. This paragon is unfortunately married to Gerda, "a stout middle-aged woman, typically German," whose prolific abuse of her husband is authorized by the "conqueror's point of view" (457–58, 800). Gerda is "allergic to Jews," dismisses Serbs as "stupid," gypsies as "dirty and stupid," Slavs as "ungrateful," the poor as "horrible people," and Yugoslavia itself as "only a mish-mash of different peoples who are all quite primitive and low" (466, 64, 507, 660, 62). "But it's precisely because there are so many different peoples that Yugoslavia is so interesting," West interrupts her, "and it is fascinating to see whether they can be organized into an orderly state." "How can you make an orderly state out of so many peoples?" Gerda persists. "They should all be driven out" (662). If the best that can be said of Constantine is that he resists his wife's aggression by

---

[44] The reviewer Stoyan Pribichevich outed Constantine, whose real name West does not herself provide. Pribichevich notes: "'Constantine' was a 'writer and a poet,' as Miss West calls him. But he was first of all Stoyadinovich's official; second, a talker; third, a writer; and fourth, a thinker" (Colquitt "Call" 89n8).

yielding to it to preserve some degree of domestic amity, West is clear that such resistance does not constitute management. When Constantine "bared his throat to Gerda's knife," West writes, "he had offered his loving heart to the service of hate, in order that he might be defeated and innocent" (916). If only, West laments, Constantine could care about himself enough to take care of his state as they both suffer German abuse. Or, to put this in the related terms offered by Adichie in *Half of a Yellow Sun*, if only Constantine and his wife could do a better job of modeling civil discussion about the administrative challenges facing Yugoslavia, even as those challenges increase under pressure of German invasion and dissident unrest.

West confirms that such arguments about how to manage a state in crisis need to be hashed out not only in postcolonies but also in bastions of stability such as England. The Yugoslavian army's battlefield prowess provides her with an exemplary demonstration that she holds up as a model to the British trying to keep things together during the Blitz. Finishing her book in a shell-shocked London, West takes inspiration from Yugoslavia's effort. There was no chance that Yugoslavia could win this fight, West willingly acknowledges, but that it was willing to undertake it regardless is what matters. "The Yugoslav Army never capitulated, although it was destroyed," she contends. "In this war, as in the one before it, they have made out of their defeats great victories" (*Black* 1147–49). "[W]hen I have thought of invasion," she writes, "or when a bomb has dropped near by, I have prayed, 'Let me behave like a Serb'" (1126). With her prayer, West threatens to demote Britain from its status as the epitome of modern nationhood and to treat it as a potentially failed state like any other.[45]

---

[45] This is but one aspect of West's reconsideration of England's geopolitical position. An "exasperated critic" of British imperialism, she identifies its primary sin as transforming colonial populations into "helpless people" and staffing offices with administrators who "regard [their subjects] as children" (1089, 1091).

It would be too much to argue that this prayer alone inaugurates the normative scheme I have identified in later fiction and political science. Yet it is perfectly reasonable to conclude that West signals a different mode of comparison than the older center-periphery scheme that made European nations the inside to their colonial outsides.

Although this brief genealogy from Adichie's novel to West's travel writing casts a focused thematic net, it might motivate a revised account of the relationship between state politics and narrative prose more broadly conceived. It is conventional to think of fiction as putting flesh on the bones of the bourgeois citizen-subject. It is, further, conventional to understand this dynamic as coming undone in the twentieth century. Canonical postcolonial tomes such as Ngũgĩ wa Thiong'o's 1977 *Petals of Blood* and V. S. Naipaul's 1979 *A Bend in the River* confirm the end of what Samir Amin calls the era of anti-imperial "Bandung regimes" and "their bourgeois national project" (*Re-Reading* 129).[46] *Petals of Blood* famously concludes with Ngũgĩ's scholar-activist Karega contemplating the possibility of working-class revolution, uncertain that he has any place in it – "Tomorrow ... tomorrow ... ," he muses (*Petals* 345).[47] The conclusion of Naipaul's novel marks the end of the line via Ferdinand, a well-schooled "évolué" and political officer who sees only bare life in his country's administrative collapse. "We're all going to hell," he reports. "Nothing has any meaning ... The bush runs itself" (*Bend* 272).[48]

By portraying what is often described as the "failure" of the postcolonial intellectual to salvage the nation, such novels also provide

---

[46] These are among the most recognizable fictions from that moment Said describes when "disenchantment" with third-world nationalism "overtook many people during the 1970s and 1980s" (*Culture* 265).

[47] The novel is set in a city undergoing what might be called industrialization without modernization. Gikandi takes up this neocolonial dynamic at length (*Ngũgĩ* 135–48).

[48] For Suleri, Naipaul's is the neocolonial novel par excellence: it displays an "uncanny ability to map the complicity between postcolonial history and its imperial past" (*Rhetoric* 156).

motivation to grant that figure a revised job description.⁴⁹ *Half of a Yellow Sun* takes up that challenge. Instead of characters whose principal function is guiding a national citizenry, Adichie's novel considers whether its protagonists demonstrate the expertise to grasp why states fail and thus, perhaps, how to manage them. A genealogical glance towards partition writing and *Black Lamb and Grey Falcon* begs questions about whether we fully understand the social function being imagined for the highly educated heroes and heroines in even earlier novels. Failed-state fiction invites speculation about whether the novel might long have been more interested in producing managers than citizens.⁵⁰

With such speculation in mind, we might better appreciate what is at stake in failed-state fiction's delegation of expert authority. When novels take up the political scientific campaign to normalize state crisis, they also ask all sorts of questions about what expert agency looks like in this context. Literature provides alternatives to the London School of Economics researcher and the United Nations policy wonk with characters like Rebecca West's Constantine, Timothy Mo's Adolph Ng, and Chimamanda Ngozi Adichie's Ugwu. These heroes are unaccredited analysts, unwilling participants in civil wars, and flawed government flacks. Fiction strives to make their expertise intelligible as specialized knowledge every bit as consequential as that of development economists and political

---

⁴⁹ That story of failure emerges out of Fanon's description of the "unpreparedness of the educated classes" in "The Pitfalls of National Consciousness" (*Wretched* 148–49). Cheah reads Ngũgĩ as positioning the postcolonial intellectual as a proxy for the nation as a whole (*Spectral* 365).

⁵⁰ Along these lines, Armstrong and Tennenhouse argue that both American and British novel traditions in the eighteenth and nineteenth centuries "registered a growing tension between 'the people' and 'the population'" ("Problem" 16). They identify a mid-nineteenth-century form of the novel that served as "the means of bringing the problem of population from the background squarely into the foreground of the novel, where it blocked and dispersed the liberal fantasy of building a nation one individual at a time" (13).

theorists. In so doing, failed-state fiction may be said to promote a dramatic revision of the division of labor that abides in policy circles. These novels do not alter the political scientific formula in which experts speak on behalf of populations rather than speaking as the people. But when fiction broaches the question of who qualifies as an expert in the first place, it identifies a problem political science has yet to fully think through. Fiction claims a special understanding of state politics by demonstrating an ability to rethink the hierarchical arrangements of meritocratic rule.

CHAPTER 3

The novelistic management of inequality in the age of meritocracy

Recent fiction that contemplates how to live with inequality reprises one of the quintessential dilemmas of liberal thought, but does so in a geopolitical context markedly different from the one described by Adam Smith. Classic liberalism frames inequality as an administrative challenge for developing nations. Civil government first emerges, according to Smith, to defend "those who have some property against those who have none at all" (*Wealth* 715). The sovereign's duty, he argues, is to ensure that the state does not sanction such unequal conditions. Smith does not imagine a state that responds to inequity by redistributing property, of course, but rather one that makes "every individual feel himself perfectly secure in the possession of every right which belongs to him" regardless of station or wealth (723).

Although contemporary governments still espouse this goal, their success is ever more understood in comparative terms. Studies including Richard Wilkinson and Kate Pickett's *The Spirit Level* (2010) and reports such as the International Monetary Fund's semiannual *World Economic Outlook* parse inequality while assessing its connection to stability and effective governance conceived on a global scale. In recent interviews and in his 2010 book *Ill Fares the Land*, meanwhile, Tony Judt identifies the collective need to "rediscover a language of dissent" capable of pressuring governments to address "inequalities of opportunity, whether between young and old or between those with different skills or from different regions of a country" (Judt and Božič "Way" 14). In addition to going global, the management of inequality has been thoroughly professionalized. The contest to administer involves the relationship between professional organizations and the populations they study and disagreements among academics and bureaucrats regarding how best to conduct surveys and to offer policy recommendations.

Fictions that grapple with contemporary professional politics often proceed by telling stories about experts from former colonies who work for international agencies and study at world-class universities. This allows them to consider two sorts of inequality. First, novels about the integration of universities and the professional workplace typically observe that increasing the diversity of the expert class alters conversations taking place in policy meetings and the hallways of academe. In these fictions, heterogeneity within education and government challenges at least some of the racist conventions of earlier imperial versions of international rule. Second, such novels also open the question of what ultimately legitimates the persistent division of labor between institutionally certified professionals and the populations they represent and administer. Michael Ondaatje's *Anil's Ghost* (2000) considers that part of the problem by staging a narrative experiment in which accredited specialists come to rely on the insights of a particularly talented layperson. In so doing, the novel does not reproduce the old anthropological mode, in which worldly professionals lean upon native informants. In this novel, to parachute in with degree in hand and the resources of an international agency is no guarantee of authority *in situ*. Instead, Ondaatje describes a temporary alliance of variously expert team members, only some of whom happen to possess university credentials. Any member of the team can redirect the collaborative project, which means that no team member's authority is absolute.

When novels improvise hierarchical arrangements in this way, they imagine what it might mean to introduce incrementally greater flexibility to the professional division of labor that structures not only science and social science research but also governments and administrations of all sorts. *Anil's Ghost*, like the rest of the novels discussed in this chapter, provides a literary counterpart to any number of other experimental approaches to administration now current in social scientific and public administrative circles. Bruno Latour, James Scott, and Anna Lowenhaupt Tsing have all published notable arguments about hierarchical relations in their respective fields. The collaborative effort *Acting in an Uncertain World* by Michel Callon, Pierre Lascoumes, and Yannick Barthe offers a particularly evocative description of "regimes and modalities of consultation" other than those currently enforced by government regulations and professional codes of conduct (259). These scholars imagine doing "without the break between representatives and represented" and establishing "more diversified, more frequent, and deeper consultation" among experts and the populations they describe and manage (259).

Fiction collaborates in this reform effort by describing interpersonal relations among researchers, bureaucrats, and laypeople in a sentimental vernacular more habitually associated with the home than with the workplace. Bruce Robbins sees the resulting "confusion of sympathy" as the most provocative aspect of fiction concerned with professionalism. He contends that by rendering the world of work in sentimental terms, novels present scenarios in which "any stranger may turn out to be a member of your family and should be treated as such" ("Very" 435). Robbins hopes such confusion will lead experts working the circuits of globalization to rethink their affiliation to members of the diverse populations they encounter. In a series of writings, he mulls over "whether this fit between professional affectivity and geographical globality ... [represents] anything other than a new social hierarchy" ("Village" 23). While Robbins hopes that it does, Timothy Brennan is convinced it does not. Brennan argues that contemporary literature promotes aesthetic discrimination that only serves to reinforce existing forms of cultural capital. The novel's global reach is best understood not as an extension of sympathy but rather as an expansionist policy in which "hermeneutically rich," formally difficult novels marginalize less obviously challenging volumes of realist prose.[1] This campaign ensures that the "best" literary product will also make apparent the need for literary scholars to interpret it (*Home* 55). Generating such demand helps in its small way to reinforce a broader distinction between specialists and laypeople that benefits all professionals (*Wars* 210).[2]

Both Brennan and Robbins consider it desirable for fiction to promote affective bonds across borders. Both imagine that even fiction that does so risks reproducing a professional division of labor. What bears noting, however, is the expectation that properly written and interpreted novels concerned with the work of experts would avoid reproducing hierarchical distinctions. This should surprise us, and the fact that Robbins and Brennan each seem to take that expectation for granted suggests a disciplinary blind spot.[3]

---

[1] The phrase "extension of sympathy" belongs to Appiah, who associates novel-reading with a revived cosmopolitanism ("Cosmopolitan" 203).

[2] Literature and literary criticism have played their part "in developing the concept of cosmopolitanism, whose ethical aura," Brennan maintains, "is largely an export from the humanities into other, more technical or policy-oriented formations, including branches of the social sciences and (outside the university) of government and business" (*Wars* 207–08).

[3] Literary scholarship about contemporary cosmopolitanism tends not to resolve this problem so much as to shuttle between the Robbins and Brennan positions. Some scholars continue to hope that literature will show the way to more egalitarian global relations

Meritocracy is built on a contradiction between entrenched inequality and an equally entrenched belief in talent, as both critics recognize. Fiction, no matter what plots it contains or how it is distributed, read, and taught, cannot simply wish away that bind. Novels such as Ondaatje's *Anil's Ghost* ask readers to tolerate the thought that literature may depict genuine friendships across geographical divides while also depicting reproducible forms of social hierarchy. From the point of view of certain orthodoxies – both liberal and anti-liberal – that proposition looks either hopelessly contradictory or politically dangerous. I am, however, convinced that it is precisely in advancing such a proposition that literature teaches us about the contemporary circumstances of, and possibilities for, global rule.

When contemporary fiction asks how recent geopolitical trends generate new possibilities for working relations, it extends a line of experimentation devoted to chronicling change in unanticipated alliances during the age of empire. *Anil's Ghost* belongs in a genealogy that includes Rabindranath Tagore's *The Home and the World* (1915/1985), the late nineteenth-century fiction of women's education and domestic reform *Kamala* (1894/1998) by Krupabai Satthianadhan, and E. M. Forster's story of class and capital, *Howards End* (1910/1985). Like *Anil's Ghost*, these novels present affective bonds that rework existing distributions of power. In all of these novels, change comes from unexpected friendships among professionals and their sometimes unaccredited collaborators. Turning to the imperial past makes it possible to see more clearly that this way of describing administration has participated in revising it. Taken-for-granted configurations in contemporary novels once had to be imagined and explained, it is crucial to recall: paradoxes that might appear incidental to recent fiction may well be rather more constitutive.

(Appiah *Ethics* 246), while others confirm that it has so far failed to do so (Gikandi "Globalization" 632, 644; Cheah "Cosmopolitanism" 486).

WE ARE ALL EXPERTS

Anil's Ghost is less prescriptive in its representation of interpersonal relations than analytic. It is less a conduct manual than a narrative laboratory, which reads as if designed to test the limits of sympathy amidst hierarchy. It offers no glimpses of shared humanity, but rather strives to understand how unequal relations can change while remaining structured by inequality. The ingredients in the novel's experiment suggest the geopolitical stakes: it brings together Anil, a United Nations (U.N.) forensic pathologist born in, and newly returned to, Sri Lanka; Sarath, a local archeologist in the employ (if not under the control) of the Sri Lankan government; Gamini, an ER surgeon ravaged by grief and addled by self-administered pharmaceuticals; Palipana, a disgraced but brilliant historian; Chitra, a young researcher who has written on the growth of pupae; and Ananda, a sculptor-cum-miner-cum-heavy-drinking-widower hired to reconstruct facial features from a damaged skull.[4] Ondaatje considers what can happen when such a catalog of worldly experts engage in a group assignment.

By foregrounding their discrepancies, *Anil's Ghost* makes the connections that emerge among these experts seem ever more noteworthy. Sarath and Gamini are estranged brothers, Palipana is Sarath's mentor, Ananda is recommended to Anil by Palipana, and, like Gamini, has lost a lover to the Sri Lankan Civil War. The book gains narrative momentum by gradually disclosing sentimental bonds that form among the members of this cast as they start collaborating on a shared task. The project of identifying a war victim is what brings them together. The novel's use of this project

---

[4] Where Siddiqi argues that the novel "privileges a personal aesthetic response to political violence" (*Anxieties* 216), it seems clear to me that *Anil's Ghost* thoroughly professionalizes the personal. For a thorough representation of the complexity of Anil's personal and professional life, see Sanghera ("Touching").

has given pause to critics who wish Ondaatje was more interested in explaining Sri Lankan violence than in imagining expert alliance.[5] Truly, the novel appears incapable of parsing the conflict. "The reason for war was war" is the tome's refrain (Ondaatje *Ghost* 43). There is a "casual sense of massacre" in Sri Lanka, the narrator reports. The country does not move forward but persists in "a rocking, self-burying motion" (283, 157). Despite its refusals to explain Sri Lankan instability, *Anil's Ghost* is far from apolitical. Civil war is simply not the scale on which its politics operates.

Instead, the novel reiterates a lesson taught by fictions of state failure: wartime is an excellent setting in which to investigate the flexibility of affective relations engendered by professional work. One set of scenes and one relationship in particular stands out from the rest in demonstrating how a sentimental idiom enables *Anil's Ghost* to begin rethinking the dynamics of expert hierarchy. About two thirds of the way through the book, Anil watches Ananda reconstruct a war victim's skull. She watches with a kind of awe. Despite their widely divergent backgrounds, despite Ananda's lack of formal training, despite the fact that just days before he had been working bent over in a cramped mining tunnel, the university-educated and U.N.-employed Anil recognizes a kindred spirit when she sees Ananda at work on the skull. Even as she notes his reliance on impoverished tools – "various household objects" such as pencil erasers – she credits his "technique" as worthy of the name (Ondaatje *Ghost* 165–66).

As she observes him, so he observes her, bending over her worktable "looking though those thick spectacles at her calipers, the weight charts, as if he were within the hush of a museum" (Ondaatje *Ghost* 170). The ability to attend closely indicates

---

[5] See Derrickson ("Untruth") and Kanaganayakam ("Defense").

a worldly "mind of science" that has made its mark on Ananda's body: "Yesterday she had noticed how delicate his fingers were, dyed ochre as the result of his work" (170). Because Anil recognizes Ananda as a fellow scientist, she is "in no way appalled" when he picks up the skeleton she has taken to calling Sailor and carries "it in his arms" (170). There had been times when, "locked in her investigations and too focused by hours of intimacy," Anil too "would need to reach forward and lift Sailor into her arms, to remind herself he was like her" (170). Sympathy, Ondaatje suggests, not only pertains among experts but also between experts and their objects. Specialized labor is saturated with sentimentality.

Once the novel trains readers to understand this, it presents the more challenging test of figuring out the appropriate context for grasping the significance of such sentiment. *Anil's Ghost* offers a series of concluding chapters, each of which promises to contain the narrative within an alternate frame.[6] Taken together, these endings constitute a form of auxesis, a gradual intensification of an aesthetic impulse that makes it clear this representation of expert work is reflexively literary. In one ending, Anil compiles her report on Sailor, which proves politically unpopular enough that it ends up costing her collaborator Sarath his life. She, however, escapes the country before the government lowers the boom. This is the stereotypical ending to a U.N. consultant's visit: "The American or the Englishman gets on a plane and leaves. That's it ... That's enough reality for the West" (Ondaatje *Ghost* 285–86).[7] This conclusion

---

[6] On the novel's multiple endings, Cook speaks for the critical majority: "It is of great significance that Anil's departure does not constitute the ending" and that "the story continues in Sri Lanka" ("Spectre" 115). For Ganapathy-Doré, this conclusion confirms that no one character's "story is more or less important than the other for the narrator" ("Fathoming" 7). See also Burton ("Archive" 49).

[7] With this and other such gestures, *Anil's Ghost* provincializes European influence, argues Daiya (*Violent* 208–09).

asserts that no amount of sympathy can overcome the basic precept that membership in the institutions of the global elite trumps any other criteria when it comes to professional hierarchy.

That some specialists are more equal than others is a lesson as old as professionalism itself. "Professional society is based on merit," the historian Harold Perkin affirms, "but some acquire merit more easily than others" (*Rise* 4). Not even Thomas Friedman's flattened world violates this axiom. Although Friedman contends that outsourcing, wireless, and other techniques and technologies enable more people than ever to capitalize on "talents that before the flattening of the world often rotted on the docks of Bombay and Calcutta," it seems equally true to him that there are specialists whose work cannot be outsourced – he calls these lucky souls "untouchables" and explains that one generally finds them in close proximity to European and American research universities (*World* 205, 43).[8] Friedman's "untouchables" are necessarily invested in the continued health of their home institutions and in the mechanisms of meritocracy those universities promote. But their self-interest is not only conservative. Belief in the value of expertise regardless of who demonstrates it furthers the demographic changes that have made the professions less preserves of white men. This belief even helps to transform social hierarchy as older class- and race-based systems give way to a political economy governed by experts around the planet.[9]

If the first of Ondaatje's endings presents this world system in terms of a stark contrast between jet-setting elites and third-world

---

[8] The paradox is neatly reproduced by Friedman's contention that such institutions are the best equipped for "nurturing individuals who can compete and thrive in a flat world" (243). See Sklair on the composition of this elite (*Transnational* 17).

[9] See Perkin (*Third*). See Spivak on one especially vexed division of labor in the work of Médecins Sans Frontiers, which finds that its doctors "cannot learn all the local languages, dialects, and idioms of the places where they provide help" and depend on translators who double as caregivers employed in the "repetitive work of primary health care" ("Righting" 524).

realities, the last of the novel's several conclusions suggests the inverse valuation. Ananda returns to yet another specialized line of work, painting the eyes on monumental statues of Buddha. As it depicts his labor, the novel shifts into a metaphysical vein. The war becomes a matter of "demons, specters of retaliation" (*Ghost* 304). The Buddha's "pure sad glance" affords Ananda a vision of the "fibres of natural history around him" (307). He sees through the statue's eyes to a reality usually obscured by the civil war's violence. He watches "rain miles away" and detects the "tiniest of hearts" beating in the birds that fly through it (307). Ananda knows that this is an idealized view: it is "seductive," he notes, and the daze it induces worries the child helping him with his painting. "He felt the boy's concerned hand on his. This sweet touch from the world" (307).

Here is escapism to parallel Anil's flight – or to trump it: it is certainly possible to read the novel as valorizing Ananda's subaltern position and his recuperative power as a figure conjoining the aesthetic and the metaphysical.[10] This interpretation is at least as well founded as one that privileges Anil's timely departure, complete with its invocation of institutional sanction. Because *Anil's Ghost* ends – at last – with Ananda's vision, we may even be tempted to read it as valorizing the underdog who beats out his more established colleagues. Plural versions of the cosmopolitan professional generate plural forms of hierarchy and lead to a contest among competing imperatives.

We might better appreciate how much play fiction has introduced to professional hierarchy by remembering how many recent novels

---

[10] Or, as Burrows does, to read the endings as thematizing "the epistemological horizons of the West," which are not open wide enough to "listen to" or "acknowledge" "the whispered histories of postcolonial subjects" ("Heteroptic" 176). See also Farrier ("Gesturing" 92). And see Marinkova ("Perceiving") on the novel's "micropolitical" answer to the global "macropolitics" of difference.

have been interested in portraying comparable experiments in expert collaboration. Examples include Tessa Quayle and her muck-raking allies in John le Carré's *The Constant Gardener* (2001); Piya Roy and her marine biology crew in Amitav Ghosh's *The Hungry Tide* (2005); the squabbling families and genetic researchers in Zadie Smith's *White Teeth* (2000); and the corporate officers, hi-tech entrepreneurs, and savvy investigators who populate *The Business* by Iain Banks (1999). Collaborators in *The Constant Gardener* range from rough and ready activists in Europe and East Africa to le Carré's typically down-in-the-mouth spies and diplomats. *The Hungry Tide* features a university-educated scientist who develops a deeply felt relationship with the illiterate fisherman who serves as her guide. Smith portrays a geneticist whose professional research becomes irretrievably intertwined with the subplots that compose an intergenerational, interracial soap opera involving no fewer than three London families. *The Business* portrays a corporation that imagines the best way to gain a seat at the United Nations is to marry off one of its upwardly mobile executives to the king of a tottering central Asian state. These varied plots demonstrate the flexibility of the premise that professional research and development can generate and solidify profoundly sentimental attachments – even across lines of subordination. They also insist to the last that renovating the dynamics of expert collaboration has unanticipated and potentially significant political effects.

REFORMING RESEARCH

It is my inclination to contextualize rather than to privilege any of *Anil's Ghost*'s endings and to do so in the name of recognizing what they share. Their discrepancies establish a paradoxical parallelism, with each form of escapism and the will to power that it invokes underscoring the profundity of the connection between Anil the jet-setting, board-certified expert and Ananda the local contract worker.[11] Together, these endings pit Anil and Ananda's professional collaboration against the violence of the novel's additional concluding chapters, which feature a Sri Lankan president's assassination and Sarath's torture and murder (Ondaatje *Ghost* 294, 88). The appearance of such self-evidently political events makes it necessary to ask whether professional relations were not themselves already fully politicized.

It can appear that we get to have it both ways in *Anil's Ghost*: we may celebrate the fact that there is no hegemony of the cosmopolitan professional in this novel while, at the same time, allow that relationships among worldly experts are stringently hierarchical. We may do so because at the very moment meritocracy has to face up to the fact that it really does distribute power and resources inequitably, the novel produces political bogeymen in the form of bloodthirsty rebels, a repressive government, and an impotent United Nations. Even if the novel makes it easy to grasp why we might feel uneasy about meritocratic inequality, in other words, *Anil's Ghost* also makes it easy to recognize why we might prefer the disparity of professionalism to the available alternatives.

The sociologists Callon, Lascoumes, and Barthe prefer that disparity because they believe expert hierarchy has democratic potential. They argue that even though protocols for research and development assure professional authority, such rules also grant a certain power to laypeople. Laypeople are objects of study (as is

---

[11] The boy's "sweet touch from the world" recalls Ananda caressing Anil's face "in a way she could recollect no one ever having touched her" and Anil's own healing touch when the distraught Ananda tries to commit suicide (Ondaatje *Ghost* 187). Holding him tight to inject epinephrine, Anil "felt she could speak in any language, he would understand the purpose of any gesture" (197).

Sailor in *Anil's Ghost*). They are the actors whose behavior provides the occasion for research (as are the combatants in Ondaatje's novel). They assist and provide support in ways small and large (Ananda's contribution may well be understood as a hyperbolically visible instance of such auxiliary input). Callon et al. note that if these contributions get downplayed in most accounts of professional methods and work habits, lay influence on expert labor is most visible in scientific experiments and sociological investigations that fail to go exactly according to plan.[12] When Sarath and Anil become aware of how risky their research has become, they find themselves more reliant on adjutants such as Ananda because they have to relocate their lab outside the university, the capital, and the company of accredited experts.

All specialists presume (or at least hope) that they have the authority and know-how to clearly define the parameters and anticipate the outcomes of their study. But invariably, as Callon et al. put it, "disconcerting events occur" (*Acting* 28). Although surprises are likely at all stages of expert endeavor, they are especially likely when research escapes the academy, the classroom, and the laboratory. In the wild, and certainly in the sort of setting dramatized by a novel like *Anil's Ghost*, scholarly investigation causes unanticipated "controversies [that] help to reveal events that were initially isolated and difficult to see" (28). Even in more banal circumstances than those represented in Ondaatje's novel, lobbying by variously interested groups can cause test results to get reevaluated, target populations can move around and create the need to alter data-gathering procedures, or protesters can burst into laboratories even as experiments enter their decisive phase. Callon

---

[12] Like Latour and other contributors to actor-network theory, Law and Callon observe that it can be easier to discern the importance of various contributions to a collaborative project when that project fails to produce the predicted results ("Life" 22).

and his colleagues argue that these and other comparable incidents are best understood not as outside interference but as particularly intrusive forms of lay participation, which help make clear that the allegedly circumscribed and exclusive field of expert research is in actuality part and parcel of a wide-open political domain. When laypeople contribute in these various ways to the "delegative" model of professional society, in which experts work on behalf of others, they shatter the illusion of specialized work as somehow "estranged ... from the world and its turmoil" (48). Once we recognize such lay participation as important, Callon et al. contend, we can stop believing in "the separation of political and scientific spheres" and start generating new models for interaction among expert and lay actors (120).[13]

Anna Tsing's 2005 account of her fieldwork on environmental activism in Indonesia provides a useful demonstration of this project. In *Friction*, Tsing describes how she learned to value the contributions of an interlocutor named Ahmad. Although he is working as a sarong salesman when she meets him, Tsing soon discovers that Ahmad "has been to college, and ... kept up particularly with natural science, philosophy, and religion" (115). Though his market stall may not indicate as much, he is "an educated man" who recognizes Tsing as "a fellow scholastic, with whom he can share serious thoughts" (115). Though she eventually comes to see him similarly, Tsing notes that Ahmad's "discussion of

---

[13] As these scholars imagine it, such reform would yield a political realm both like and unlike the public sphere as conceived by such figures as Arendt, Habermas, and Rawls: "Like the public spaces of Habermas and Arendt, it privileges debate ... Like that of Rawls, it puts on the stage actors who are not solely concerned with their own interest ... But, unlike the public spaces described by these three authors, it does not specify that the participants be persons or individuals divested of every particular quality and detached from their networks of sociability, having bracketed off everything they value and everything to which they are attached, that is to say, everything that makes up their irreducible identity, including their bodies, genes, and emotions ... " (262).

nature conservation would not be recognized by environmental activists" (116). "[T]hey would consider him countrified, quirky, and out touch," despite the fact that their ideas "are consonant in many ways" (116).[14] Ahmad "does not share [the activists'] access to international circuits of environmental information and action," Tsing observes, and she implies that a desire to monopolize such access makes "better recognized intellectuals" reluctant to acknowledge Ahmad's lay opinion (116).

Tsing does not share this reluctance, which allows her to see how lay participation influences environmental science and politics in one corner of Indonesia. Even as she observes how local and international experts constrain the participation of non-specialists, she also finds numerous examples of Ahmad-like contributors to environmental thinking, research, and activism. By providing Ahmad and his ilk with new visibility, and in documenting various ways that local environmental politics and science depend on lay collaboration, Tsing might be thought of as having democratized her research procedures. She could further be thought of as having revealed democratic potential in the hierarchical arrangements governing social life in the region she researches. In a small way, then, her work might be thought of as exerting a democratizing influence on Indonesian environmental study and, to the extent that the state makes decisions about the environment that are influenced by experts, Indonesian politics as well.[15]

---

[14] Both are interested in the "confluence between modern science and Islamic precept," Tsing argues, and seem convinced that these two presumably discordant bodies of thought can be said to "reveal the same truth" (116).

[15] As an indication that Tsing is not so sure how to evaluate the significance of Ahmad's participation, however, it is worth noting that he makes his appearance not in one of the main chapters of her study, but in an interstitial section on "popular environmental knowledge" (116).

As James Scott observes, there are "ironies" involved in efforts to smooth relations among accredited professionals and those possessing the kind of practical skill or seemingly idiosyncratic expertise displayed by Ondaatje's Ananda or Tsing's Ahmad. The first irony, he notes, is that neither practical skill nor specialized knowledge is ever evenly distributed across a population. Even the kinds of know-how that anthropologists call "folk wisdom" or "indigenous technique" depend on a knack or touch "that may not be common" as well as on access to ways of thinking and modes of practice that "may be restricted" (J. C. Scott *Seeing* 334). Tsing's Ahmad and Ondaatje's Ananda are not representatives of some undifferentiated mass or people, although Scott believes that the relative status of such figures can tell outside observers a great deal about the social structures in which they live and work. A second irony is that although the forms of discrepant specialization Scott labels *metis* may appear to be analogs, allies, and competitors of professional disciplines, some of those forms of expertise "depend on key elements of preindustrial life for their elaboration and transmission" (335). Democratizing relations between the likes of Tsing and Ahmad, Anil and Ananda can imperil, or so Scott suggests, the very specialization that unaccredited experts bring to the table.

When he weighs the stakes of reimaging relations between specialists and more or less talented laypeople, Latour comes to the resounding conclusion that, whatever the peril, "[p]olitics is too serious a thing to be left in the hands of the few" (*Reassembling* 253). That said, he also contends that as academics broaden their understanding of who exactly contributes to the expert analyses that inform governmental policy, they ought not to imagine that they are trading the narrow confines of academe for the universal realm of "the Total" (252). Instead, to understand "what it is for a social science to have political relevance" entails new attention to the small groups, "weak ties," and "surprising connections" that experts forge with actors in the course of their labor (252). The definition of "what it is for a social science to have political relevance" depends on how social science (or science, or humanities scholarship for that matter) understands the interpersonal dynamics involved in scholarly research (253).

In gauging the impulse to reform professional privilege, then, it is worth remembering that such revision can make for strange bedfellows. Peter Miller and Nikolas Rose observe that since the 1970s expert authority has been under notably strident attack from a variety of sources on the left as well as the right. Latter-day liberal arguments on behalf of a smaller state have tended to resonate with populist complaints about "the arrogance of government overreach" (*Governing* 210). Social democratic concern about the "lack of effectiveness" of existing administrative programs is surprisingly complemented by the widespread fear that "welfare services actually destroy other forms of social support such as church, community and family" (210). In any number of states around the world, observers have witnessed the emergence of a "new pluralization of 'social' technologies" that have little to do with democratizing authority but rather bespeak a liberal idealization of the "responsible individual and their self-governing community" (212). Instead of centralized decision-making, administrative responsibility has been privatized and disseminated in ways that grant local control to the loudest critics of big government. Callon et al. surely would wish to distinguish their vision of democratic collaboration from an approach in which experts teach laypeople "techniques for active self-management" (Miller and Rose *Governing* 106–07). But it is important to recognize what these differing efforts to undermine the unquestioned authority of experts share. Both conceive of the state as an ongoing experiment, one that can accommodate shifting patterns of authority. Both, further, value small changes in professional practice as well as the sort of minor but telling institutional realignments that might escape the notice of political commentators who care only about revolutionary overhauls of social orders and governmental regimes.

The difference between Callon and colleagues' reform program and that of liberal thinkers resides in how they confront the persistence of hierarchy. Liberalism answers inequality with measures to inculcate a general freedom of opportunity but "social transfers . . . of a very limited character," Foucault notes (*Birth* 143). Wilhelm Röpke spoke of "shifting the center of gravity of governmental action downwards" and of "decentralization in the widest and most comprehensive sense of the word," which Foucault understands as an argument on behalf of a democratization of enterprise, not a redistribution of expertise (cited in Foucault *Birth* 148, 157n61). Despite its populist rhetoric, liberal governance, both classical and neo-, relies on intervention from above to reproduce the entrepreneurial behaviors of individuals below. The reform proffered by Callon et al. is also top down, but it has nothing to do with extolling individual agency. Instead, it involves greater awareness of "attachments and entanglements," myriad modes of collaboration, and "relations of reciprocity" among specialists and laypeople (*Acting* 265). By renovating professional hierarchy, Callon et al. hope, experts and their subject populations might work together to redefine the very terms of social organization, including the liberal categories of the individual and the market.[16]

That their collaboration may be infused with sentimentality seems as self-evident to Callon and company as it does to the characters in

---

[16] "Markets and delegative democracy work hand in glove," they argue, and if one changes the way delegating to experts operates, one changes the way in which market society operates too (237).

Anil's Ghost. Instead of dispassionately hierarchical arrangements between lay populations and the experts employed by governments, corporations, and universities charged with their management, Callon et al. envision entanglements that combine reciprocity and inequality reminiscent of relations "between parents and the children they care for, who often are unable to articulate well-formed sentences" (*Acting* 265). If this comparison makes it appealing to imagine that select fictions and particular social science studies may be allied in an effort to generate a more sympathetic dynamic of professional administration, it also begs questions about the historical precedence that makes such familial figures of sentimentality available in the first place – and, further, about fiction's ability to offer an analogical model that does not smack so much of paternalism.

IMPERIAL FEELING

By granting the professional's cold, calculating gaze a sympathetic aspect, novelists and social scientists alike make it easier to talk about what different sorts of specialists share without undermining the imperative to organize specialized work hierarchically. Although *Anil's Ghost* contains its representation of professionalism in a story about one group of experts in a singular location, it also introduces a more general rule about the professional woman as the very ideal of the sympathetic expert. Anil appears not as a contradiction – the woman doing the man's job – but as an upgrade – the woman who demonstrates how the job should be done. Anil models a combination of specialized technique and sympathetic care – with the stereotypic connotation of femininity that such caregiving retains – and other characters reproduce this synergy. She finds "the tenderest of all discoveries" at an archeological site and whispers "Honey, I'm home" to a corpse on her lab table (Ondaatje *Ghost*

55, 19). Gamini is a surgeon notable for being "tender" on the job (224). When Ananda soothes Anil he does so "tenderly and formally" in a manner so neatly recalling his skill at facial reconstruction that she feels "as if hers was a face being sculpted" (187).

Before a woman like Anil could seem to represent the exemplary instance of cosmopolitan expertise, professional authority had to be understood as wanting a sentimental supplement. Its dispassionate analyses had to be portrayed as deficient, in other words, before the benefits of a soft touch could become apparent. Specialized knowledge had to be seen as potentially anyone's property, moreover, and not the possession of men alone. Postcolonial novels such as *Anil's Ghost* have reason to behave as if these steps have already been taken. Early twentieth-century novels completed much of the work decades ago, when they retooled the married couple of domestic romance. Their refashioned marriage plots treated the sexual division of labor abiding in the household as if it provided the means to critique and ultimately reform the professional division of labor emerging as the new norm in world politics and business.

When novelists as admittedly diverse as Tagore, Satthianadhan, and Forster overhauled domestic romance, they retained certain properties of the genre while revising others. True to the tradition of Austen and the Brontës, these writers valued women of wit, intelligence, and refined aesthetic sensibility. They repurposed such conventional novelistic attributes, however, and developed a feminine sensibility as cosmopolitan as it was critical of the world of professional work. Where Tagore offers a narrative that depicts the challenges of generating a model of femininity to contest expert authority, Satthianadhan describes a woman whose bookish learning turns her into an activist, and Forster formulates a feminine counterpoint to the hierarchical structure of labor in London's imperial firms. Read together, these three writers demonstrate how fiction relied on a conjoined femininity, education, and cosmopolitanism to critique imperial social organization.[17]

Because these writings work against particular versions of professional privilege while holding onto the possibility of a defensible expert hierarchy, their approach can only appear as a kind of compromise. A compromise appearing, moreover, at a time when the structural inequality of imperial rule must make it seem even more questionable than contemporary globalization makes the compromise entailed by the incremental reform represented in *Anil's Ghost* and in Callon et al. If tacitly accepting certain features of a division of labor risks seeming like a major political concession today, the necessary limits of any effort to democratize expertise can only appear more glaringly apparent in imperial formulations. Although we may be ready to credit the professional ambition to mediate among the world's populations as "admirable," Ackbar Abbas allows, we also should remember that such affiliation is most straightforwardly evocative of social change "where the encounter with other cultures is a matter of free choice" ("Cosmopolitan" 771). In the contrasting "situation where 'divergent cultural experiences' are not freely chosen but forced ... as they are under colonialism," he cautions, the worldly relations formed by professionals risk appearing more "compadorist" (771). This is precisely the risky political terrain of Tagore's *Ghare-Baire*, written in Bengali in 1915 and translated into English in 1919 as *The Home and the World*. This novel exemplifies an early twentieth-century aspiration to present the reform of expertise as providing the impetus for wide political reform. It also demonstrates the period interest in recruiting the figure of the domestic woman for this endeavor.

---

[17] Such a "critical cosmopolitanism" resonates with what R. L. Walkowitz describes as the "idiosyncratic expressions of culture and the conditions of international sympathy or reparation" discoverable in a range of modernist writings (*Cosmopolitan* 18).

Commentary by Martha Nussbaum and others observes that *The Home and the World*'s benevolent landowner, Nikhil, models the worldliness of the intellectual while his interlocutor, Sandip, tends to fit the stereotype of the nativist nationalist (*Love* 3–5).[18] Most readers agree that the contest between these two focuses attention on the decision-making of Nikhil's wife, Bimala, forced to choose between her husband's cool universalism and her would-be-lover Sandip's hot nationalism. Even as the novel invites such a reading, however, it also insists that Bimala's two suitors have a good deal in common. They are recognizable members of the Bengali elite, which Sumit Sarkar explains was "not really characterized by any association with capitalistic enterprise ... but by education (of the new kind introduced by the British, with English as a medium at higher levels)" (*Writing* 169). Their opposing positions require this shared education. The English school gives these two a political scientific vernacular in which to debate. It further provides them with a storehouse of cultural knowledge that enters the novel in the form of interpolated fragments of verse.

Scholars have latched onto this poetic conceit as a clue to Tagore's politics. Dipesh Chakrabarty contends that eruptions of poesy have a typical function in turn-of-the-twentieth-century Bengali writing: they complicate historical narratives of national self-definition (*Provincializing* 155). Poetry "transports," and thus gestures to a world beyond the realist representation of social history.[19] Rosinka Chaudhuri contends that Tagore's poetic

---

[18] The list of scholars who make this novel a reference point in debate about cosmopolitanism and expertise includes Nussbaum; Brennan (*Home*); Robbins (*Feeling*); and Spivak ("Ethics").

[19] Nandy argues that Tagore's "poeticized" novel is affiliated with the "upakathas, fairy-story-like narratives surviving in the public memory, often as morality tales" and with the novel's South Asian history of taking up "issues and themes that were peripheral to traditional forms of literature" (*Illegitimacy* 18).

emphasis represents the essence of his modernism as well as his antagonism towards non-literary modes of representation.[20] This debate is complicated by the range of Tagore's experimentation. He composed poetry featuring prosaic content as well as lines he called "prose-poetry." The range of verses cited in *The Home and the World* alone is extensive. Nikhil and Sandip quote lines from the Upanishads and Vaishnava lyrics as well as Bankim Chandra Chatterji's anthem *Bande Mataram* and the stanzas of Milton and Browning. When a Browning verse can appear cheek by jowl with a nationalist anthem or "a song in the Bhairavi mode," poetry is not merely a means of transportation but also of pluralization (Tagore *Home* 158). Patriotic rhetoric built of such heterogeneous textual matter invokes a nation of "irreducible pluralities" and a nationalism that is also a species of cosmopolitan art (178–79). Tagore's poetic play taught readers not to oppose nationalism and cosmopolitanism, but rather to subsume politics in an elevated aesthetic.

The Home and the World leans across oceans towards European modernism, forward towards postcolonial prose, and back into the history of Indian fiction. It does so most emphatically through the character of Bimala, who, like so many leading ladies of domestic fictions from the nineteenth through the twentieth centuries, appears poised to decide her nation's future place in the world order. Just as it will for a parade of heroines in anticolonial novels set around the globe, nationalist resistance proves as exciting to Bimala as it does dangerous. Sandip's songs, speeches, and poems turn her on. When "his eyes, like stars in fateful Orion" look her way, she becomes "utterly unconscious"; his words make her "blood dance" and her heart glow "with living fire" (Tagore *Home* 31, 74, 177). Her choice

---

[20] A point missed, Chaudhuri argues, by the subaltern studies scholars who "seem to all be returning to Tagore" ("Flute" 104, 119)

to stay with Nikhil in the end might appear to squelch such lust and secure her loving marriage. Readers who recognize in Bimala touches of a modernist leading lady, however, know better than to believe this ends the tale. Her speculation that there are "two persons in me" invites readers to identify her as a sort of New Woman struggling with the barely repressed desire symptomatic of that type (178).

"She was called 'Novissima,'" Ann Ardis says of this character type, "the New Woman, the Odd Woman, the Wild Woman and the Superfluous Woman" (*New* 1). She was "a resonant symbol of emancipation," writes Rita Felski, "whose modernity signaled not an endorsement of an existing present but rather a bold imagining of an alternative future" (*Gender* 14). She was the unlikely heroine and the bête noire of journalism, genre fiction, and social scientific prose. Her default narrative forms were the *Bildungsroman* and the marriage plot – both dramatically altered by her presence.[21] Although perhaps still thought of primarily as Anglo-American, in truth this figure circulated farther afield. Tani Barlow, Madeleine Yue Dong, and the other scholars associated with "The Modern Girl around the World Research Group" chart her movement from "Beijing to Bombay, Tokyo to Berlin, Johannesburg to New York" (245). In all of these locations, "what made the Modern Girl distinctive was her continual incorporation of elements drawn from elsewhere," the members of the research group argue (246).[22]

---

[21] Marriage was "the source of the heroine's problems" rather than the culmination of her development (Pykett *Engendering* 57). The New Woman story of development emphasized process over product (Joshi *Another* 188). Ardis considers such generic experimentation a signature of "New Woman novelists [who] anticipate the reappraisal of realism we usually credit to early twentieth-century writers" (*New* 3).

[22] "Often, the Modern Girl combined and reconfigured aesthetic elements drawn from disparate national, colonial and racial regimes to create a 'cosmopolitan look'" (246).

When Tagore recycled aspects of this character type he drew on a substantial South Asian tradition that included the late nineteenth-century writer Krupabai Satthianadhan. Priya Joshi explains that Satthianadhan's literary focus on "female subjectivity as both the source and substance of reform aligns her work most immediately with New Woman fiction in Britain, to the extent that the Madras Presidency *Catalogue of Printed Books* describes her work as 'showing the native new Woman beside the old'" (*Another* 187). If New Women in the writings of Sarah Grand, Dorothy Richardson, and H. G. Wells tended to fling themselves into scandalous affairs and transgressive forms of paid labor, New Women in the Indian tradition tended to need more coaxing. To wit, Nikhil finds himself having to persuade Bimala: "Merely going on with your household duties, living all your life in the world of household conventions and the drudgery of household tasks – you were not made for that!" (Tagore *Home* 23). Bimala resists. "The outside world may want" *her*, she credits, but it is not clear that she wants *it*. "If the outside world has got on so long without me," she contends, "it may go on for some time longer" (23). Sangeeta Ray considers Bimala's ambivalence indicative of the "indeterminacy" that afflicted women in period South Asian fiction, indeterminacy of the "individual woman (when am I a woman?) . . . political indeterminacy (what can 'women' do?) . . . [and] historical indeterminacy (what do women mean, and when?)" (*En-Gendering* 113).[23]

Not all writers treated this situation as a muddle. As early as the 1890s, Satthianadhan was encouraging readers to take the opportunity to rethink the position of women and their attraction to reform-minded intellectuals and experts of various sorts. Her

---

[23] In India, nation-building presented women in new ways. For two competing accounts see Sarkar (*Beyond* 115) and P. Chatterjee (*Nation* 203). See too Majumdar ("Nationalizing") on the problem of "nationalizing the woman" in *The Home and the World*.

eponymous heroine Kamala faces a rather different choice than does Tagore's Bimala. Kamala, widowed in the novel's second to last chapter, receives a proposal from her longtime friend Ramchander in the novel's final chapter. He pleads "most eloquently – 'It is the land of freedom I want you to come to. Have you not felt the trammels of custom and tradition? Have you not felt the weight of ignorance wearing you down, superstition folding its arms round you and holding you in its bewildering and terrifying grasp?'" (154). If it is jarring to find talk of transgression in a marriage proposal, it may be useful to note that widows had been able to remarry lawfully in India only since 1856. Having invoked this British measure, *Kamala*'s narrator clarifies that though she has no love for the "old rooted prejudice in the Hindu mind against women," neither does she equate marriage reform with Anglicization (133).[24]

Instead, the novel links romantic entanglement with education. The men in Kamala's life perceive her as a student. She spends her childhood listening to "learned talk" uttered by her father, "a recluse and a scholar" who teaches that courtship and education go hand in hand (Satthianadhan *Kamala* 24). "Your mother read with me," he tells Kamala, "books that are never put into women's hands, and she was delighted when difficult portions were explained. Nothing came between her and me, and as her understanding unfolded, her love for me increased" (120). When her father-in-law discovers that Kamala is literate, he agrees that "it was right that the daughter of a reading man should learn how to read" and strokes her head as she sits in his well-stocked library (43).

---

[24] Brinks argues that "Satthianadhan's strategic flexibility helps us to understand the ways that some commonly held ideological ends such as the reform of child marriage allowed for unforeseen alliances between different groups as they critiqued patriarchal practices" ("Gendered" 149). The stereotypic plotting in Kamala's household is grist for critique of nineteenth-century South Asian domestic fiction. Sangari meticulously unpacks the sort of stock material involved (*Politics* 257–64, 311–17).

Her husband, Ganesh, meanwhile, with his government job and "his English idea ... regarding women's love and education," contemplates "striking out on a new line and developing Kamala's mind and so training her to be a real companion to him" (73). Ganesh is recognizable as "modern" and "educated," which makes him the authority in a marriage that mimics the inequality of higher education and, by extension, the professional hierarchy it engenders.

In *Kamala*, women as a class fight against this model of professorial husband and undergraduate wife by supporting the "Hindu home" dominated by a mother-in-law (Satthianadhan *Kamala* 62). But individual women such as Kamala and her competitor for Ganesh's affection Sai threaten the established order by demonstrating that the student can become the master. Sai's "knowledge of the world is great," the narrator avers, and that knowledge is reciprocated: "The whole world knows Sai," one of her many male admirers intones. "I should like to study her character" (124, 52). Learning makes women public authorities, which can only diminish their interest in reproducing the "Hindu home."

Kamala's decision not to remarry confirms that being a wife is but a stage in the process of generating a revised version of women's authority according to the terms of specialized knowledge. The novel presents her choice as an ambivalent one: it is both a "victory" for "her religion, crude as it was," against the "freedoms" of colonial rule, and an act of defiance against local treatment of widows, who typically find themselves "despised ... and degraded in the sight of the little world in which she lived" (Satthianadhan *Kamala* 155–56).[25] Satthianadhan leaves her heroine in a position readers of English

---

[25] Mukherjee describes this as a triumph over domestic romance: "this may be read as a truly feminist ending where a woman's happiness is not necessarily dependent on her relationship with a man" (*Perishable* 86–87). Lokugé interprets the novel's not-always-so-loving

fiction know well from defining instances of the genre. She spends her days "in unselfish works of charity" caring for those whom Samuel Richardson's Pamela might have called "the honest and worthy poor" (Satthianadhan *Kamala* 156; Richardson *Pamela* 516). Unlike Pamela, however, Kamala performs this work without a husband. After presenting marriage as a form of schooling, Satthianadhan concludes with Kamala's bittersweet graduation. Having crafted a narrative of reform that can take or leave elements of British colonial social development, Satthianadhan's novel describes a discrepant but well-educated authority, damaged but sainted – the narrator notes the building of "a shrine and chuttram bearing the name of Kamala" (156).

Kamala's trajectory from student to reformer is shared by any number of British modernist heroines. Virginia Woolf's Lily Briscoe from *To the Lighthouse* and D. H. Lawrence's Ursula Brangwen from *The Rainbow* are among those who demonstrate the new clout of educated women to critique and even overturn existing hierarchies in their specialized fields. To the last, these women exercise their power not only by drawing on expertise in a chosen discipline but also by forging interpersonal connections. Modernist fiction thereby established a link between expertise and the creation of sympathetic bonds. The logic that makes such linkage appealing is clarified by *Howards End*. Like his South Asian counterparts, Forster is concerned with the future of the nation and its women. Even more clearly than they, perhaps, Forster contrasts the poverty of professional relationships in male-dominated firms with bonds created by his New Women, the Schlegel sisters. Their intelligence and vast reservoir of cultural capital combines with a keen sympathy that allows them to understand others in a way the novel's male experts simply cannot. With this gesture, *Howards End*

approach to local custom as a function of "Satthianadhan's private ideological conflict" ("Introduction" 15).

completes my truncated genealogy of imperial-era precursors to the sympathetic bonding that *Anil's Ghost* presents as the hallmark of postcolonial professionalism.

While Tagore and Satthianadhan represent education as disrupting conventional femininity and sparking the renovation of feminine authority, Forster's signal innovation is a further revision to the marriage plot that establishes competing yet complementary masculine and feminine varieties of expertise.[26] Class governs these relationships, but as in Tagore the class that most interests *Howards End* invests in cultural capital. The relation of that class to land and property is precisely the issue in the novel's central trope of inheritance.[27] The estate that Forster places under Margaret Schlegel's ownership is composed of atavistic elements to be sure – the wych-elm on its grounds, for instance, has notoriety for the pig's teeth embedded within it. But Howards End is also rapidly becoming part of "London's creeping" sprawl and, through metropolitan London, "part of something else" (*Howards* 268). "Howards End, Oniton, the Purbeck Downs, the Oderberge, were all survivals," Margaret thinks, "and the melting-pot was being prepared for them" (268). English culture as it appears in this list of relics is a native essence in the midst of increasingly cosmopolitan terrain. The Schlegel sisters are embroiled in a "battle

---

[26] Though he denounced Tagore's novel as a "boarding-house flirtation" masked "in patriotic talk," Forster was never above taking on geopolitical subject matter in the form of domestic romance (cited in Desai "Introduction" 7). He also employed the same characteristic love triangle formulation with all it portends for sentimental bonds among men – where Tagore offers us Nikhil and Sandip, Forster's *A Passage to India* offers Cyril Fielding and Dr. Aziz.

[27] The plot thoroughly embroils the Schlegels with the property and as it does so demonstrates that none of the Wilcoxes are fit to inherit it: they are all afflicted with hay fever. "The house lies too much on the land for them," its caretaker reveals (Forster *Howards* 216). Trilling provides the classic account of the house as a figure (*Forster* 118).

against sameness," an attempt to hold onto "[d]ifferences" that may preserve a bit of "colour in the daily grey" (267).[28]

And yet these same sisters also famously connect the human representatives of difference that move about the novel. These include a plurality of worldly individuals: Margaret and Helen's father – "countryman of Hegel and Kant ... whose Imperialism was the Imperialism of the air" (Forster *Howards* 21);[29] Henry Wilcox, whose imperialism is that of commerce executed at the Imperial and West African Rubber Company (154);[30] and Leonard Bast who loves the world of the arts but who lacks money and schooling. Leonard's presence in the novel invokes a question of hierarchy directly anterior to that of *Anil's Ghost*. When Henry Wilcox looks at Leonard and his clerical kin he is looking at fellow professionals embroiled in the work of international finance, but from where he sits atop the administrative ranks such staff may as well be a separate species: "I look at the faces of the clerks in my own office, and observe them to be dull, but I don't know what's going on beneath," he confesses (115). Helen Schlegel sees deeper and recognizes something in Leonard's pretension that is difficult to articulate but is powerfully felt. Along with her sister, she aspires to form attachments across social divides.

The arts provide them with the opportunity to meet Leonard – at a Beethoven recital – and with the metaphor that captures their

---

[28] For a taut reading of salvage work in this novel, see Outka ("Buying").

[29] The same passage makes plain that the elder Schlegel was a literal as well as literary soldier, active in campaigns against "Denmark, Austria, France" (21). But "Germany with colonies here and a Forward Policy there" was not interesting to him, so he settled at a "provincial" university and waited for the "clouds of materialism" to part (21).

[30] Worldliness of this economic bent appears first via Margaret's speculative strategy of "taking her money out of the old safe investments and putting it into Foreign Things" (9). Though Charles Wilcox runs Margaret down as a "cosmopolitan," and though he distinguishes that term from its competitor "imperialist," *Howards End* weighs up whether those two categories are at all compatible (79).

awkward attempts at communication – "One little twist, they felt, and the instrument might be in tune" (Forster *Howards* 95). From the beginning, the Schlegels see Leonard as a charity case. The novel roughly equates a difference in advanced education with economic disparity. But Forster assures us that such inequality does not thwart sentimentality. During her brief, unfortunate, yet reproductively successful affair with Leonard, Helen "loved him absolutely, perhaps for half an hour," but her note dismissing him, a note she "intended to be most kind" but which "hurt her lover terribly," leaves Leonard feeling guilty for his part in the affair (250). The narrator recounts Leonard's thoughts: "It was as if some work of art had been broken by him, some picture in the National Gallery slashed out of its frame" (250). "I ought to remember Leonard as my lover," says Helen. "I tempted him and killed him, it is surely the least I can do" (266). Shared guilt is but one lasting sign of a complex, fraught, and highly charged affinity between two characters whom Forster in no way portrays as equals.[31]

The novel's other couple is marked by a different inequality: Forster uses Margaret and Henry Wilcox to spell out the social implications for his gendered division of labor. "It is impossible to see modern life steadily and see it whole," the narrator tells us, "and [Margaret] had chosen to see it whole" (*Howards* 127). A man with a profession, such as her husband, in contrast "saw steadily. He never bothered over the mysterious or the private. The ... chauffeur might conceal all passion and philosophy beneath his skin. They knew their own business, and he knew his" (127). One wants both ways of seeing, or so it seems from the novel's demand to bind people through associations that nevertheless preserve their

---

[31] On the relationship between "advocacy for recognition" and "advocacy for redistribution" in *Howards End* and Forster more generally, see Shirkhani ("Economy" 212).

distinctive outlooks on life. When it comes to calculating power in such associations, the balance tilts towards sentimental women and their less steady, thus more flexible, approach. The novel compares Margaret and Helen to London, whose "continual flux" is "emblematic of their lives" (84). Margaret finds herself equally at home in the city and at Howards End, where she takes charge of the Wilcox estate, and Helen, despite her countercultural leanings, thrives in the very environment that undoes Leonard. The cultural capital that elevates Forster's heroines buries Leonard when he dies, grabbing at a bookcase as "[b]ooks fell over him in a shower" (256).

Forster's demand that the Schlegels both preserve distinction and bring different sorts of people together strikes Paul Armstrong as demonstrative of a "community based not on unity or solidarity but on ... relationships of mutuality that do not erase difference and heterogeneity. Such a vision," he comments, "is inherently contradictory" ("Narrator" 307). We can go farther: these are relationships that preserve inequality even as they produce mutual affection. By modeling this dynamic, they anticipate the attachments that *Anil's Ghost* finds in professional affairs. The inherent contradiction that Armstrong identifies is the abiding truth of the professional workplace, which encourages bonding that does not threaten hierarchy. In *Howards End*, a company run by Henry Wilcox and staffed by Leonard Bast lacks the means to generate such ties among its managers and workers. The Schlegels' desire to bring people together is what masculine professionalism needs. In fact, given the dysfunctional households Forster, Satthianadhan, and Tagore describe, it is not too much to contend that the domestic models offered by such late nineteenth- and early twentieth-century fictions were better suited for the boardroom than the bedroom. Though generated in homes, these depictions of deeply felt relationships that preserve inequality were cut to the measure of a professionalism that would flower decades later in the pages of postcolonial fiction.[32]

HUMANITIES AMIDST HIERARCHIES

The novels I have considered in this chapter refuse to separate two different types of relationship, one based on common feeling and the other on institutional standing. This refusal is bound to vex readers reluctant to imagine that inequality and companionship could go together. And yet the novels do not collapse the difference between friendships and hierarchies. They instead offer stories that exploit the tension between fellow feeling and workplace arrangements to pose this question: what would be a desirable professional hierarchy? I have argued that asking this question can help us own up to the reality of meritocratic power. This is what is at stake in the plots I have reviewed about what happens to one rural Indian widow or one U.N. investigator.

To understand these novels as modeling ways of being professional is to think of them as reforming, rather than overturning, the abiding inequality of meritocracy. There is a common thread that runs through these narratives that calls attention to their suspicion of at least some versions of actually existing hierarchies. *Howards End* is surely the most overt in expressing such misgiving. *Kamala* is the most explicit in its invocation of a contending hierarchical

---

[32] With an eye on this anticipatory glance, it is worth recalling *Howards End*'s sweeping verdict: "the imperialist is not what he thinks or seems. He is a destroyer. He prepares the way for cosmopolitanism" (256). Professionalism, we might say, is the vehicle the novel employs to test what Jameson calls the novel's linking of local English settings to the "Great North Road . . . suggestive of infinity" (Forster *Howards* 10) and other motifs connoting the empire beyond. Jameson focuses on what the novel does not or cannot show, on "the representational dilemmas of the new imperial world system" ("Modernism" 59). And yet, what it does show of its characters' worldliness teaches a good deal about the relationships that system might abet.

arrangement organized around the likes of its sainted heroine. The ambivalent endings of *Anil's Ghost*, meanwhile, direct readers to treat administrative reform as a transnational matter.

Dipesh Chakrabarty is among the contemporary scholars to take a long view of literature's investment in reform of the professional division of labor. In the Mumbai-based journal *Economic and Political Weekly*, Chakrabarty recounts a discussion that emerged out of the conference of newly independent Asian and African nations held in Bandung, Indonesia, in 1955. "Anti-colonial thinkers," he notes, "devoted a great deal of time to the question of whether or how a global conversation of humanity could genuinely acknowledge cultural diversity without [relying] on a hierarchical scale of civilization" ("Legacies" 4812). Chakrabarty calls this urge "the dialogical side of decolonization" (4812) and finds one particularly powerful expression of it in the polemical writings of Leopold Senghor.

For Senghor, one way that diversity could be harnessed ... was by deliberately creating a plural and yet thriving tradition of humanities in the teaching institutions of the world. The way forward was a world of multi-lingual individuals who would appreciate language both as means of communication and as repository of difference. (4817)

What began promisingly enough at Bandung has not fared so well in the long haul: "The humanities have generally suffered in the newly emergent nations," Chakrabarty reports. "[M]y generation of Indians could testify to the cult of engineering and management ... [I]t may very well be ... that it is only in the west that modern, non-western humanities are pursued with some seriousness ... [and] the west has seldom performed this task in a manner that transcends its own geopolitical interests" (4817). Though there may be an element of hyperbole in Chakrabarty's dismissal of humanities study outside the

West, his assessment remains bracing. It reinforces, first, the belief that the expertise represented by work in literature and the arts can serve to mediate dialogue across hierarchical divides and, second, the disappointment felt when the dissemination of such work fails to nurture conversations among equals. We scholars of literature need to come to grips with the fact that cosmopolitan sympathy and professional inequality complement one another in the academy. It is not unexpected that as humanities professors help along the worldwide circulation of literature and art, they also reinforce the difference between trained and untrained interpreters that empowers them in the first place.

Entrenched though this hierarchy may be, it is not the same as an imperial divide between the West and the rest. The brain drain enabled by the relatively low cost of air travel and the growth of an international market in higher education means that scholarship in the "non-western humanities" may end up being paid for by institutions in the West but staffed by scholars from the East and vice versa. Because careers as well as fields are shaped by such phenomena of uneven development, the humanities scholars who might displace imperial talk of "civilization" are best thought of as allies bound not by a culture, a nation, or a hemisphere but an educational apparatus, a host of competing and collaborating professional institutions, and most importantly by the meritocratic ideal of the academy itself. In this context, dialogue among critics about literature cannot help but be structured by the same inequality that structures all professional discussion.

Novels can and do mediate dialogue in and outside the academy in all sorts of important ways, but the stories they tell and the manner in which they circulate remain symptomatic of professional hierarchy. That said, all professional hierarchies are not the same. In place of Chakrabarty's narrative of decline, therefore, in this chapter I have sketched an account of the novel's participation in a project spanning more than a century, which involves telling stories that explain and inspire different versions of affiliation among unequals. Instead of an imperial North–South, core and periphery schema, these fictions represent the hierarchical arrangement of experts and expertise held together by sentimentality that crosses specializations, disciplines, and even national borders. In so doing, novels model ways of reimagining inequality and managing its effects. There are no global revolutions nor prospects for universal humanism in novels such as *Anil's Ghost* or *Howards End*. But there is considerable and potentially significant change on the highly resonant if small scale of professional collaboration and interpersonal relations.

CHAPTER 4

Entrepreneurship and imperial politics in twentieth-century historical fiction

Contemporary fiction that investigates relations within and among groups, interpersonal politics, and collaborative practice reworks the problem of individual development bequeathed by nineteenth-century novels. Contemporary fiction focused on groups cares little for the question of how individual sovereignty can be cultivated through a dynamic of maturity, autonomy, separation from setting, environment, and community. It cares far more about individuals whose actions depend on contributions from others. It strives to figure and explain the support systems that help individuals act, and it rethinks the problem of subjectivity in these terms. The narrative point of such works is not to arrive at a condition of maturity that can appear universal, but to investigate how social organization affects the production and reproduction of individuals. Novels thereby demonstrate an investment in the workings of civil society every bit as serious as their investment in the workings of states.

Civil society went global in the twentieth century, any number of commentators have observed, and it also came under ever more comprehensive professional scrutiny as social workers, anthropologists, and specialists in public security lay claim to the authority to supervise popular assembly. The individuals described as composing civil society could not help but change as a result. Fiction and social science portray them as subjects of expert intervention, to be sure, but equally as enterprising types eager to appropriate expert authority for themselves. Entrepreneurs abound in recent accounts of civil society, extremely adaptable sorts always alert for opportunities to take greater charge of their lives and to increase their human capital. A good deal of scholarship on these would-be experts is struck by the novelty of their enterprise culture. Updated versions of the historical novel take a longer view. Like Sir Walter Scott's classic iteration of the genre, contemporary historical fiction offers a prehistory of the present, the better to fathom managing the highly unstable civil society of the twenty-first century.

Enlightenment historian and philosopher Adam Ferguson stipulated in his 1767 *Essay on the History of Civil Society* that "[m]ankind are to be taken in groupes, as they have always subsisted" (6). Taking the group as a given makes it clear that to understand how human beings tick requires understanding the associations they form. "The history of the individual," Ferguson wrote, "is but a detail of the sentiments and thoughts he has entertained in the view of his species: and every experiment relative to the subject should be made with entire societies, not with single men" (6). Before engaging in experiments designed to better the lot of individuals, Ferguson argued that it was prerequisite to have some comprehension of the ways people organize themselves into civil societies that nurture and protect individuals as they live and work. Humans do this according to an "order established by nature," Ferguson believed: "Prior to any political institution whatever, men are qualified by a great diversity of talents, by a different tone of the soul, and an ardour of the passions, to act a variety of parts. Bring them together, each will find his place" (95). The challenge before political institutions is to reproduce this dynamic in the modern day, to figure out how to govern in a manner that provides every individual with the opportunity to find her place and exercise her talents. In this classic liberal formulation, civil society is both the object on which the state acts and a realm that must remain separate from the state if the human species is to thrive.

When contemporary fiction reveals the support systems that engender individual activities, it contributes to an ongoing project of imagining civil society. Fiction does so at a moment when, as Partha Chatterjee observes, the idea of civil society has expanded to "include virtually all existing social institutions that lie outside the strict domain of the state" (*Politics* 39). International financial firms offering microcredit, non-governmental aid agencies providing welfare services, and communal organizations offering educational programs present themselves as "the precious flower of the associative endeavors of free members of civil society" (39). The "polyvalence" of contemporary civil society is part of its appeal, argue the anthropologists Jean and John Comaroff: "its ineluctable unfixability is intrinsic to its power as panacea," "the ultimate magic bullet" especially attractive to experts overseeing populations who live in failing states ("Millennial" 334).

The notion that civil society must take over governance when the state falters is not a new idea. Mitchell Dean explains that it has long been the habit of liberal rule to connect wherever possible "interventions of the state with the agencies, regulations, expectations, values and obligations embedded in the processes of society" ("Liberal" 45). What has changed over the past one hundred years or so is the proliferation, professionalization, and specialization of those agencies charged with picking up where the state leaves off. Civil society today is composed less of self-organizing coalitions like those imagined by Ferguson, more of hierarchical institutions that compete with one another to recruit and to teach and to advise. The individuals that civil society now inculcates are used to being pulled first in one direction and then in another. They are well habituated to an ongoing flux Zygmunt Bauman calls "liquid life," a state of being in which every person makes himself over again and again as he moves in and among institutions of education and welfare, as well as from job to job (*Life* 11).

Michel Foucault supposes that this version of the individual is best understood as "an entrepreneur of himself," possessed of "human capital" as opposed to classically liberal, quasi-natural powers of rational decision-making (*Birth* 225–26). Gilles Deleuze describes this individual as being engaged in a kind of "permanent training" to develop and supplement the capital he accrues ("Postscript" 7). Success depends on canny "educational investments," Foucault relates, "whether this involves school instruction strictly speaking, or professional training, and so on" (*Birth* 229). The range of what can be considered "educational investments" appears ever more expansive, including "the number of hours a mother spends with her child, even when it is still in the cradle," "cultural stimuli" of all kinds, and even migration for work (229–30). The notion that enterprise depends on life-long learning – and conceives of learning as an investment in human capital – makes clear that today's entrepreneur is not the quasi-natural being of liberal political economy but something else, more of an expert or even a professional.

The challenge of explaining the history of this entrepreneurial subject provides literature with a new but not entirely unanticipated challenge. Narrating the historical emergence of the classical liberal subject was the project of the fictional form described in Georg Lukács's defining study *The Historical Novel* (1937/1983) and exemplified by the writings of Sir Walter Scott. "What is lacking in the so-called historical novel before Sir Walter Scott," according to Lukács, "is precisely the specifically historical . . . derivation of the individuality of characters from the historical peculiarity of their age" (19). Contemporary historical fiction differs from the work of Scott both in the civil society it describes and in the individuals acting out its plots. However, recent historical novels follow Scott, first, in seeking to correlate individuality with historical situation and, second, in treating the past as precondition for the present. As a result, contemporary historical fictions appear every bit as committed as their nineteenth-century antecedents to representing social change in prose narrative form.

When it updates the individual, recent fiction makes redundant the bourgeois hero whose domestication concluded Scott's *Waverley* (1814/1985) and who served as the pivot around whom history moved in Lukács's *The Historical Novel*. Works such as Amitav Ghosh's *The Glass Palace* (2000/2002) trace the movements of an entrepreneurial subject who appears incapable of settling down, lest he cease acquiring the human and economic capital that allows him to thrive. That this subject has a history may be discerned in the way heroes from contemporary fiction recall the hyperactive bourgeoisie of Marx's *Manifesto* (as opposed to the ordinary Englishman of Scott and Lukács). Like Marx's agents of commerce, Ghosh's actors are chased "over the whole surface of the globe," driven to "establish connexions everywhere" (K. Marx *Selected* 162). Given the prevalence of such types in recent prose, the contemporary historical novel appears less interested in the Lukácsian mission of distinguishing capitalist from pre-capitalist social relations and more invested in the dissemination and elaboration of capitalist knowledge.[1]

---

[1] Writing on Lukács's other great work of novel criticism, *The Theory of the Novel*, Cunningham offers the comparable hypothesis that, "in a context in which, more clearly than ever, it is precisely global capitalism rather than either the bourgeoisie *or* the proletariat which seems to drive any revolutionizing of 'the whole relations of society,' it raises the question of whether, if we are to revisit *The Theory of the Novel*, it is perhaps – against the grain of Lukács's own rereadings – not as an epic of the bourgeois 'people', but

This shift in emphasis suggests the need for a genealogical alternative to the nineteenth-century rise and fall provided by Lukács's account of the genre. Contemporary historical fiction's interest in stories set during the final decades of European empire further suggests that revision is warranted. This was the very era that Lukács considered the moment of the historical novel's obsolescence; the period when, he argued, bourgeois art degenerated along with the European bourgeoisie and historical fiction was reduced to "archeologism," to the representation of the past as exotic and foreign rather than determining and explanatory, and to the depiction of characters as "purely private" beings engaged in "intimate and subjective happenings" (*Historical* 198–99). Familiar though it may be, Lukács's contention that modernist fiction turned away from history would require us to ignore early twentieth-century antecedents for the historical novel of our present day. At the end of this chapter, I focus on two novels in particular, *Nostromo* (1904/1985) by Joseph Conrad and *Prince of Destiny* (1909) by Sarath Kumar Ghosh. As for Lukács's contention that fiction after Scott became more interested in privacy, I suggest that it makes greater sense to argue that the historical novel turned away from nation-centered publicity. Although the novel never forgot national history, with all that entails for class relations and dynamics of sovereigns and peoples, its increasing attention was on the administration of an expansive, seemingly global civil society well populated with highly adaptable enterprising sorts and their flexible networks. I flesh out this change with reference to a plurality of contemporary fictions – including Amitav Ghosh's *The Glass Palace* (2000/2002), Abdulrazak Gurnah's *Desertion* (2005), Ahdaf Soueif's *The Map of Love* (1999/2000), and M. G. Vassanji's *The*

> as a displaced account of 'the system of capitalism itself' that the latter's engagement with the novel's impossible epic form is best understood today" ("Capitalist" 13).

Gunny Sack (1989) – while briefly noting two anticipatory mid-century works – Attia Hosain's *Sunlight on a Broken Column* (1961) and Venu Chitale's *In Transit* (1950).

When they seek to discover precedents for the civil society of today, fiction writers work alongside a host of researchers in disciplines ranging from history to anthropology. Some historians have found echoes of present-day commercial networks in world-spanning systems dating back to the thirteenth century, while others have compared contemporary transnational organizations with the sprawl of more recent European empires.[2] In contrast to the thesis of history as epochal change that Lukàcs found confirmed in the fiction of Scott, many scholars and fiction writers today are allied in emphasizing affinities and puzzling over intricate but far from revolutionary shifts within and among group affiliations past and present. In truth, this approach is both contemporary and reminiscent of Ferguson's treatment of change: he presented civil society as a busy place wherein men were forever getting enlisted "on the side of one tribe or community" (*Essay* 16). History as he describes it is a record of vacillating bonds, the struggles of "small and infant establishments" and the corruptions of "barbarous nations" (371). Historical fiction updates this liberal formula when it seeks to discover what the liquid life of enterprise society owes to imperial governance. With this revisionist approach to the past, recent historical novels share a common denominator with their Romantic precursors. As Scott did before them, historical novelists still provide readers with accounts of the past attuned to the problems of governing in the present.

---

[2] See Abu-Lughod's *Before European Hegemony*, Frank's *ReOrient*, and Arrighi's *Adam Smith in Beijing*. Also Bayly (*Birth*), Bose (*Hundred*), and Hobson (*Eastern*). For a polemical assessment of the impact such arguments have had on work in world history, see Northrup ("Globalization").

WORLD-HISTORICAL NETWORKING

With plots that are veritable how-to manuals for establishing connectivity, fictions like *The Glass Palace* explain which life supports help to maximize entrepreneurial behavior. The heroes Ghosh's novel follows are dedicated to seeing projects through and are exceedingly flexible in their techniques for doing so. Against conventional wisdom, they thrive in the colonial South Asian settings *The Glass Palace* depicts. Instead of getting pushed around by History with a capital "H," as do the heroes of the historical novel theorized by Lukács, they ride History's currents. They seize opportunities. They adapt. They anticipate. They are able to do so, the novel shows, because these innovators never act alone: all of them share the defining attribute of being supremely well connected.

Such fictional protagonists are reminiscent of the heroes who feature in recent economic scholarship and commentary. Hernando de Soto begins his influential 2000 polemic *The Mystery of Capital* by depicting a "Third World ... teeming with entrepreneurs. You cannot walk through a Middle Eastern market, hike up to a Latin American village, or climb into a taxicab in Moscow without someone trying to make a deal with you," he relates. "The inhabitants of these countries possess talent, enthusiasm, and an astonishing ability to wring a profit out of practically nothing" (4). It has become so common for swarms of entrepreneurs to appear in writing about global economy that they have generated a new problem: how to distinguish among enterprising actors and thus figure out which ones to study. The futurist Malcolm Gladwell concentrates on entrepreneurial predators like the notorious hedge-fund manager John Paulson, whom he finds notable for making the biggest of scores by acutely managing risk ("Sure" 25). Saskia Sassen peeks into middle management to discover specialists working in "the most innovative, speculative, internationalized service sectors," coordinating the "mobility of capital" from their "intermediate position between the subnational and the global" (*Territory* 301). The legal scholar and social theorist Roberto Unger affirms the twentieth-century rise of a "productive vanguard" always ready to "exchange ideas, practices and people as well as technologies and services" (*Free* 99–100). The comparative literature scholar Ackbar Abbas directs attention to "arbitrageurs" "with a difference," ordinary "men and women ... in the transnational space[s]" of Shanghai and Hong Kong "trying to make sense of ... spatial and temporal contradictions" ("Cosmopolitan" 786). The researcher of Cameroonian informal economy Margaret Niger-Thomas asks whether "female entrepreneurs [who] have accumulated capital and become economically empowered through smuggling" "encourage or deter development" ("Women" 66). Although these commentators differ in their objects of study, all agree that contemporary capitalism privileges agents who thrive amidst fluidity and unanticipated change.

The surge of entrepreneurship in popular and scholarly comment has altered thinking about economic administration. Alan Liu's analysis of business writing shows that corporate managers increasingly organize their employees into "teams," which appear to be the units of "ephemeral identity that most flexibly fuse technologies and techniques into skill sets (called 'innovation,' 'creativity,' or 'resourcefulness') adapted to the changefulness of the global economy" (*Laws* 47). According to Richard Sennett's *The Culture of the New Capitalism*, the administrative goal of encouraging flexible associations has all but eclipsed the older hierarchical priorities of "military, social capitalism" (23). Instead of an economy dominated by the "bureaucratized imposition" of corporate culture with its "gift of organized time," Sennett argues, the "new-business world" of "impatient capital" demands managers willing "to destabilize [their] own organization" and employees with "a thick network of social contacts" to smooth their relentless shuttling from project to project and job to job (23, 40, 46–47).[3]

For all the fuss about teams and networks made by business commentators, big governmental bureaucracies and robust corporate hierarchies never went away. It is possible that this was hard to remember in the halcyon days of 2006. Since the "new-business world" shot itself in the head, however, the role that large institutions play in cultivating and shepherding entrepreneurial activity has been a little more difficult to miss. According to Arjun Appadurai's pithy survey of recent trends, the largest of corporations (not to mention governments) embraced the notion of the flexible worker and the project-specific team in the last decades of the twentieth century, thus making apparent capitalism's "split personality" (*Fear* 27). Global economic activity still relied on what Appadurai calls the "vertebrate features of the nation-state system" but it also proliferated laboratories "for new forms of cellularity, de-linkage, and local autonomy" (28). The dynamic nature of these two features – stability and bureaucracy on one side, flexibility and local-area networking on the other – is not only a defining characteristic of recent economic commentary, but also a constituent element of earlier twentieth-century revisions to liberal governance. Foucault argues that beginning in the 1930s, the "art of

---

[3] The professor of management Angelo Kinicki describes the criteria of "employability" now used by human resource administrators: "Individual characteristics that predispose people to be more proactively adaptable are clearly beneficial, as individuals now are required to negotiate a never-ending series of workplace changes and transitions" ("Hiring"). The organizational ecologists Monique Girard and David Stark study firms in which "adaptability is promoted by the *organization of diversity* within an enterprise," which itself appears less a unified company than an agglomeration of "multi-disciplinary project teams" (Girard and Stark "Heterarchies" 80).

government" propagated by German "ordoliberals" and American "neoliberals" sought to orient society "towards the multiplicity and differentiation of enterprises" (*Birth* 149). De Soto and his ilk update a tried-and-true program, in other words, when they prescribe bureaucratic means to encourage independent risk-takers. Without a state apparatus to guarantee "legally enforceable transactions on property rights," de Soto contends, much of the world's enterprise will remain "dead capital" (*Mystery* 16). By endorsing the notion that stimulating entrepreneurship is and should be the goal of governments worldwide, de Soto and a host of political allies and strange bedfellows succeeded in updating the classic formula for liberal rule. They imagined an ever-watchful state capable of ensuring its subjects' ability to take on risk.

When economic historians explain how thinking about the state and civil society transformed in the twentieth century, they tend to focus on developments in Europe and North America. The usual tale begins with the founding of the Mont Pelerin Society by Friedrich von Hayek in 1947, touches upon the Economics Department of the University of Chicago in the 1950s and the London School of Economics in the 1980s, from which it migrates into Thatcher's 10 Downing Street, Reagan's White House, and the rise of institutions of Anglo-American capital including the International Monetary Fund (IMF). Although this account makes sense as intellectual history, it is poorly equipped to describe the origins of de Soto's "Third World ... teeming with entrepreneurs," much less such widely touted phenomena as the 1980s rise of Asian Tigers and the twenty-first-century innovations of the Hawala remittance system. To explain the diversity of contemporary capitalism requires a supplement to the usual story with its emphasis on Anglo-American ingenuity, command, and control.

Where de Soto presents third-world businessmen and businesswomen waiting to exploit property reforms modeled on those of the United States, fiction portrays a plurality of additional origin stories for Asian and African enterprise. Some of these tales turn on the influence of colonial rule, while others trace the ebb and flow of pre- and para-colonial networks. Instead of desperate would-be men and women of commerce craving the intervention of structural adjustment programs from the IMF, fiction populates the world with trading clans and entrepreneurial teams that figure out how to thrive during the age of empire and the postcolonial period alike.

For all that imperial governance was engineered to corral populations in castes and tribes, *The Glass Palace* suggests that it also had the effect of facilitating competition. The fantasy of one massive regulatory body overseeing markets that spanned continents made it possible to imagine that investors might raise capital in one colonial holding, move labor to another, and launch a development project in a third. Ghosh's novel introduces just the sort of businessmen to make such ventures happen: Saya John, who looks "to be Chinese" but speaks "Hindustani" while wearing the "clothes ... of a European," and Rajkumar, an orphan who arrives in Rangoon mere days before British forces take over the city and send the king into exile (*Glass* 8). These two compete ably with more established English companies by responding with the flexibility of a network. Rajkumar earns money by ferrying migrant workers from India to Burma and spends it donating to temples, developing friendships with clerks, and cultivating associations that not only yield insider knowledge but also facilitate smooth transactions. Just so, when he and Saya John arrive at the Chartered Bank to make their pitch for a deal, they are ushered into the boardroom by a cashier who greets Rajkumar and whispers, "Everything is arranged" (113). These friendships and associations enable Rajkumar to prosper: they compose the support system that allows a character marginalized by imperial racism to epitomize the entrepreneurial spirit of colonial capitalism.

The seeming paradox of a repressive governmental apparatus that provides openings for free enterprise is best expressed in a set piece from one of the novel's opening chapters. Waiting on the boat that will take him into exile, Burma's king gazes down at the "busy mass of things" on Rangoon's waterfront and marvels at empire's "incomprehensible power, to move people in such huge numbers from one place to another – emperors, kings, farmers, dockworkers, soldiers, coolies, policemen" (Amitav Ghosh *Glass* 43–44). As much as the "furious movement" on the docks testifies to British imperial might, it also anticipates Rajkumar and his colleagues cutting deals and signing contracts amidst "all this moving about" (44).

In that early scene and throughout, *The Glass Palace* recounts historical change at two scales of magnification. A panoramic view captures the kind of broad governmental reorganization that accompanies the collapse of a kingdom or the spread of an empire. A tighter focus reveals commerce, communication, and the buzz of networking that anticipates, responds, and persists as regimes fall and rise. The novel's story reproduces this twinned structure as it runs from the late nineteenth to the late twentieth century, switching between the scale of imperial conquest and eventual decolonization, on the one hand, and the detailed depiction of exchange and association, on the other. Although the novel is a revisionist account of South Asian colonialism, it is not anything like an apology for empire. It may be better understood as a novelistic record of enterprising activity that empire engendered in spite of itself, which notably included nationalist organization.[4]

---

[4] See Forter on the way contemporary historical novels offer what he calls "counterfictions," which "retrieve and transmit from the dustbin of history the stories of people arranging their lives" in alternate patterns ("Unsworth" 781).

The Glass Palace imagines postcolonial politics as an uncanny corollary to imperial economics. The novel's nationalist subplot features Uma, the former wife of a district collector. She has a habit of opportunistic connection reminiscent of Rajkumar's own. Her nationalist campaigning emerges out of global travel and exchange that extends the circuits in which Rajkumar makes his wealth. Uma forges ties with such figures as Kadambari Dutt (a cousin of the poetess Toru Dutt, who travels on the same ship Uma takes to Europe) and Madame Cama (who welcomes Uma into her London circle) (Amitav Ghosh *Glass* 162, 65).[5] One connection begets another. Madame Cama introduces Uma to Irish activists in New York. The "Irish resistance" leads her to "a small Indian contingent" that marches in the St. Patrick's Day parade, which clues her into "a newsletter published from the University of California in Berkeley by Indian students," who hook her up with Saya San's rebels in Burma. When their popular uprising is summarily crushed by Indian Army troops, it takes but a letter for Uma to join yet another team: "She wrote to the Mahatma offering her services, and he, in return, invited her to his ashram" (222).

Whether labeled commercial or political, the teams and networks that adapt to, and precipitate change in, *The Glass Palace* are recognizably different from the world-historical individuals nudged along by History in Scott's *Waverley*. Heroic passivity finds formal expression in what Lukács calls a "retrogressive motif" in Scott's fiction, "an uninterrupted chain of obstacles" that thwart Edward Waverley and thereby direct him towards a goal predetermined by the "proper hero" of the novel, "life itself" (Lukács *Historical* 148–49). What Waverley does is subordinated to what History wants. "Historical necessity," Lukács calls this, of "the most severe,

---

[5] See Gandhi (*Affective*) on the sort of affective community Uma joins.

implacable kind" (58). Read this way, Ian Duncan notes, Scott's fiction presents "the revolutions of history" as "a vast, dispersed, impersonal machinery without regard for individual identity and its (after all but local) strategies of accommodation" (*Modern* 55).

Where *The Glass Palace* shows how association enables individuals to build a network, in Lukàcs's account *Waverley* uses its hero "as an external central hub round which the events unfold" (*Historical* 35). What significance Waverley has accrues from being in the right place at the right time. His neutrality allows the novel to present all sides of a conflict: through him "opposing social forces can be brought into a human relationship with one another" (36). Lukács understands Scott's characters as demonstrating why historical events such as the development of the modern British nation came to appear necessary; whereas *The Glass Palace* relies on its characters to demonstrate how the British Empire generated unintended possibilities.[6]

The contrast between the conclusions of these two novels helps clarify the stakes involved in their differing approaches to history. Ghosh's novel closes with a kiss between the much older Uma and Rajkumar, now a couple living out their days in Calcutta. The two have just woken up, and their dentures have interlocked while resting overnight in a glass. Unwittingly, Rajkumar puts both sets of teeth in his mouth and it is only by fastening "her mouth on her own teeth" that Uma extricates them. As she does so, their "mouths cling to each other and they shut their eyes" (Amitav Ghosh *Glass* 470). Lest we hesitate to be stirred by this image, the narrator points the way. This is "the most tender, the most moving sight I have ever

---

[6] Rajkumar's son Dinu captures the balance that *The Glass Palace* is after when he contends that, although there is no denying empire's might, "the greatest danger" is that if "in resisting the powers that form us, we allow them to gain control of all meaning; this is their moment of victory; it is this way that they inflict their final and most terrible defeat" (447).

seen," she affirms (470). That narrator's nudge indicates how much is riding on a kiss, but readers of historical fiction probably do not need the prompt to begin speculating on its significance. They are surely familiar with the precedent of Rose Bradwardine and Edward Waverley's marriage at the end of Scott's genre-defining plot. "By wedding English core to Scottish periphery," Nancy Armstrong observes, "Scott appears to fulfill the progressive mission of the novel to imagine a more inclusive social body" (*Novels* 65). Not entirely a mission accomplished, Armstrong argues, since neither Scott's novel nor the British nation succeeded in assimilating the Celtic fringe.[7] Like the ambivalent union between Edward and Rose in *Waverley*, the coupling of Uma and Rajkumar at the end of *The Glass Palace* invokes antagonism the novel cannot actually resolve. Just as there is little room for Highland freedom in the modern British household, there is no way to accommodate what Uma sees as Rajkumar's comprador activity with what he understands as her political naïveté.[8]

The difference is that Ghosh's tome makes resolution appear unnecessary.[9] There is no need to explain precisely how former nationalist and former comprador capitalist sort their differences

---

[7] *Waverley* produces this ambivalence, as Armstrong notes, when "Rose emerges as the morally superior woman" but "Flora [Mac-Ivor] remains the locus of the novel's aesthetic investment" and its nostalgic affection for the Highland culture Britain subsumes (*Novels* 67). This divided allegiance epitomizes what Armstrong calls "the limited definition of community that ushers in the age of realism," limited because it requires "the loss of expressive individualism" associated with Highland life, as well as "the sacrifice of the heroic genres from an earlier literary tradition" (78).

[8] *Waverley* provides superficial containment by transforming "ontological and ideological differences between England and Scotland" into "so many elements of interior decoration," Armstrong suggests (67).

[9] And unexplained. "The legacy of Rajkumar's quarrel with Uma was forgotten," the narrator tersely reports (Amitav Ghosh *Glass* 414). Tension is replaced by cohabitation, which as a result takes on a pragmatic before romantic quality: Rajkumar has lost all his money in World War II, so it "was understood by everyone that their connection was one of charity" (469).

because it is abundantly clear that accommodation is what these two are good at. Negotiation is each character's calling card: they are both known for getting along with disparate individuals and managing competing interests, thereby enlarging their respective spheres of influence. Though Rajkumar and Uma bring their work home with them, moreover, their relationship is not structured by a sexual division of labor. They may rely on different sorts of cultural and economic capital as well as different kinds of expertise, but these are not explicitly gendered.[10] It is fair to say, in sum, that they come together as equals, as teammates rather than as husband and wife. By ending up with what amounts to one more instance of teamwork, *The Glass Palace* avoids not only *Waverley*'s concluding figure of a couple burdened by national allegory but also any sense that it has reached a conclusion at all. Uma and Rajkumar's domestic arrangement invokes a series of associations that stretches out before and after this one example.

Although Ghosh's novel discovers teamwork in all manner of states and in all sorts of political situations, it is clear that not all teams and not all states produce enterprise of the same sort or scale. Consider, for example, a late episode that takes place in 1990s Myanmar. There, Rajkumar's son Dinu launches a small business, "The Glass Palace: Photo Studio," "the only place in Yangon where you can see ... contemporary art" (Amitav Ghosh *Glass* 437). His labor yields a seminar among a "motley mix of people" including a "student in a black cap that said *Giorgio Armani*" and

[10] Roy provides terms for understanding this distinction: the bhadralok "were broadly divided into the abhijat bhadralok, who had acquired their fortunes in the late eighteenth and nineteenth centuries as business agents of the British, and the grihasta or madhyabitta bhadralok, a middle-income group characterized by English education, professional occupations, and salaried (rather than entrepreneurial) status" ("Bhadralok" 1). Although, "the latter group has come to be associated most powerfully with the term bhadralok," Roy notes that "considerable heterogeneity" remained the social category's paradoxically defining feature through the late colonial period (2).

"three monks in saffron robes." They meet for weekly discussions of politics wrapped in the "secret language" of photography (436–38). Dinu relies on his interlocutors' discretion as much as they require his expertise in photographic aesthetics – reproductions of pictures by Weston, Cartier-Bresson, and Raghubir Singh line the studio walls.

Different though the photo studio and its coded mentoring may be from the nation-building efforts in which Uma is involved or the speculative investments that Rajkumar and company undertake, Dinu's covert pedagogy shows that project-specific collaboration emerges in Myanmar as in colonial Burma and postcolonial India. *The Glass Palace* registers state repression by the way it affects the agency of packs and networks. Myanmar does not appear to be a state interested in understanding its population as an aggregation of adventurous groups whose enterprise it might wish to nurture. As a result, it represents an outlier to the forms of governance Ghosh finds in the colonies. In Myanmar, it is nearly impossible to tell with certainty where the state ends and civil society begins: "there are always spies, everywhere," Dinu cautions, indicating that it is best to behave as if one is always being watched (Amitav Ghosh *Glass* 438). In the totalitarian state, civil society appears close to unthinkable, which has a surprising upside: "You have to understand that their brutality is of a strangely medieval ilk," Dinu explains. "[T]hey are not so advanced as to be able to perceive a threat in what we do in this room" (438).

The Glass Palace tells the history of Burma's transformation into a British colony and then into postcolonial Myanmar from the standpoint of a resilient civil society that sometimes figures prominently in the state's vision of itself and sometimes does not. Distinctions among precolonial, colonial, and postcolonial states matter in this novel, but they matter in as much as they afford or restrict the activities of what Foucault calls those ever-shifting "limited ensembles" that liberalism dreams of setting in motion (*Birth* 308). The history of the social so conceived is a tale that does not stop and start at the epochal breaks of colonization and decolonization. Civil society, Foucault writes, generates "a never-ending history without degeneration, a generation which is not a juridical-logical sequence but the endless formation of new social fabric, new social relations, new economic structures, and consequently" the possibility for imagining "new types of government" (308). The historical novel that contributes to this kind of history has an episodic form, and like *The Glass Palace* tends not to conclude with a neat resolution but rather to promise further episodes and new instances of collaboration.

The Glass Palace is hardly alone in its approach. Ghosh himself has an even more sweeping historical fiction about the agency of groups under way in his Ibis Trilogy, the first volume of which is entitled *Sea of Poppies*.[11] Burma and Malaya have proven particularly rich territory for this sort of revision to the conventions of historical fiction, as demonstrated by the publication of *The Piano Tuner* by Daniel Mason (2002), *The Harmony Silk Factory* by Tash Aw (2005), and *The Gift of Rain* by Tan Twan Eng (2008).

Although the episodes that compose Ghosh's novel tend to focus on members of three intertwined families, the form of the novel compels questions of how professional collaboration takes on the character of kinship relations. The novel is interested in individual characters with a proclivity towards association and the states that appear to encourage (deliberately or not) networking tendencies among their subject populations. When Rajkumar or Uma's

---

[11] I write elsewhere about *Sea of Poppies* as an exemplary instance of the historical novel after Lukács (J. Marx "Historical").

associations reproduce family or ethnic ties, those sorts of associations appear to be versions of, rather than departures from, the more explicitly economic or political bonding in which the two characters engage. This is to say, although *The Glass Palace* notes the family and caste and ethnicity of its entrepreneurial characters, and although it explains how racism affects its characters' ability to forge connections and even the kinds of connections they forge, the novel does not stare down the relationship between economic freedom and communal discipline within British Empire. There are novels that do so, however, and turning to them will allow me to thicken my description of how fiction seeks to explain contemporary capitalism when it provides globalization with a colonial precedent.

GLOBAL CLANS

Popular commentators have zeroed in on "global tribes," as Joel Kotkin calls them, migrating collectives and well-networked ethnicities that appear both as privileged contributors to a "new pattern of human coexistence" and a reminder of a communal past (*Tribes* 4).[12] Such enterprising groups owe a paradoxical debt to imperial administration that defined populations in communal terms. As Gyan Prakash explains, Britain in particular imagined that its colonies "could never accept civil society as an arena of freedom, as a domain of free individual citizens" ("Civil" 28). The categories of race and ethnicity Britain used to divide and rule also guided the colonial state in cultivating commercial activity among

---

[12] No "relic of a regressive past," Kotkin argues, transnational communities with their "peculiar influence" guarantee a multicultural ideal of "the entire enormous richness and range of the human experience" and also spark economic growth worldwide (12–13, 255). On the contemporary attention to global multitudes, groups, and crowds, and on the political sticking points that appear to trap philosophical and social scientific treatment of communal "habit[s] in motion," see Mazzarella ("Myth" 726).

its subject populations. So long as the members of certain groups continued to conform to the ethnographic traits ascribed to them – to remain, as it were, in their place – the colonial state could be more benign than usual, even offering to provide security and allowing certain communities to profit. There are any number of histories documenting such arrangements between British government and various ethnically defined commercial organizations, some of which predated empire and some of which were generated by it.[13] Familiar though their stories may be, tales of Parsi financiers and Swahili traders can still seem anomalous. They can appear to indicate a devolution of economic decision-making that we more readily associate with postcoloniality and globalization than with imperial administration.

Not surprisingly, therefore, novels that represent trading diasporas tend to mess with the usual chronology of epochal transformation in which precolonial social order yields to colonial domination only to be supplanted by postcolonial rule. Vassanji's *The Gunny Sack*, to take one important example, notes but downplays the significance of those breaks by treating them as among the myriad political shifts that force businessmen to alter their plans. Vassanji's plot is the record of a commercial clan that takes the episodic form I have also observed in *The Glass Palace*. As in Ghosh's novel, characters in Vassanji's tome evaluate the difference among regimes by considering what kinds of opportunities for networking and exchange they make available.

"Among the trading immigrant peoples," the narrator of *The Gunny Sack* relates, "loyalty to a land or a government, always

---

[13] See, regarding South Asian populations and British imperial commerce, such works as Luhrmann's *The Good Parsi* and Niranjana's *Mobilizing India*. For a longer view on the relationship between diaspora, colonialism, and postcolonial nationalism in South Asia and around the Indian Ocean, see Engseng Ho's *The Graves of Tarim*.

loudly professed, is a trait one can normally look for in vain. Governments may come and go, but the immigrants' only concern is the security of their families, their trade and savings" (Vassanji *Gunny* 52). *The Gunny Sack* employs an ethnographic vernacular when presenting the Shamsi collective as a "small overseas community" with a shared religion and "some history" – namely, a conflict with another group that propelled them out of the Indian village of Junapur and across the Indian Ocean (3, 7). Once mobile, the Shamsis never stay still for long. They do their best to become indispensable to the denizens of the regions they inhabit, but they also stay out of local politics. In East Africa they dodge the Maji-Maji revolt, lie low during World War I, and keep their distance from the Mau Mau rebellion. When independence comes, they monitor events by "sitting quietly around the ancient Philips oracle" (156–57). After independence, they cope as best they can with new challenges: Idi Amin's expulsion of Uganda's Asian population "cracked [their] world open like an egg," while Tanzanian nationalization schemes leave Shamsi shopkeepers "washed out" (246, 42). When a character like Hassan Uncle loses his business, however, he is able to fall back on his last assets, "five children, three of them overseas," including Mehboob who runs an Indian cinema in Toronto (247).

The Shamsi appear to be as if at home in a liquid modernity. As Hassan Uncle's recourse to the Canadian wing of his family suggests, moreover, their civil society is pointedly global in scale. While *The Gunny Sack* observes how the Shamsis respond to changes in state administration, therefore, it is even more attentive to showing how they extend a communal network. The key example for one family's idiosyncratic method of extending itself involves the patriarch Dhanji Govindji, who breaks the Shamsi mandate to privilege endogamous relationships when he fathers a son with a woman from outside the clan. After being disciplined for his wayward desire, Dhanji Govindji shuns his son who, in turn, runs away. Dhanji Govindji feels remorse and goes after him, funding his search by stealing from his neighbors. Although he betrays the clan again in stealing from it (and will be punished for doing so), Dhanji Govindji also firms up the Shamsi network as he searches up and down the East African coast. His travels teach him how good colonialism has been for the bottom line: "Our people are doing well under the British" (Vassanji *Gunny* 31). *The Gunny Sack* is full of episodes like this one, wherein breaking with group norms produces both a disciplinary response and a seemingly inadvertent extension of the community's reach.

Rosemary Marangoly George observes that the novel's characters routinely "enter into relationships that leap over political and social chasms" without their trans-ethnic contacts and "impossible loves" ever "bringing together different communities" (*Politics* 181). The episode that best demonstrates this tendency involves the novel's eponymous piece of luggage and Dhanji Govindji's great-grandson Kala, who falls in love with the "small and attractive, fair and African" Amina (Vassanji *Gunny* 210). Kala betrays his lover, wife, and family like, he says "my grandfather Huseni … and even his father Dhanji Govindji" (263–64). He flees to Boston, where the novel finds him holed up in a basement with the gunny sack containing his family's records. This tidy figure for the communal baggage Kala cannot leave behind is equally a trope for the familial ideology he exports to North America.[14] Kala, like his

---

[14] Given the pull of the past, it is perhaps not surprising that the book ends with Kala dreaming of "redemption" in the "banal present" (268). His brother Sona, meanwhile, has a slightly different take, and one that might be said to anticipate the salvage operation of *Desertion*. Like the bevy of historians in Gurnah's novel, Sona is an academic. And like Gurnah's researchers, he is "so excited" at the prospect of analyzing the history contained in "three fragile books" his family has passed down (268).

predecessors, demonstrates his membership in the Shamsis by moving overseas while remaining connected. By meticulously chronicling the persistence of family ties that paradoxically rely on exogamous desires, *The Gunny Sack* offers an alternative to the more typical stop-and-start narrative of anticolonial resistance and postcolonial nation building. It helps us to envision a world composed of competing and occasionally intermingling groups and a world history that chronicles changing patterns of movement among such groups and their shifting patterns of exchange.

The pleasure and danger of exogamy is equally a theme in social scientific accounts of how mobile ethnicities reproduce and grow.[15] Aihwa Ong describes the "flexible ... discipline" of transnational Chinese "family governmentality" as a gambit to generate a distinctive "habitus" that remains coherent as it moves, "finely tuned to the turbulence of late capitalism" (*Flexible* 136). Although, she argues, there "may not be anything uniquely 'Chinese'" about migrant Chinese communities, they have managed to retain an ethnic type nonetheless, and one whose association with commerce might make it the source of "the ideal *homo economicus* of the next century" (136, 34).[16] Mamadou Diouf describes the Murid trade diaspora as engaged in comparable adaptation as it embraces "possibilities offered by globalization" ("Senegalese" 682). As it spreads, the Murid brotherhood modifies "its strong Wolof coloring" and reorganizes "its apparatuses with a view to globalizing Muridism"

---

[15] As is the establishment of institutions like the Shamsi Boys' Secondary School that Vassanji describes his trading clan building in Dar es Salaam. Tölölyan spells out the role of such institutions for the Armenian diaspora, whose communities "have necessarily and inevitably developed local, host country-specific 'ethnic' features" ("Elites" 108).

[16] The recipe for this stereotype, she contends, involves a mix of "Confucian cultural triumphalism," "the endless capacity to dodge state regulations, spin human relations across space, and find ever new niches to exploit," with the result being that the image of "the border-running Chinese executive with no state loyalty has become an important figure in the era of Pacific Rim capital" (136).

(700). Even as the brotherhood becomes an "integral part of the process" of globalization, it reproduces communal distinction, which Diouf thinks can help explain "what is at stake in the debates regarding modernity and cosmopolitanism, ways of being that are too often perceived as incorporation into Western universality" (702, 683). For Ong and Diouf, such transnational communities appear major players in contemporary social life.[17] For other scholars, they are but a reminder that communities of capitalists have a long history. Sugata Bose describes the Indian Ocean "bazaar nexus": an "Indian and Chinese chain of trade and finance" that includes "Gujarati communities," "Baghdadi Jewish, and Chinese specialist communities" whose activities link locations as distant as Zanzibar and Singapore, and who form "a distinct international system that never lost its identity in the larger dominant world system of the West" (*Hundred* 13, 27–28).

As Appadurai observes, scholarship on these and other such groups and systems breaks with "the dominant, Weberian prophecy about modernity in which earlier, intimate social forms would dissolve, to be replaced by highly regimented bureaucratic-legal orders" (*Fear* 5). In Fernand Braudel's version of that narrative, longstanding networks of Armenian merchants and South Asian brokers precede but do not contribute to the eighteenth-century rise of capitalism as a world system. "[T]he fact is that this high-tension trading activity was only present in certain places" outside Europe, Braudel argues; "huge areas were quite untouched by it" (*Wheels*

---

[17] And that means giving up the notion that all "diasporas and cosmopolitans are liberatory forces against oppressive nationalism, repressive state structures, and capitalism" (Ong *Flexible* 15). A further reason to do so: twenty-first-century thinkers inside and outside the academy are so drawn to the idea of global family and clan, DeHart argues, that the likes of Microsoft and Verizon engaged in a "transnational development" plan for conjuring up the "notion of a Latino diaspora" as a means for first defining and then recruiting "Latino elites" ("Hermano" 254).

585). Although he documents commercial traffic in and around the Indian Ocean and the Pacific Rim, in terms of overall economic development Braudel finds those regions most comparable "to Europe in the thirteenth and fourteenth centuries" (585). "A minority ... was a solid and ready-made network," he confirms, but because diasporic partnerships and commercial connections remained the property of minorities, Braudel finds little grounds to credit them with contributing to broader changes in social organization (167).[18]

The Romantic historical novel largely affirmed that account.[19] In *Waverley*, the clan is the social model that modernity displaces, imperialism crushes, and the rise of the English bourgeois household privatizes. In fact, the clan's disappearance is what demonstrates that a historical shift has appeared in *Waverley*'s pages. As Walter Scott puts it in his postscript, that a Scottish "race has now almost entirely vanished from the land" is testament that there "is no European nation which, within the course of half a century, or little more, has undergone so complete a change as the kingdom of Scotland" (492). Duncan observes that treating the clan's obliteration as evidence of historical transition assures later readers that they live in a contrastingly peaceful era of "purely economic progress ... without the extremity of a wholesale structural transformation of social and political relations" (*Modern* 53). Duncan argues further that this was not Scott's formulation alone, for in general "Scots writers articulated their period

---

[18] Braudel's model features classes of "powerful families" like those "which had existed in India – that of the merchants, manufacturers and bankers which had traditionally, father and son, controlled both the economy and the administration of the trading cities" (598). But he does not see these as so much integrating with global changes as engaging in a dynamic wherein they "corrupt the invader" from Europe who seeks to tie them into a larger economy and get "corrupted in return" (598).

[19] This is, as Trumpener and others have shown, one of its notable differences from the Romantic national tale (Trumpener *Bardic*).

consciousness by looking back at the preceding epoch ... covered in the first trilogy of 'Waverley novels,' in which the drastic if uneven modernization of Scottish life provided a material context for the Enlightenment conception of history as wholesale social change" (*Shadow* 23).

Our much revised, contemporary form of historical fiction is not ignorant of wholesale social change, but its approach to context differs. Rather than setting a local stage for the clash of epochs and the groups that inhabit them, migrant populations move through time as well as space. The community abides in and through historical and geographic changes. The genealogical approach taken by a book like *The Gunny Sack* is so effective in capturing this clan tendency to endure that a novel such as Soueif's *The Map of Love* can employ it to provide an imperial origin story for a multiethnic cohort of jet-setting professionals. Like that of *The Gunny Sack*, the repository of family history in *The Map of Love* is a piece of luggage: "a story conjured out of a box; a leather trunk that traveled from London to Cairo and back" (*Map* 11). What the box reveals is a bond linking three generations of intellectuals and experts.

Instead of the cohesion of ethnicity, the members of this novel's clan share the experience of extensive education. To be fair, not every member of *The Map of Love*'s family is university trained, but all are extremely well read. A breadth of education makes it possible for Lady Anna Winterbourne to communicate, the better to fall in love with Sharif Basha and befriend his sister Layla al-Baroudi in early twentieth-century Cairo. Like all good female adventurers, Anna visits the souk in drag. Mistaken for an Englishman by radicals with ties to Sharif, she gets kidnapped. When they take her to their leader, she has little Arabic and Sharif has little English, but they share knowledge of French, a tongue that "makes foreigners of us both" (Soueif *Map* 281, 157).[20] In the present-day portion of the novel, another affective and intellectual triangle forms against the backdrop of national ferment (this time the aftermath of the Oslo peace accords). This connection is also mediated by translation: Isabel Parkman is directed by 'Omar al-Ghamrawi to ask his sister Amal to translate the documents that turn out to contain their shared family history.

Waïl Hassan is surely right to describe *The Map of Love* as providing a nearly comprehensive "map of translation practices," but it is also true that the novel privileges a particularly elevated linguistic mode ("Agency" 757). Amal recognizes her skill in translation as a source of cultural capital, as she suggests with an efficient analogy:

How do I translate 'tarab'? How do I, without sounding weird or exotic, describe to Isabel that particular emotional, spiritual, even physical condition into which one enters when the soul is penetrated by good Oriental music? A condition so specific that it has a root all to itself: t/r/b. Anyone can be a singer – a 'mughanni' – but to be a 'mutrib' takes an extra quality. (Soueif *Map* 332)[21]

Although a cluster of tough-to-render terms – "tarab," "mutrib," "shabby tereb" – lead Amal to conclude that translation is "almost impossible really," her work on the trunk full of diaries and journals suggests otherwise (515). Amal succeeds, Mariadele Boccardi supposes, not only in bridging Arabic and English, Egypt and Britain, but also in the "re-establishment of continuity" between the

---

[20] Hassan calls theirs an "amour bilingue" or more accurately "trilingue." The term is Abdelkébar Khatibi's, and in Hassan's usage it captures the novel's articulation of "the relation among ethnics, love, and translation" (756–57).

[21] For passages such as this, Hassan considers *The Map of Love* a "paradigmatic translational novel," including modes of translation that range from "from literal to literary ... from domesticating to foreignizing ... and from epistemically violent ... to loving translations that surrender to the experience of alterity" ("Agency" 757).

Global clans 153

seemingly radically discontinuous periods of colonization and globalization ("History" 193). Skilled translation makes it possible to grasp that the civil society of colonial Egypt is not so different from the globalized social life of today, filled as both are by expert team-builders. *The Map of Love* reaffirms, furthermore, that throughout the twentieth century civil society served as a realm where fellow feeling might overcome the differences of race and ethnicity, even as states both colonial and postcolonial exploited those differences for national ends.

The Map of Love presents the historical novel's generic capacity as one of its central themes: Amal "has translated novels – or done her best to translate them," and she treats the translation of historical documents as a comparable task (Soueif *Map* 515). She works through Anna Winterbourne's journal, satisfying as she goes a "need to fill in the gaps," to "piece a story together" (26). "That is the beauty of the past," she argues: you can see where people were headed; "you can tell the story that they, the people who lived it, could only tell in part" (234). Research at the British Council Library, at Dar al-Kutub, and the second-hand bookstalls allows her to smooth the fragmented accounts she finds in Layla and Anna's diaries. The result has historical substance because it is so thoroughly literary: Amal says of Anna, "She has become as real to me as Dorothea Brooke" (26).[22] By personifying fiction's desire to

---

[22] As much as *The Map of Love* relies on a theme of translation, it also recycles tropes of adaptation. Massad notes that the novel narrates "certain sections in a way reminiscent of both a traditional *hakawati* (Arab storyteller) style and that of Trollope, Dickens, and especially Thackeray's *Vanity Fair*" ("Politics" 81). In addition to these, Hassan spots a *Heart of Darkness* rewrite ("Agency" 760). Soueif herself notes in an interview that as she prepared to write the novel she was "thinking along romantic lines," thinking of Sharif as "the Byronic hero," and in general composing the novel of "very odd, pastichey things like that" ("Talking" 102). Finally, as they read Anna's prose in the present day, Amal and Isabel critique it as "a little self-conscious perhaps, a little aware of the genre – *Letters from Egypt, A Nile Voyage, More Letters from Egypt*" (*Map* 58).

narrate a prehistory of the present, Amal also provides an explanation about why writers and readers may want novels that do so. She seeks in the social interactions of the past some indication that the future "can't be that bad," that there "must be a way" to cope with a changing world even if we "can't see it yet" (234). By relating to past personages as fictional characters and by composing a plot with the seamless narrative of a realist novel, Amal imagines that literary techniques can help give us a sense of a manageable present by representing a manageable past.

Fiction that imagines colonialism might have diversified entrepreneurship interrupts the more usual story about the derivation of present economic instability. Instead of routing the current crisis through a tale of Anglo-American liberalism – briefly interrupted in its march to global dominance by socialism before splintering into various and sundry techniques of neoliberal rule – these novels find examples of enterprise culture everywhere. The contrastingly Eurocentric account treats early twenty-first-century "liquid life" as a departure from mid-twentieth-century stability – to borrow Zygmunt Bauman's phrase once again. But contemporary historical fiction of the sort I have been reading does no such thing. Instead, it details an unstable past that holds lessons for an equally unstable present.

Management, as opposed to, say, usefulness, is the right word for this attitude towards the past because of the sense of risk and unruliness inherent within it. "Most polite, mainstream interests recoil in horror," writes Paul Gilroy, when faced with "the prospect of colonial history providing an opening onto the multicultural promise of the postcolonial world" (*Postcolonial* 143). Understanding multicultural society as part of our imperial inheritance challenges what Gilroy calls "fantasies of the newly embattled European region as a culturally bleached or politically fortified place" (141). Recognizing the "little-known historical facts of Europe's openness to the colonial worlds it helped to make" also threatens existing accounts of social life during the age of empire (141). For Soueif, it appears newly possible to imagine colonial Egypt as a place where one could engage in interracial romance and start transnational families that would survive for generations. Gurnah's *Desertion* presents a comparable account of the possibilities afforded by colonialism and goes one step further by posing the seemingly impossible challenge of living up to the risk-taking precedent of our early twentieth-century predecessors.

Like *The Map of Love* and *The Gunny Sack*, *Desertion* features a family tree and a contemporary investigator who discovers its imperial roots. Gurnah's genealogist is Rashid, a Swahili professor of literature who works in Britain and writes about "race and sexuality in settler writing in Kenya" (*Desertion* 257–58). He investigates the impossible love between a British explorer named Martin Pearce and a South Asian woman named Rehana Zakariya, who lived in an East African community very much like the one depicted in *The Gunny Sack*.[23] Rashid is gobsmacked by the enormous risk these two took in hooking up. He wonders what it was about them and about their era that made such risk-taking seem appealing. "What would have made an Englishman of his background – university, colonial official, a scholar – begin something like that with the sister of a shopkeeper in a small town on the East African coast?" (117). Rashid wonders similarly about Rehana: "Perhaps she thought she had nothing to lose, that all that remained for her was a life in that bright yard behind the shop, making clothes for women who only paid her a pittance" (118). Rashid is stumped. His

---

[23] As in Vassanji's novel, so too in *Desertion* it is axiomatic that "wherever Indians went … there prosperity followed" (39).

narration of *Desertion* comes to a full stop on page 110. "An Interruption," proclaims the header on that page, followed by Rashid's confession. "I don't know how it would have happened." And yet, "it did happen, that Rehana Zakariya and Martin Pearce became lovers" (110–11). This aporia maddened Gurnah's reviewers, but it makes the best sense for a novel invested in renovating our understanding of imperial history.[24]

Rashid's account does recognize that empire divided populations into ethnic peoples and regulated their interaction. But it also adds that Britain's habit of encouraging certain individuals and groups to move around the planet inadvertently created opportunities for intimacy among the most daring representatives of those peoples. Rashid knows that this was so. He is so daunted by the might of colonial and communal discipline, however, and so persuaded by the conventional wisdom that they must only have limited rather than also occasionally abetted crosscultural intimacy, that he thinks of Martin and Rehana's risky business as "miraculous" (Gurnah *Desertion* 110).

In *Desertion*, one couple's risk-taking produces a family that ultimately incorporates South Asians, Mswahili, and Britons. This family spans from colonial Tanganyika to Zanzibar, Kenya, and England. As in *The Map of Love*, many of the members of *Desertion*'s clan are intellectuals and professionals of one sort or another, teachers and antiquarians, professors and government administrators. Instead of feeling empowered by this heritage, however, Rashid feels guilty. His family had the capacity to make sure he was educated and sent to school overseas right before the bloodiest period of Zanzibar's postcolonial history. As a result, he experiences

---

[24] "The reader is robbed of the opportunity to witness the affair through the eyes of the protagonists," complains Laila Lalami in *The Nation*. "Gurnah himself can be charged with a form of literary desertion," argues Adam Mars-Jones in *The Observer*.

mobility as a mode of betrayal. Like Kala in *The Gunny Sack*, moreover, Rashid discovers that he is linked to a whole series of betrayals, including Martin's abandonment of Rehana, whom he left behind at their home in Mombasa while she was pregnant with their daughter.[25] As much as *Desertion* posits the colony as a place of heroism, it also expects heroes to fall. Martin's betrayal of Rehana is predictable, or at least it seems so to Rashid. Far from lowering Martin in his eyes, however, this failure only increases Rashid's admiration for his initial willingness to take a real risk.

Rashid thinks of the recovery of his family history not as reassuring, as Amal does, nor as immobilizing, as Kala does, but as an instigation to take a risk of his own. When he presents his research at a conference, in the audience is a woman named Barbara Turner, who reveals that her mother was Martin's daughter, not by Rehana but by his later, English wife. Barbara and Rashid decide to collaborate on a project the novel frames not just as the reconstruction of their shared family but also of the planet. "Everything is scattered," Rashid says to Barbara, "dispersed to the farthest corners of the world. No one can find anyone" (Gurnah *Desertion* 261). They treat this difficulty as a dare, and head off to Zanzibar on the last page of the novel, "starting again," Rashid says, ready to bridge "different customs, discomforts" just like their ancestors (261). *Desertion* in no way encourages its readers to doubt the challenge that Rashid faces in going home to see his family and in coming to grips with his guilt at leaving them behind when he went to school. Still, the "comedy" he and

---

[25] Martin and Rehana's daughter has her own children, among them Jamila, who becomes well known on Zanzibar for having a grandmother who "was a dirty woman who lived a life of sin with an Englishman" (Gurnah *Desertion* 235). Rashid's brother Amin falls in love with Jamila just before independence, but his family frowns on the relationship and he leaves her, as Martin left Rehana before him. Introducing a variation on this theme, Rashid feels guilt for abandoning his family by going to school in England (221).

Barbara anticipate if Rashid's family asks them, unmarried couple that they are, to sleep in separate rooms makes clear that they risk comparably little by getting on a plane (262).

I imagine that few readers would be likely to disagree with the contention that Martin and Rehana's coupling would have required genuine bravery, or even with the idea that non-European traders in the mold of Rajkumar from *The Glass Palace* or Dhanji Govindji from *The Gunny Sack* were ingenious in taking advantage of what colonialism afforded them. When historical novels seek to connect these actors and their actions with more contemporary lives, however, questions remain about what exactly such heroes, rebels, and sly compradors stood for. Those were especially vexed questions for mid-century fiction writers seeking to explain what decolonization did to familial networks of the kind that thrived during the colonial period. Attia Hosain's 1961 *Sunlight on a Broken Column* tells a story in which the partition of colonial India involves the dismantling of one Muslim *taluqdari* family in Lucknow, along with the social networks that landlord clan helped to organize. These include quasi-feudal arrangements between estate owners and peasants as well as, Muneeza Shamsie observes, a range of less formalized connections that entailed "the blending of cultures and ideas, which enabled people of different beliefs to respect and participate in each others' festivals such as *Holi* and *Diwali*, *Shubraat* and *Eid*" ("Sunlight" 143). The novel's ambivalence about the decline of that colonial multiculture is nowhere clearer than in its final retroactive section. Hosain's heroine Laila, who throughout the novel has been critical but supportive of nationalism, returns to Lucknow after Independence to discover that "[t]attered settlements for refugees had erupted on once open spaces. Ugly buildings had sprung up, conceived by ill-digested modernity and the hasty needs of a growing city" (Hosain *Sunlight* 270).²⁶ If Venu Chitale's 1950 *In Transit* is less nostalgic, it nonetheless follows a similar narrative arc, observing the decay of a Pune *wada* and the dissolution of the family it housed, as the fractious decades before Independence see familial disputes gradually overwritten as political differences.²⁷ At the same time that the homestead decays and the family travels away, bonds remain that tie characters living in Pune, Bombay on the coast, and abroad in England. The *wada* eventually transforms into a privileged point in an international familial network as well as the site for ongoing nationalist activism (498). Although Hosain's and Chitale's novels tell tales of loss, they equally belong in a genealogy of stories about history's victors, durable clans of landlords and pioneering members of a transnational professional class. In aggregate, these mid-century books and the more contemporary novels they anticipate remind us how much that transnational class owes its multifarious composition to imperial contact.

COLONIAL RISK

Contemporary fiction can imagine British Empire the way it does because a variety of novels published during in the early decades of the twentieth century were already engaged in framing colonial enterprise in liberal terms. They too portrayed Britain as inadvertently providing the tools for its own undoing, where its own undoing meant extending the ability to take risks and forge transnational social networks to the most enterprising and most educated factions of colonized populations. Characters in a novel such as

---

[26] See Needham on the complicated politics of the novel's nostalgia ("Multiple" 103).
[27] On this narrative arc in other Indian decolonization novels, see Kabir ("Gender").

Sarath Kumar Ghosh's *Prince of Destiny* (1909) or Joseph Conrad's *Nostromo* (1904/1985) anticipate the portrayal of incipient professionalism among traders and activists who populate more recent historical fictions. These books provide points of departure for later experiments and start the process of transforming the historical novel from a genre focused on epochal change within nations to a form more attuned to the management of increasingly global civil society.

Nostromo situates its plot at a moment of transition from one species of colonization to another, with the intimation of a further change in the future. The fictional South American territory of Costaguana swaps Spanish for Anglo-American domination, which brings with it a more rapid development, a "second youth, like a new life, full of promise, of unrest, of toil ... Material changes swept along in the train of material interests" (Conrad *Nostromo* 417). Critics have found stereotypic representatives of a British Empire dependent on American capital in the teamwork of the Englishman, Charles Gould, driven to salvage the mine his father first established, and the San Francisco investor, Holroyd, who influences local events from afar. Holroyd's declaration, "We shall run the world's business whether the world likes it or not," even strikes some as articulating the Americanization of global capitalism (94–95).[28] As ever, imperialism appears all-encompassing in this Conrad novel: there is no promise of postcolonial independence. But that does not mean that what happens in colonial society is predictable or that colonial rule goes unchallenged. Benita Parry argues that Conrad plays up empire's unevenness with his novel's

---

[28] See C. Miller on this imperial allegory ("Holroyd's" 16). Fothergill argues, "Through the figure of arch-capitalist Holroyd, we have a sense of the acuity with which Conrad was already articulating what we now call 'globalization,' specifically a modernity under the aegis of U.S. domination" ("Connoisseurs" 142).

"deferrals, digressions and temporal displacements" ("Narrating" 235). "A notoriously devious chronology, together with the dramatization of the barriers to imperialism's supremacist goals," she contends, distinguish *Nostromo* from other period texts (237).

Conrad's plot largely turns on the question of how events conspire to place one unique character in a position to appropriate the colony's wealth. The novel's last third famously zeroes in on Nostromo's gambit to grow "rich very slowly," selling off the silver that he stole from a ruling faction, in a process that quietly transforms him from local champion into international trader (*Nostromo* 432).[29] The silver is a textbook example of the commodity fetish. It makes Nostromo the "slave of a treasure," destroys "the genuineness of his qualities," and convinces him that "everything was a sham. But the treasure was real" (432). "Commodities cannot themselves go to market," as Marx reminds us, and true to form the silver sets Nostromo in motion as much as it weighs him down (K. Marx *Capital* 178). He devises a plan that involves digging up a few bars at a time under cover of darkness. Even as he continues to play the part of the loyal servant, he also becomes the "unquestioned patron of secret societies," "a revolutionist at heart" funding a workers' movement "under the presidency of an indigent, sickly, somewhat

---

[29] For Jameson, the trope of getting rich slowly indicates the novel's aporetic theory of historical change. Although *Nostromo* portrays the arrival of full-on capitalist development in Sulaco, it portrays this epochal shift absent some singular event to herald transition from "one state of things (fallen nature) to another (genuine society)" (Jameson *Political* 278). Such a "decisive shift" occurs – "capitalism arrives in Sulaco" – "not as an event that can be narrated, but rather as an aporia around which the narrative must turn" (278). "This is clearly the sense of Nostromo's warning to himself: 'Grow rich slowly!' Such a watchword offers all the paradoxes and puzzles of diachronic thinking," Jameson argues: "at what 'point in time' do the minute accretions of coin, dropping one upon the other like the slow dripping of a faucet, suddenly become riches? How in the measurable world is time ultimately possible? How do things come into being, how can they possibly 'happen'?" (278).

hunchbacked little photographer, with ... bloodthirsty hate of all capitalists" (Conrad *Nostromo* 434, 436). Playing both sides is "difficult to keep up," but he manages to do so by trading increasingly "far afield," stretching his network of trusted middlemen to "distant ports" (435, 433). An opportune marriage proposal seems likely to provide further cover for his business affairs, but instead precipitates his accidental death and the abrupt end to a short, unplanned, and seemingly successful transnational business.[30]

There is more than a little of the dynamic Homi K. Bhabha terms "mimicry" in Nostromo's behavior. With his illicit commerce hidden behind a legitimate trading concern, it becomes difficult to distinguish the Nostromo who performs what Bhabha calls an "authorized version of otherness" from the more "inappropriate" criminal version (*Location* 88). He remains to all appearances a "dog of the rich," even as he surreptitiously disrupts colonial authority (Conrad *Nostromo* 391).[31] He disrupts that authority, however, by reproducing the logic of colonial capitalism and displaying the sort of entrepreneurial streak that the novel otherwise associates with the likes of Holroyd and Gould.[32] Foreshadowing Rajkumar's canny management of colonial

---

[30] "The search for a restored family is an underlying motif in Conrad's fiction," Schwarz notes, denied here as so often in Conrad's work by the demands of economic and political plotting that appear incompatible with domesticity ("Quarrel" 566).

[31] Bhabha's *Nostromo* example of this formulation is Decoud, the "scene-setter of the *opéra bouffe* of the New World," the propagandist for the colonial republic who so believes the hype he spouts that, in the end, he entertains "doubt of his own individuality" (*Location* 88). He so fully loses "all belief in the reality of his action past and to come" that he commits suicide (Conrad *Nostromo* 413).

[32] Parry suggests that Nostromo mutates in "schizoid fashion" into "the thief who mimics imperialism's (im)morality" ("Narrating" 237). This mimicry is funded by imperialism, and in more ways than one: Nostromo plies his stolen silver from a boat purchased for him as a gift by his former boss and the matriarch whose family owns the silver mine. They seem unsurprised when "he paid all the price back within the next three years." After all, "[b]usiness was booming all along this seaboard" (Conrad *Nostromo* 406).

opportunities in *The Glass Palace*, Nostromo rebels and becomes complicit simultaneously.[33]

This formulation appears elsewhere in late nineteenth- and early twentieth-century prose, Meenakshi Mukherjee observes, describing how the "flaunting of subjection" coexisted comfortably with "fierce cultural pride" in many colonial-era South Asian fictions ("Beginnings" 96). Among the titles on her list is K. K. Singha's *Sanjogita or The Princes of Aryavarta* (1930) and S. K. Ghosh's *Prince of Destiny*. Partha Chatterjee adds the Bengali classic *Anandamath or The Sacred Brotherhood* (1882) by Bankim Chandra Chatterji, which he describes as executing a "reversal of the Orientalist problematic, but within the same general thematic" (P. Chatterjee *Nationalist* 73). That novel generates "a cultural ideal in which the industries and the sciences of the West can be learnt and emulated while retaining the spiritual greatness of Eastern culture" (73). Elite, nationalist, but also cosmopolitan: Bart Moore-Gilbert discerns a common theme of "transnational mediation and interaction" in such novels, as characters travel "periphery–periphery" axes, especially between India and Japan ("Imagining" 124).[34] For Alex Tickell, the account of India proffered in *Prince of Destiny* smacks of nothing more than contemporary globalization: the novel's depiction of "imperial transport networks [used] to gather political and technological know-how from Japan, Germany and America" makes its "feudal

---

[33] As Mongia observes, in making such a comparison it pays to be aware that arguing that later fiction shares a problem set with *Nostromo* risks binding the likes of Amitav Ghosh to a literary historical "narrative of the West" that defines Conrad "at the center" ("Between" 89, 98). Risks, she contends, mitigated by the fact that Conrad's writing is as often thought of as part of "high literature" as it is "associated with the 'third world,'" a schizophrenic positioning that makes it hard to conflate his fiction with imperial or Western representation per se (98).

[34] Ghosh's *Prince of Destiny* is Moore-Gilbert's privileged example, for even as it "centers on the divided political, cultural and emotional loyalties ... of a young ruler of a nominally independent Indian 'native' state" who has a deep affinity for Britain, it also treats Japan as the inspiration for "'new' Indian nationalism" (126).

setting seem more like an international transit-zone than a culturally-unified homeland" ("Writing" 531).

Ghosh's protagonist is Barath, heir to the throne of Barathpur, born in the year that Queen Victoria was proclaimed empress of India. He is a "sweet boy," according to the queen, and according to *Prince of Destiny*'s narrator is a perfect mimic who possesses the "capacity to be an Eastern or a Western at will, as required for the moment" (*Prince* 229, 17). At university in Britain, Barath demonstrates a disciplinary flexibility as well, succeeding wildly in English history, mathematics, and poetics (177, 262, 275). Barath's adaptability makes him the perfect teammate: he collaborates with the poète maudit Francis Thompson on "[a]n accurate yet truly poetic translation of" the Sanskrit masterwork "Sakuntala," which Barath trusts will "remove a mountain of misconception between Great Britain and India" (295–96). In addition to poetry, the two conspire on topics of urban planning. After Thompson shows him around a London slum, a "deep yearning arose in [Barath's] heart that some day a great personage," a "new Haroun-el-Raschid ... who had walked at night ... through the streets of Delhi and Lahore and Benares," "might come forth and study London ... for its weal" (251). As it elaborates a list of Barath's various projects, *Prince of Destiny* spins mimicry into social reform: "The best way for a man of keen perception to know England objectively – that is, truthfully – is to be born outside, and then to come in and become an Englishman" (158).

The second half of the novel reproduces the episodic structure of the first, as Barath turns his attention to improving social life in Barathpur. He imagines a campaign to increase coal production, grow the local iron works, "open a technical institute" to educate a generation of engineers, and instruct "our thakurs and zemindars not to let their wealth lie idle, but to bring it out and use it for their own benefit and for the welfare of our people" (S. K. Ghosh *Prince* 385). Barath dreams of development, of wooing new British investment, and of engaging everyone in the excitement of trade. He imagines Barathpur as a land where new sources of commercial wealth are lying around on the ground, waiting for someone with the ingenuity to exploit them. "Here is a vegetable product growing in abundance everywhere," he announces, "a part of which we use in our households, but the rest is eaten by wild monkeys: and yet in a liquid form it would make an excellent red wine, of which millions of gallons could be exported to Europe; in a solid form, with suitable adjuncts, it would make perhaps the purest soap for preserving the skin ... and in a condensed form as a pill it would be a simple and wholesome blood purifier" (386–87). Because "there seems to be no capitalist in Europe with imagination enough to start works in India" and thereby launch these various product lines, Barath calls upon his fellows to become entrepreneurs themselves and help turn Barathpur into a thriving export economy (386).

Although his schemes garner initial praise, when it becomes clear that he is not interested in developing a militarized state to accompany a reinvigorated economy, Barath finds he is opposed by the high priest, Vashista, who bridles at talk of Britain and India as economic partners and spiritual "brothers" (S. K. Ghosh *Prince* 366).[35] *Prince of Destiny* stages the debate between Barath's attempt to build civil society and Vashista's attempt to resist colonial rule as a contest between competing networks and competing styles of administration. Vashista sends members of his posse to the United

---

[35] He has none of Barath's confidence that "peace ... guaranteed by the presence of the British" will engender the emergence of an Indian "Galileo, a Newton, a Pascal" or a reincarnation of the likes of Kalidas or Valmikhi (595). "All that is based on India's Independence," Vashista counters. "And when Britain voluntarily grants independence to India we shall all be dead" (597).

States and Germany, where they learn cutting-edge techniques in steel and iron manufacturing as well as military tactics and strategy to build on their knowledge of Rama, Arjuna, and Ghengis Khan (388–89). Vashista also brings in Japanese drill masters to train an army in jiu-jitsu, which "makes a man out of the lowest wreck of humanity," and he clothes that force in military uniforms "of Japanese pattern" hidden under their "saffron robes" (471, 551).[36] Barath's network includes contacts made during his studies, such as Lord Melnor, a "genial, hearty Englishman" and the brother of Lady Ellen, who was a mother to Barath in Britain (62). Nora, his English sweetheart, reappears as well, promising an alliance that would "be but a symbol of the bond between Britain and India" (538). When *Prince of Destiny* introduces Nora's local competition, named Suvona, it borrows a trope as likely to be familiar from the tradition of nineteenth-century Indian historical fiction as that of Walter Scott – whose "story of young Lochinvar has been frequently enacted" in India, the narrator reports (98). "Verily thou art the one true Cosmopolitan," Suvona woos, while also cautioning Barath that he has "forgotten the customs of his people" (499, 553).

Inevitably, girlfriends and networks clash and revolution threatens, but all is quickly diffused when Barath finds no support for his appeal to "forgive the West" and Vashista's army is dispirited that "[o]ur Prince has failed us – for the love of the British" (S. K. Ghosh *Prince* 598, 610). Though the stakes were high, it is as if the tumult never happened: because all communication lines with Barathpur were cut, "[t]he imperial government never heard of the intended revolution" (621). After this anticlimax, and establishing a pattern routinely recycled in much later historical fiction, *Prince of Destiny*

[36] See both Tickell ("Writing") and Moore-Gilbert ("Imagining") on how *Prince of Destiny* draws attention to the significance of the Japanese model of resistance for other anti-colonial efforts.

leaves its hero on the move, "awaiting his call" (621).[37] The novel promises a "New Buddha," "one who will turn the armaments of West and East of our generation from instruments of carnage into instruments of industry" (629). *Prince of Destiny*, like the journalism that Ghosh also published at the turn of the twentieth century about Parsee "millionaires of the orient," anticipates a future that rewards flexibility in political as well as commercial allegiance. One 1902 column in particular is worth noting. There, Ghosh comments on the news that Bombay businessman and cotton trader Nowojee Manockji Wadia was "about to convert a million pounds, his entire fortune, into a public trust for charitable purposes" ("Millionaires" 11). Wadia was but one of the Parsee "millionaires of the orient," Ghosh explains to his readers in London and New York, whose "public service to all India" lies in demonstrating that "in the twentieth century it is wealth that makes the man – not caste or lineage" (11). The Parsees testify to that "subtle law of economics," he contends, "which postulates that 'in a conservative community minorities must rise to the surface'" (11). After migrating to India, the Parsees bided their time, "ever looking for an opportunity for material progress," until that "opportunity came at last with British rule" (11). Just as Barath awaits a day more propitious for his mode of transnational collaboration, so the Parsees suggest the possibility that "a generation hence, when the armies of Europe are booted with the skin of the sacred cow from some factory in the heart of India, perchance a high-caste Brahmin will be found at the head of it. Ye shades of Manu," Ghosh concludes, "what a revolution!" (11).

---

[37] When it seems clear neither Vashista's revolutionary networking nor Melnor's incompetent imperialism offers an alliance that facilitates Barath's mediation, he drops out. Instead of a domestic arrangement suggestive of a new historical era, Barath marries Suvona but instructs her to "adopt an heir" while he heads "out of the palace, into the world . . ." (629).

With stories of colonial networking and economic innovation, the novels in my necessarily brisk genealogy of twentieth-century historical fiction convert empire into a setting for portraying risk-taking entrepreneurs and intellectuals, experts and activists. There is no mistaking these heroes with the "more or less mediocre, average English gentleman" Lukács finds in Scott's defining instance of the genre (*Historical* 40, 33). These novels do not conform, moreover, to Lukács's account of a post-1848 tendency to exoticize history à la Flaubert's *Salammbô*. Instead, like Lukács's "classical historical novel," they endeavor to provide a "concrete prehistory of the present" (296). They seek to explain where what we might call a global civil society came from, and to explain how imperial contact might have precipitated a multicultural professional-managerial class. Twentieth-century historical fiction does rely on the sort of "friendships and love entanglements" that for Lukács served to humanize "bourgeois revolution" (37, 24). But as its investment in describing the support systems that afford entrepreneurship suggests, twentieth-century historical fiction is less concerned with describing affairs among self-governing citizens embroiled in what Lukács called "the formation of the national character" (54). Instead, the historical novels I have described tend to portray agents whose mobility and desire to network is reminiscent of Karl Marx's description of a capitalist class that gives a "cosmopolitan character to production and consumption in every country" (*Selected* 162).[38] This process starts with colonial businessmen such as Rajkumar, social reformers such as Barath, bazaar traders like Dhanji Govindji, and adventurous heroines like Anna Winterbourne. By delineating the bonds that tie such early

---

[38] Harvey observes of Marx's line, "If this is not a compelling description of 'globalization' as we now know it then it is hard to imagine what would be" ("Geography" 54).

twentieth-century innovators to their postcolonial brethren, the historical novel provides a prehistory for globalization that is also an origin story for the social organization we might call, for better and worse, global meritocracy.

Contemporary historical fiction differs from the neoliberal theory of development offered by the likes of de Soto, in that it understands entrepreneurship less as an untapped resource – the vital ingredient in the production of a universalized individual subject – than as the result of education systems and kinship networks. Entrepreneurs are not loitering on the docks of Mumbai and in the slums of Lima waiting for de Soto's Institute for Liberty and Democracy to intervene on their behalf. According to contemporary historical novels, such enterprising subjects are propelled into action by reproducible sentimental bonds, familial networks, and education systems. The characters in these novels are the sorts who mediate between labor and capital, affirming in various ways the foundational definition of the professional-managerial class offered by Barbara and John Ehrenreich. Fiction reveals global civil society to be a professional-managerial formation – just as Scott's novels allowed readers to see early forms of European civil society as a bourgeois formation – and in so doing offers a different account of liberalism after liberalism than one finds in the work of neoliberal thinkers.

CHAPTER 5

Women as economic actors in contemporary and modernist novels

Researchers studying women's labor know how much the terms for political and economic participation have changed over the course of the twentieth century. Reports issued by the United Nations, studies undertaken by feminist economists, and news coverage of women in the economy locate gender in a history less focused on extending the franchise than on explaining what happens when women become a new majority in the workforce. *Homo economicus* is no longer masculine, they reveal. Headlines proclaim "The End of Men" and magazine covers reveal the sorry lot of "The Beached White Male": "He Had a Big Job, a Big Office, a Big Bonus. Now He's All Washed Up" (Rosin "End" 56; *Newsweek* cover). Scholarship, meanwhile, turns more soberly to the "thoroughly contemporary" question of women's "new access to a wide range of leadership roles" in business and government (Eagly and Carli *Labyrinth* 184, 1). It is unclear, however, whether women's heightened visibility in management offices, on assembly lines, and in higher education means the end of liberalism's durable sexual division of labor. The library of scholarship on eighteenth- and nineteenth-century political economy reminds us that the self-governing actor who stepped off the pages of *The Wealth of Nations* required feminine support at home to enable his calculated participation in the market.¹ Talk of the 2008 recession as mostly a "mancession," combined with pronouncements about the feminization of work, and migration, and even globalization, certainly appear to indicate that arrangements between men and women are shifting away from an older liberal division of labor, even if sexism has yet to disappear.²

Fiction has contributed to this shift by generating new tales to supplement the old stories of domestic women and rakish men who added literary substance to classic liberal economy. In this chapter, I focus on two novels that purport to explain what women want today and to show what they can do once they leave the house and become breadwinners. William Gibson's *Pattern Recognition* (2003) and Monica Ali's *Brick Lane* (2003) present the world as viewed from the standpoint of professional and working-class women, respectively. *Pattern Recognition* features a jet-setting advertising consultant; *Brick Lane* concentrates on two sisters working in different wings of the garment industry. That working women come in two classes has given scholars pause. For all their differences, I argue, these two categories of women (middle managers and wage laborers) have interested scholarly and popular commentators for the same reason: they beg the question of whether paid labor is *all* that women want today. As if to provide an answer, *Pattern Recognition* and *Brick Lane* offer literary reassurance that women

---

¹ As W. Brown puts it, "the autonomous subject of liberalism requires a large population of nonautonomous subjects, a population that generates, tends, and avows the goods, relations, dependencies, and connections that sustain and nourish human life" (*States* 156). Brown is hardly alone in arguing that a sexual division of labor underwrote what Adam Smith called the "natural course of things" (*Wealth* 380). See also Dillon (*Gender* 11–12) and Bodkin ("Agency" 47).

² The term "mancession" is habitually attributed to Perry, who noted in a blog post in November 2008 that 82 percent of the job losses from November 2007 to November 2008 in the United States were jobs held by men ("Recession?"). Although that first post called it a "male recession," by January 2009 Perry had switched to "mancession," and the term was rapidly appropriated by the economic press.

who work will not become as doggedly focused on economy as men have been. Women who work are not, these novels suggest, latter-day versions of the masculine rational actor whose single-minded self-interest allowed him to pursue his advantage in Adam Smith's market.

It may seem puzzling that anyone would worry about women turning into rational actors. Misogynistic claims of feminine irrationality aside, conventional wisdom has it that after modernism the entire option of rationality is off the menu. Who, after Freud and Weber, still thinks that any human consistently acts reasonably, and especially when it comes to money? Economists hope they can, is the short answer to that question. Scarcely any economic report issued or policy implemented does not reflect the believe, or at least the hope, that consumers and producers can be taught to act rationally. "*Homo oeconomicus* is the one island of rationality," Michel Foucault explains, "within an economic process whose uncontrollable nature" is a given for scholars working in the tradition of Smith and John Stuart Mill (*Birth* 282). Gary Becker and Kevin Murphy allow that in the "short run" individual choice can be "seriously constrained" by various barriers and mediators of knowledge, among them "common culture, norms, and traditions" (*Social* 22, 24).[3] Mitchell Dean submits that liberal government strives to help populations overcome such barriers, to develop "capacities for autonomy . . . including the practice of exercising 'ethical despotism' upon themselves where necessary" ("Liberal" 48). Governments want populations that know how to repress, the better to embody the self-governing, aspirational norm of twenty-first-century social

---

[3] But they also argue that even taking such constraints into account, the notion of "individual rational choices in a society with strong cultural influences is not an oxymoron, but rather . . . the interaction of choice and culture produces novel, important, and neglected behavior" (26).

order. "The freedom offered and defended by liberal rhetoric is a freedom that is entwined with these images of a subject whose integrity is an impossible perfection," Vikki Wells explains, "a subject who can be calculated and predicted into the future at the same time as he or she has a clarity of thought and will that directs these very promises and predictions" ("Promise" 82). Self-governance is as essential to rule now as it ever was in the past, but rational calculation is also more clearly thought of as an effect of social administration rather than its foundation.

By portraying working women who struggle to gauge their own interests, set career goals, and put their plans into action, contemporary fiction treats women as a source of stories about what it means to calculate now. To the extent that novels such as *Pattern Recognition* and *Brick Lane* describe characters who cannot make decisions on their own, they present figures akin to research subjects, employees, and clients both male and female who depend on social scientists, bosses, counselors, and case officers for help in becoming self-governing. That fictions like those of Gibson and Ali focus on women does not disqualify them from contributing to an interdisciplinary debate about economic actors in general. To the contrary, these novels confirm social scientific hypotheses that patriarchy no longer exiles women to the margins of economic life. Sexism persists in the workplace even so, as Gibson and Ali observe, which is one reason why it can be difficult to see how women have altered the market.

To provide genealogical context for this problem, between my treatment of *Pattern Recognition* and *Brick Lane* I read three earlier twentieth-century fictions. Jean Rhys's *Voyage in the Dark* (1934/1985), Virginia Woolf's *To the Lighthouse* (1927/1981), and Elizabeth Bowen's *The Heat of the Day* (1948/2002) helped convince readers that the Victorian model of domestic femininity was in the process of being thoroughly revised. Although these novels take different approaches, all agree that the ramifications for women moving out of the domestic realm are as wide-ranging as they are uneven. With their radically different narrative arcs, these novels presage contemporary uncertainty about whether working women are better understood as the victims of social change or the incipient managers of yet-to-be-determined social order. Before turning to fiction, I frame the debate about working women and their futures as it has appeared in recent scholarship.

THE FEMINIZATION OF GLOBALIZATION

"The logic of feminization is complex and contradictory," writes the professor of women and gender studies Mary Hawkesworth, casting her eyes back at nearly two decades of claims about how global economy shaped and was shaped by the activities of women at work. "Women are simultaneously hailed as resourceful providers, reliable microentrepreneurs, and cosmopolitan citizens and positioned as disposable domestics, the exploited global workforce, and as displaced, devalued, and disenfranchised diasporic citizens" (*Globalization* 23). Given such widely divergent associations, it is little wonder that the world's working women have developed into a multifarious object of study in disciplines ranging from economics to sociology, political science to women's studies.[4] As often as they get defined by their differences, however, working women appear joined by their shared testimony of sexism on the job. They register as the paradoxical effect of centrifugal and centripetal forces; they anticipate a woman-dominated future and recall a recalcitrant

---

[4] The counterpart to assessments of "women's" multifariousness is the notion of a more or less monolithic "women" that globalization promises simply to liberate, on which see Grewal and Kaplan (*Scattered* 17) as well as Spivak ("Diasporas" 104).

patriarchal past. They seem still more contrary, furthermore, when as interview subjects and employees they openly disagree with the experts who wish to describe and manage them.

The urgency that drives much current study stems from the conviction that women are vital players in the most important tendencies of contemporary globalization. When Gayatri Chakravorty Spivak asked in 1997, "[A]re the new diasporas quite new?" she saw only one answer: "The only significant difference is the use, abuse, participation, and role of women" ("Diasporas" 92). Writing in the disciplinary vernacular of development studies, Amartya Sen made a related claim in 1999: "Nothing, arguably, is as important today in the political economy of development as an adequate recognition of political, economic and social participation and leadership of women" (*Development* 203).[5] In 2003 Barbara Ehrenreich and Arlie Hochschild went so far as to maintain that no appraisal of globalization was possible without considering its "female underside ... the global transfer of the services associated with a wife's traditional role – child care, home-making, and sex – from poor countries to rich ones" (*Global* 4–5). Though one could easily adduce further instances, these examples suffice to identify a critical trend: at the dawn of the twenty-first century, scholars and general commentators made women a key index of global economic and political change.

To turn women into such an index meant explaining their mixed status as both globalization's winners – privileged professionals consulting in the administrative centers of capital – and its apparent losers – consigned to the lower ranks of service work and industrial

---

[5] "[T]he limited role of women's active agency seriously afflicts the lives of *all* people," Sen contends, which lends a certain urgency to attempts to use "an agent-oriented approach to the women's agenda" when reconsidering strategies for development in general (191). Koggel offers the case against, arguing that "[h]aving 'paid work' may do little to promote women's agency" ("Globalization" 171).

labor. Ehrenreich and Hochschild argue that "the globalization of child care and household work brings the ambitious and independent women of the world together: the career-oriented upper-middle-class woman of an affluent nation and the striving woman from a crumbling Third World or postcommunist economy" (*Global* 11). Spivak further enjoins "[f]eminists with a transnational consciousness" to recognize that their own upward mobility provides "alibis for the operation of the major and definitive transnational activity, the financialization of the globe, and thus the suppression of decolonization" ("Diasporas" 93). Beverly Mullings's research on Caribbean professionals provides support for such arguments when it shows how "liberalization has allowed middle-class women to disrupt the eurocentric and patriarchal gender order of professional and managerial workspaces," while at the same time making their "organizational success ... even more dependent on the existence of a cheap army of domestic labor" ("Rule?" 22–23). That the very changes launching some women up the ladder doom others to servitude and sweatshops makes it crucial to study both groups together, scholars agree.

This approach is further affirmed by scholarship that finds women's gains in institutional authority mitigated by the persistence of an unnervingly transnational sexism. Case histories of white-collar women tend to start promisingly enough by noting, for example, how they have benefited from shifts in education policy and practice. According to the United Nations Development Fund for Women, education systems worldwide saw sizable decreases in gender gaps in the last decades of the twentieth century.[6] The economist Lourdes

---

[6] "A majority of countries cited in the [*Progress of the World's Women 2002*] report have achieved gender equality in secondary school education or have more girls enrolled at the secondary level than boys" (UNIFEM *Progress* 14).

Benería notes, "there are clear indications that women's higher education levels and rising labor market participation have contributed to a gradual increase in women's participation in managerial and professional occupations" (*Gender* 121). Such participation has led to altered philosophies of administrative style and altered workplace dynamics. Deborah Kidder's study of "organizational citizenship behaviors" suggests that feminized capacities previously excluded from the world of business are being incorporated into managerial discourse ("Influence" 641). Her research shows that firms increasingly value the "altruism behaviors" of managers with a "high feminine identity" (641).[7] That the very stereotypes formerly justifying women's domestic roles are now valued in the workplace suggests how the story of professional women's upward mobility typically goes awry. Researchers agree that professionalization has failed to disrupt binary thinking about gender. The management scholars Marc Cardano, Robert F. Scherer, and Crystal Owen testify to this point when they show that "women managers on international assignments ... can expect to find negative stereotypes from males around the world" ("Attitudes" 58). Public policy researchers Alice Hendrickson Eagly and Linda Lorene Carli concur, arguing that female leaders face a familiar double bind: "The prescriptions for the female gender role stipulate that women be especially communal, and the prescriptions for most leadership roles stipulate that leaders be especially agentic" (*Labyrinth* 101). The historian Harold Perkin sums up the dynamic, arguing that "growth in ability, qualification, and expertise" has provided women with a "ticket to ride, but it often does not take them very far" (*Third* 13–14).

---

[7] "Altruism is characterized as helping behavior," she writes, "implying sensitivity" in contrast to the more masculine "civic" behavior characterized by "speaking out and challenging the status quo" (631–32).

Scholarly studies of women on assembly lines also document updated forms of sexism. Helen Safa observes that globally "the male breadwinner model" and its expectation of feminized, unpaid domestic support "is being eroded," since women now represent half or nearly half of the paid workforce in many places ("Questioning" 12).[8] At the same time, however, a new gendered division of labor has emerged. Because women represent considerably more than half of the workers in export processing zones, feminization leads to what Teri Caraway describes as "the mixed blessing of increased integration and continued marginalization" ("Political" 425).[9] A case in point: the Chinese managers interviewed by Melissa Wright describe themselves as "factory fathers" and supervise their female line workers "according to the ... widespread assumption that their reproductive cycles and sexual desires will eventually turn their productivity into waste" (*Disposable* 29).[10] When women migrate to Europe or North America, Laura M. Agustín recounts, they find that "few of the jobs available to them are in the formal sector, many pay miserably, and working conditions are often semi-feudal" ("Migrant" 391–92).[11] Valentine Moghadam sums up these uneven developments:

At the macro level of analysis, the capitalist world-economy is maintained by *gendered* labor, with definitions of skill, allocation of resources, occupational distribution, and modes of remuneration shaped by asymetrical gender

---

[8] See UNIFEM (*Progress* 30–37) and United Nations (*Survey* 8).

[9] See also Freeman's scholarship on how gender stereotypes "permeate" the hi-tech field in Barbados (*High Tech* 119).

[10] These managers see themselves as empowered to monitor the menstrual cycles, sexual behavior, and "moral impurity" of their disposable employees (29). "Their parents trust us to protect their daughters from the trouble they can find in this city," reports one supervisor. "That is part of my job too" (34).

[11] For the first time in British history, according to Yeo, "women with jobs almost equal men in the paid workforce ... [b]ut this apparent parity conceals tremendous disparity in their terms and conditions of employment" ("Conflicts" 140).

relations. Moreover, gender ideologies define the roles and rights of men and women and the relative value of their labor. But the effects of this incorporation have not been uniformly negative, for there have been unintended consequences of women's economic participation. (*Globalizing* 76–77)[12]

Analysis of working-class and professional women alike regularly takes this shape: having documented how women fall short of becoming full and equal participants in the economy, researchers still maintain that women's more substantial participation in paid sectors of the labor market has potentially radical consequences. What makes the multifarious category of working women coherent in contemporary scholarship, we may conclude, is the certainty among academics and researchers that such women represent the future.

Women serve this forward-looking function in a remarkable variety of ways, many of which do not emphasize anything like an overthrow of patriarchal authority. Wright shows that women workers are so integral to state-of-the-art economic rhetoric that they appear to embody the ideal of flexible labor. "In the tale of turnover that is told by maquila administrators," she recounts, "the Mexican woman takes shape in the model of variable capital whose worth fluctuates" as workers are hired and fired at will (*Disposable* 72). Rosalind Morris finds that Thai sex workers prove similarly evocative to observers who treat them as rhetorical touchstones for the promiscuity, the "transience and indiscriminateness" of transnational capital ("Failures" 47). J. K. Gibson-Graham tracks analogical thinking that equates emerging national economies with starving female bodies desperate for the sustenance of speculative

---

[12] See too Padavic and Reskin, who note that for "educated women with professional skills or access to capital, globalization has created better-paying opportunities and more autonomy" and yet, they argue, because "the most powerful institutional actors in the global economy ... do not hold gender equity as a goal ... little basis for women's equal integration into the new economy has been laid" (*Women* 34–35).

investment (*End* 125, 97).[13] The very idea of an informal market is inextricable from the notion of a feminized working class, according to Shirin Rai, who argues that neither existed as objects of study before the 1970s, when the International Labor Organization began to "define 'informal' labour markets" as such, and to affirm the importance of working women to their growth (*Gender* 94).

Given the ubiquity and flexibility of working women's capacity to connote futurity, it is important to remember that this rhetorical habit has a history. Denise Riley observes that since the nineteenth century at least, women have "lean[ed] forward" in social scientific writing "into a future which is believed to sustain them" (*"Am I"* 47). Women's experiences served as a measure of social conditions in the writings of Marx and Fourier. Riley quotes Engels, who described them as "true bearers of a moral future," and some earlier enlightenment thinkers too "included 'women' as indices of civilisation, as a kind of social leaven" (47–48). Riley is right to suggest that this use "echoes through feminisms today," although now women are just as likely to signify a future of ongoing and difficult-to-interpret change as they are to indicate the direction of teleological progress (47).

There are sound methodological as well as more explicitly political reasons why commentators might want to avoid understanding women as indicators of progress or decline. Elizabeth Grosz cautions that there "is a paradoxical desire at work" in any gesture "to think the new," for such anticipation always "entails some commitment to and use of the past and the present, of what prevails, what is familiar, the self-same" ("Duration" 214). We

---

[13] Gibson-Graham also attends to a broad range of "left discussions in which globalization is represented as the penetration ... of capitalism into all processes of production," and argues that this tropic tendency feminizes territories and treats peoples as victims according to a "rape script" (120–22).

judge progress and decline as if the criteria for doing so remained constant, with the result that we risk "being stuck in political strategies and conceptual dilemmas that are more appropriate to the past" (230). Even so, there are also risks to taking Grosz's advice and asking instead what "politics would be like if it were not directed to the attainment of certain goals, the coming to fruition of ideals or plans, but rather required a certain abandonment of goals" (Grosz *Becomings* 11). To concentrate on "life itself, which unfolds without a ready-made script, with no program, goal, or aim," is to inadvertently echo contemporary political economy's habitual accounts of change without development (Grosz *Nick* 242).

Jacques Donzelot describes a "substitution of the theme of change for that of progress" in recent strategies of governance, which rely on what he calls "a new relation of society to time" ("Mobilization" 177). No longer constrained by a telos that dictates "actions that must be taken and actions that must not be taken," administrators free themselves to experiment, Foucault argues, and to formulate ever more innovative versions of "governmental style" (*Birth* 133). Social policy detached from the evaluative measure of collective progress has but one criterion – namely, that it accord "everyone a sort of economic space within which they can take on and confront risks" (144). Zygmunt Bauman describes the society that results from this strategy as one "in which the conditions under which its members act change faster than it takes the ways of acting to consolidate into habits and routines" (*Life* 1).[14] Change without progress means mobility without the "postulated orders of

---

[14] In Bauman's analysis of the current conjuncture, "'[p]rogress,' once the most extreme manifestation of radical optimism and a promise of universally shared and lasting happiness ... now stands for the threat of relentless and inescapable change that augurs not peace and respite but continuous crisis and strain" (68).

superiority/inferiority" that would allow anyone or any polity to know whether they were changing for better or for worse (31).[15]

The concern that women's lives may be altering without improving ought to make scholars as wary of new models of change as they are of older criteria for progress. If it seems clear that increased mobility grants women possibilities they did not have fifty or even twenty years ago, it seems equally clear that women would do well to be critical of what that opportunity costs. Appropriate as awareness of such complication may be, however, it can lead social scientists into methodological quandaries when they encounter research subjects who are simply excited by their accomplishments. Summing up her research in West Bengal, Ruchira Ganguly-Scrase evinces alarm that, "[a]gainst the overwhelming evidence of the negative impact of economic liberalization ... women do not perceive themselves to be the victims of neoliberal policies" ("Paradoxes" 547). According to every economic measure she can imagine, structural adjustment has left locals poorer and less certain of their prospects than they were before reform began in the 1980s. Still, the women that she interviews show none of the strain and disequilibrium that Bauman equates with a life of uncertainty. Instead, the forty-something Mrs. B speaks for her peers when she declares, "Work gives women freedom" (558). Ganguly-Scrase can only interpret such an utterance as indicative of how thoroughly women have been duped by a "current cultural transformation [that] continuously subverts and appropriates discourses of female emancipation to promote a prowoman market" (562).[16]

---

[15] The implications of the displacement of a "ladder of development" are ably captured by James Ferguson ("Decomposing" 176–77).
[16] When they ventriloquize "the neoliberal state's rhetoric of female empowerment in its structural adjustment policies," women "assert their senses of self and personal agency" in terms that are by definition those "of patriarchal ideologies of the neoliberal state" (563).

Leslie T. Chang's Pearl River Delta migrants similarly struggle to represent themselves in language that contemporary scholarship would find easy to credit. These women intone the keywords of the Chinese boom: Wu Chunming narrates everything from her migration to Dongguan to her registration with a dating agency as part of a campaign to "give myself more opportunities" (*Factory* 208). Chunming's fellows act decisively, possess a "tolerance for risk" Chang finds "astonishing," and so thoroughly absorb the logic of a city in which everything is "reduced to numbers" that they know the important economic news before just about anybody else: "in early 2005, some workers told me that the minimum wage would rise, before it was officially announced" (25, 345, 27). Unlike Ganguly-Scrase's Mrs. B, however, Chang's Chunming yearns "for something that couldn't be measured," for "quality" rather than quantitative improvements to her salary or the size of her apartment, and for "new kinds of happiness" (345–46). Such goals prove elusive in an environment where to survive a woman must be "moving too fast to correct herself," and where the tactical mantra "Keep moving" makes long-term strategy impossible (266, 368).

The economic subject who emerges from this confluence of studies acts without appearing to be able to calculate the larger stakes – personal and more widely social – of her actions, at least to the satisfaction of the scholars who observe her. She participates in events that are changing the world, but she does not and seemingly cannot direct them, much less evaluate their import. She represents herself, but in borrowed language that requires interpretation by skeptical social scientists. Her limitations demonstrate the need for further study, for more and better analyses of the fast economies and boardroom politics in which she works. Fiction demonstrates this need as much as social scientific research does, and its narratives of women in the workplace provide further evidence that the feminized subjects of global economy wield authority with little ability to say how they do so.

WOMEN WHO NETWORK

Gibson's *Pattern Recognition* contributes to the picture I have been sketching by telling a story about an advertising professional named Cayce Pollard who knows she has a knack for her work but cannot explain where, exactly, that talent comes from or how, precisely, it allows her to do her job. Although Cayce's version of this problem is highly particular, *Pattern Recognition* also treats it as symptomatic. To act in self-interested fashion is challenging for everyone in this novel, and not only for Gibson's protagonist. Even loners discover that their decision-making is shaped by networks of actors whose scope can be difficult to ascertain. As a result, no one in this book can claim to fully understand how their actions affect others, or how their actions are affected by others in return. *Pattern Recognition* historicizes such social interaction by embedding it in a present day whose uncertainty and flux echo reports from recent social scientific research. Instability that scholars often present as cause for alarm, however, appears to Gibson as the perfect environment for a thriller.

More than a thriller, perhaps: Fredric Jameson is among those to discover "reliable information about the contemporary world" in Gibson's well-paced plot ("Fear" 105). He describes *Pattern Recognition* as "a kind of laboratory experiment in which the geographic-cultural light spectrum and bandwidths of the new system are registered" (107). According to this reading, *Pattern Recognition* does far more than depict the perils of a professional woman caught in a cutting-edge plot of corporate espionage: Gibson's novel provides its readers with new data.

Pattern Recognition begins its presentation of that data by introducing a heroine with a hyperbolically acute sensitivity to branding, which proves indispensable for her profession of "cool hunter." A "dowser in the world of global marketing," Cayce consults for ad agencies on several continents (Gibson *Pattern* 2). "What I do is pattern recognition," she explains. "I try to recognize a pattern before anyone else does . . . [and] point a commodifier at it" (86). Her ability to facilitate the commoditization of trends would appear to make her the perfect candidate for calculative agency, if only Cayce thought rationally about her reactions to brands. Instead, the novel reveals that Cayce "has no way of knowing how she knows" about the icons that she consults on, and as a result she begins to appear a particularly gifted puppet (12). That, at least, is her fear: as Gibson's story begins, Cayce feels as if "inhabited now by something single-minded, purposeful, yet has no idea what it plans, or wants" (25).

Michel Callon suggests that for "an agent to be able to calculate . . . she must at least be able to draw up a list of actions that she can understand, and describe the effects of these actions on the world in which she is situated" ("Embeddedness" 4). Cayce cannot do this. Instead, she is hyper-aware of being used. She "knows that she is, and has long been, complicit. Though in what, exactly, is harder to say. Complicit in whatever it is that gradually makes London and New York feel more like each other" (Gibson *Pattern* 194). At the close of Gibson's novel, Cayce senses the world "rearranging itself according to a new paradigm of history" (340). She grasps that she has been instrumental in this, but has difficulty seeing how. "[T]he actual conspiracy is not so often about us," she muses; "we are most often the merest of cogs in larger plans" (341). If, as Georg Simmel famously observed, modern capitalism transforms "the world into an arithmetic problem," Gibson's novel features a protagonist whose importance is paradoxically complemented by an inability to do the math ("Metropolis" 14).

Instead of analyzing the market and coming to reasoned conclusions about which brands will sell and which will not, Cayce relies on a heightened responsiveness she describes as an "allergy, a morbid and sometimes violent reactivity to the semiotics of the marketplace" (Gibson *Pattern* 2). She is a "woman of affect, not of feeling," Lauren Berlant clarifies: "the empress of the amygdala" ("Intuitionists" 855).[17] This title fits the theory offered by her current employer, Humbertus Bigend, who argues that our responses to branded goods derive not from rational thought but from impulses generated in our "limbic brain. The seat of instinct ... That is where advertising works," he argues, "not in the upstart cortex ... [and] I hire talent on the basis of an ability to recognize that, whether consciously or not" (Gibson *Pattern* 69). In this account of commodity culture, Cayce's failing is representative. No one can do the math. But some people are more comfortable with that fact than others.

Bigend, for his part, is completely at ease with uncertainty. He embraces the endlessly changing circumstances of global commerce via his London-based, "globally distributed, more post-geographic than multinational" ad agency called Blue Ant, which bills "itself as a high-speed, low-drag life-form in an advertising ecology of lumbering herbivores" (Gibson *Pattern* 6). He has hired Cayce not to sell a product but rather to find the person or persons disseminating a series of filmic fragments that he considers indicative of a new mode of connectivity. "The footage," it is called, and Cayce knows it well: she is a charter member of the usenet group "Fetish:Footage:Forum."

---

[17] Her namesake is Edgar Cayce, the "Sleeping Prophet of Virginia Beach," a seer with a transnational following and the web site to prove it. You can visit him at edgarcayce.org.

She has a professional interest too: the film's images suggest a fluency in the language of fashion that rivals her own. The footage contains images stylized in such a way as to suggest timelessness: any potentially datable referents are so neatly reworked that they appear unmarked by the history of commerce, which gives the footage a quality that Cayce "understands to be utterly masterful" (23).[18]

If Cayce's appreciation for the footage indicates a desire to escape (or at least imagine some place outside) the system that affects her so deeply, Bigend is trying to get more securely inside that network. Both get their wish when Cayce finds the footage's "maker," Nora, and her sister Stella, who acts as the film's distributor. Humble in her declaration that "[t]he one who finds an audience is not so great a talent," Stella is in Cayce's line of work (Gibson *Pattern* 286). She too has her bills paid by a Bigend-type, a Russian magnate named Andrei Volkov. Watching Bigend and Volkov together, one character observes, is "like watching spiders mate" (330). Volkov has his hand in manufacturing, investment, and, intriguingly, the creation of post-Soviet civil society. He runs a private prison where inmates render the footage. Like the Russian economy itself, Volkov has had difficulty integrating with the global system, which is why he is overjoyed to make Bigend's acquaintance. Bringing these two together was never Cayce's goal, but it is among the most suggestive outcomes of her search.

Bigend and Volkov and Cayce contribute to a network of experts and administrators whose sprawl across Europe into Russia recalls the inaugural events in many popular accounts of globalization – namely, the collapse of the Berlin Wall, the end of bipolar

---

[18] Jameson elaborates on this sentiment, writing of "the Utopian anticipation of a new art premised on 'semiotic neutrality,' and on the systematic effacement of names, dates, fashions and history itself, within a context irremediably corrupted by all those things" ("Fear" 111–12).

geopolitics, and the opening of Eastern European markets. As if to ensure that Cayce appears most tightly tied to this watershed, Gibson gives her a CIA agent father and access to a spy network that has profoundly touched the creator of the footage as well.[19] Lodged within Nora's head is a piece of shrapnel, a T-shaped arming mechanism from a Claymore that somehow made its way into the hands of a violent Russian group, which set off the mine that killed Nora's parents and left her brain damaged.[20] The maker of the footage is, it turns out, as talented and impaired as Cayce. She is the perfect producer to pair with Cayce's consumer. Where Cayce receives images affectively, Nora's work is the product of a "wound, speaking wordlessly in the dark" (Gibson *Pattern* 305).

The footage may be crafted in the shadow of the Kremlin, but its images represent a dream of unfettered movement through digital media that have long escaped the grasp of the intelligence administration that spawned them. Instead of international men of mystery, *Pattern Recognition* portrays a planet in which women with idiosyncratic specializations enable parallel networks to converge. These gifted experts only belatedly grasp their role in solidifying a network of capitalist men.[21]

---

[19] The Cold War may have paved the way for globalization, but its new models of conflict lead old spooks to disappear. Cayce's father vanished in lower Manhattan on September 11, 2001. Her mother speculates that "when the second plane hit ... his ... professional mortification ... would have been such that he might simply have ceased, in protest, to exist" (351).

[20] Volkov's colleagues toast "men like Wingrove Pollard, [without whom] Andrei Volkov might languish today in some prison of the Soviet state" (341). A drunken former intelligence officer and Harvard mathematician provides Cayce with vital information about how to contact the footage's creator, in whose brain lies "one specific piece of ordnance, adrift perhaps since the days of the Soviets' failed war with the new enemies ... And from it ... there now emerged, accompanied by the patient and regular clicking of her mouse, the footage" (Gibson *Pattern* 305).

[21] Hayles and Wegner read *Pattern Recognition* as locating the genre of the novel itself in such a belated position vis à vis its object of study. Hayles argues that "*Pattern Recognition* is a self-referential fiction, for its ability to create a narrative about creating a narrative

If this seems a vexed division of labor, the novel's conclusion only makes it worse. After Cayce finds Nora, she gets drugged by her competitor in the search, an industrial spy named Dorotea Benedetti. This has the side effect of suppressing Cayce's trademark allergy. She responds neither to a Louis Vuitton attaché given to her as a gift, nor to "a section full of Tommy in Galleries Lafayette" (Gibson *Pattern* 355). Even the Michelin Man – who used to give her panic attacks – now "registers as neutral" (355). To cap its eradication of the talent that made Cayce such a highly paid professional, *Pattern Recognition* closes with its heroine falling asleep in a new boyfriend's bed. Having ensured that she is incapable of working, at least in her previous capacity, the novel concludes by transporting Cayce from the exciting literary terrain of the corporate thriller to the pacific realm of domestic romance.

As much as this conclusion seems unexpected given all that has gone before it, the final scene featuring Cayce and her newfound beau suggests a reading of *Pattern Recognition* in which it reprises the social function Catherine Ingrassia attributes to domestic romance. Ingrassia presents Samuel Richardson's prose as a literary tool for stabilizing early protocols of speculative investment. By portraying his heroines as "domestic stock-jobber," Richardson stoked existing "anxiety about a woman's use of her sexual, financial, and textual capital" (Ingrassia *Authorship* 143, 62). By concluding *Pamela* with such a volatile heroine safely ensconced in the home, he reassured his readers that a keen-eyed speculator could also be a good wife. By such means, Ingrassia concludes, "*Pamela*

> through code reflexively points back to the role of code in its own production as a material artifact" ("Traumas" 147). Wegner, meanwhile, contends that "in fact, this older machinery ... continues to dominate our present: the social, technological, and literary possibilities of the new media and globalization remain at best potentialities in a world still in the thrall of the 'undead' forms of the novel and ... the nation-state" ("Recognizing" 194).

contributed to the cultural 'domestication' of paper credit and the narrative demands of speculative investment" (142). One may say something similar about *Pattern Recognition*'s treatment of Cayce: what she experienced at work as an allergic response to the rapidly changing signs of commerce becomes considerably less alarming when she retreats to the home. The safety and security of heterosexual domesticity appears capable of making the speed and instability of contemporary capitalism appear less threatening.

If Cayce teaches us this lesson, of course, she does so only by giving up the talent that made her a successful professional, which is in its way as difficult a plot point to swallow as the reinvigorated private/public division that the novel's conclusion portrays. Even before she gets home, however, Cayce's story might strike readers as a bizarre narrative leftover from the age of classical liberalism. If Cayce's contract job ends by enabling Bigend and Volkov to grow their respective commercial networks and strengthen their ability to compete, her job may seem structurally little different from that of the virtuous wife called upon to support her husband's economic activities. If such wives were at one time themselves signifiers of "a new (commercial) version of masculine autonomy," as Elizabeth Dillon explains, Cayce's professional woman may similarly signify as today's most innovative support for manly capitalist (*Gender* 158). When Nancy Armstrong taught readers of eighteenth- and nineteenth-century novels to acknowledge the authority that women of wit and feeling acquire in domestic fiction, she also showed that because feminine characters in the plots of Austen and the Brontës end by facilitating a sexual division of labor, it is difficult not to have a certain ambivalence about their empowerment. "Because women have been written," Armstrong shows, "they have become visible as such, and writing as women has made it possible for a distinctively female voice to be heard. It is the way in which we are visible, then, and the conditions under which we are heard – and not silence – that now seem to constrain us, even though these limitations initially empowered women to write" (*Desire* 255). If Cayce and her affective sensibility update femininity for contemporary capitalism, and if *Pattern Recognition* ends by affirming that she is most comfortable at home, this might offer a tidy parable for how professional women get written into commerce today in a manner that still yields ambivalence about the sexism that limits them.

It can be difficult to judge how much should be extrapolated from the singular example of Cayce Pollard. As the chronological gap between *Pamela* and *Jane Eyre* and *Pattern Recognition* suggests, a good deal of conceptual territory gets left out when we leap from the sexual division of labor in eighteenth- and nineteenth-century domestic romance to Gibson's twenty-first-century thriller. Even if it seems plausible to imagine that something like a classically liberal dynamic gets reprised in this later novel, we know full well that much has changed both to women and to work in the intervening centuries. To explain how liberal domesticity may still be relevant to contemporary gender relations, therefore, it behooves me to explain how earlier twentieth-century writing laid the conceptual groundwork for later literary experiments like that of Gibson.

AFTER THE DOMESTIC WOMAN

To enable working women to represent the future, fiction had to clarify their relationship to the past. Neither Rhys's *Voyage in the Dark*, nor Woolf's *To the Lighthouse*, nor Bowen's *The Heat of the Day* promises a clean break from Victorian precedents, but collectively they clarify the need to manage domestic femininity's continued influence. By considering these novels and their relationships to nineteenth-century stereotypes and themes, I aim to provide a rhetorical bridge between the classic liberal model of feminine authority and a more contemporary dynamic. Although published in 1934, Rhys's novel drew on some of her earliest prose and was set in 1914. I read it as an argument that working women required new skills if they were to survive in rapidly changing early twentieth-century society. I understand Woolf's fiction as an effort to fulfill this need and Bowen's novel as anticipating more contemporary discussion about the contingency of the choices that working women make.

The backdrop for modernist fiction and feminist commentary alike is a nineteenth-century notion that, as Riley explains, women were the privileged actors in a realm of activity called the "social." This "society" took shape in the eighteenth and nineteenth centuries as a "blurred ground between the public and the private" where the "empathies supposedly peculiar to [women] might" be put to "fresh" use mediating all sorts of interactions (*"Am I"* 47–49).[22] That "social" life engendered a seemingly intractable double bind, for it empowered women while requiring they remain feminine. As a result, when twentieth-century writers set out to rethink the relationship between women and sociality, they confronted what Riley calls "the dilemma of modern feminism; the impossibility of moving out from the recuperable reiterations of 'women' to the fullness of an unsexed humanity, without either getting stuck in the collectivity, or

---

[22] As Poovey recounts, one point of emergence for ideas of the social and sociality was eighteenth- and early nineteenth-century moral philosophy, especially Scottish, which imagined a world in which public and private lives were newly and somewhat paradoxically joined ("Liberal" 54). As the privileged agents charged with mediating these spheres, English women were called upon to "humanize the public" in Europe and to "help in raising the moral standard of the Hindoo female" abroad (Riley *"Am I"* 47, 54).

bypassing it completely" (65). Feminist writers of the period were in an "uneasy state," critical of femininity but jealous of the authority associated with it (65). Modernist fiction began to seek a way out of this dilemma by revamping femininity, and few writers engaged in that project more deliberately than Rhys.

Anna Morgan's inability to fathom the English society to which she emigrates in *Voyage in the Dark* can seem overdetermined. Jilted by lovers she never suspected would dump her, willing to give up everything including her job to be with a promising man, Anna is often sick, frequently drunk, and always confused. Although she keeps telling herself, "You've got to make a plan," she proves incapable of doing so and worries, rightly so, that she is "going to be one of the ones with beastly lives" (Rhys *Voyage* 92, 15). What she knows about these "ones" comes from reading, which has also taught her about the possibility of upward mobility – this she learns about, curiously enough, from Zola's *Nana* (it is unclear whether she gets far enough in the novel to discover Nana's death). Unfortunately, Anna finds little actionable intelligence in her literary education. When a beau dumps her, she writes to say, "My dear Walter I've read books about this and I know quite well what you're thinking," but her familiarity yields no canny tricks to win him back. Instead, her letter trails off into pleading to "see you just once more listen it needn't be for very long" (64). His refusal to reconnect leaves Anna with no potential husband, no idea how she might "get on," and, thus, fear that she will inevitably have to "get out" (46).

Voyage in the Dark portrays Anna as struggling to understand a social world whose tendencies she paradoxically also embodies: as a migrant to England, she is part of what is remaking modernist cities and towns into ever more multifarious locales. She brings with her from the West Indies a Creole family background rife with racial ambiguity and "unfortunate propensities," both of which hint at

Rhys's much later revision of *Jane Eyre* in *Wide Sargasso Sea* (*Voyage* 40). Anna feels fondly for her clan and misses the black playmates with whom she grew up. Her unwillingness to let them go generates a powerful fantasy life, which causes her to lose situational awareness. "Sometimes it was as if I were back there and as if England were a dream," she narrates. "At other times England was the real thing and out there was the dream, but I could never fit them together" (3). Anna, it would seem, can no more distinguish core from periphery than could Marlow in Joseph Conrad's "Heart of Darkness," with his conviction that England had also been one of the dark places of the earth. Anna's inability to distinguish England from a more tropical isle becomes even more pronounced as she falls into prostitution. After a botched abortion, she collapses in bed, woozily reliving her West Indian past while a doctor assures her that she'll be "[r]eady to start all over again in no time" (115). In the novel's original ending, which Rhys was forced by her publisher to change, there are several additional pages of foggy reminiscence that complete Anna's degeneration before "blackness comes" and she bleeds out (Rhys "Original" 389).

Urmila Seshagiri discovers a "metacommentary" on modernist aesthetics in this tale of a fallen chorus girl ("Ashes" 498). In the early twentieth-century metropolis where Raymond Williams and others found immigrants shaping a rich venue for artistic experiment, Rhys locates a crisis of "Metropolitan perception" (Williams *Politics* 45; Seshagiri "Ashes" 498). What served as the "creative fount of Rhys's literary predecessors," Seshagiri explains, appears reworked in *Voyage in the Dark* as a frightening mélange that Anna "fails to transform ... into gratifying artistic form" (498). Anna fails, we may reason, because she is no artist. She is but a woman in

After the domestic woman 195

search of love and marriage, and sentimentality provides no accurate guide to the glorious chaos of modernist social life.[23]

To the Lighthouse is set in the same messily heterogeneous milieu. Critics after Erich Auerbach largely agree that Woolf's novel elaborates the challenge of ordering an "always changing, more or less radically, more or less rapidly" "world in which we live" (Auerbach *Mimesis* 549).[24] Like *Voyage in the Dark*, *To the Lighthouse* tasks a young woman with sorting things out. Unlike Rhys's Anna, however, Woolf's Lily Briscoe is equipped with more than the usual domestic heroine's skill set. The novel's last third famously finds her painting an abstract landscape that serves as what Alex Zwerdling calls the "classic" instance of Woolf's use of "art as a force for unity and permanence" (*Real* 315). Although Lily's painting fills in for Mrs. Ramsay's domestic strategies of organization, which were on display earlier in the novel, her state-of-the-art techniques still draw on the influence of her Victorian predecessor.[25]

To set the stage for Lily's appropriation of Mrs. Ramsay's authority, Woolf presents daily life as a puzzle requiring a semiotic

[23] Seshagiri shows how Rhys relies on modernist mixtures of "the psychic and experiential merging of England and the Caribbean" as well as "the linguistic shifts from English to French to Creole patois" to elaborate a social world its domestic heroine cannot put in order (498). Esty describes such admixture as typical in modernist revisions of *Bildungsroman*, which do everything they can to show how the stalling out of a British hero or heroine's development analogically suggests imperial disarray as well ("Colony").
[24] R. L. Walkowitz finds in Woolf's tendency to zero in on the smallest of domestic details an attempt to ground the large scale of history and to remember "what 'happens' while war is happening or while war, in its violence and its precedency, keeps one from noticing that anything else does happen" (*Cosmopolitan* 89). Laurence finds in the "pausing" and "flickering" and "dancing rhythmical movement" of Lily's painting a reminder of the emphasis on artistic process favored by the Chinese artists and writers whom Julian Bell brought into Woolf's circle, and whose influence might also be glimpsed in the repeated motif of Lily's "little Chinese eyes" (Woolf *Lighthouse* 157–58; Laurence *Lily* 352–53).
[25] Here is the famous passage that establishes this correspondence: "Mrs. Ramsay bringing them together; Mrs. Ramsay saying, 'Life stand still here'; Mrs. Ramsay making of the moment something permanent (as in another sphere Lily herself tried to make of the moment something permanent)" (Woolf *Lighthouse* 161).

solution. Lily must cope with a "strange morning" in which "words became symbols" and "wrote themselves all over the grey-green walls" (*Lighthouse* 147). Lily's fellows evince skepticism about her ability to process the symbolic raw material of the Ramsay vacation home and its environs: Charles Tansley's remark ("Women can't paint, women can't write") echoes in Lily's head, and makes her fear she is "wasting her time ... playing at painting" a canvas that will only be "rolled up and flung under a sofa" (48, 149, 179). Once she starts, however, Lily proves entirely able to manage the "innumerable risks" of painting, and unflinchingly makes the "frequent and irrevocable decisions" necessary to complete the work, to have her "vision" (157).

To the Lighthouse only hints at what Lily's painting looks like, which implies that its appearance is less significant than its effects.[26] The painting has the power of what Douglas Mao calls "intersubjective mediation by the object" (*Solid* 54). Her canvas calls up a whole set of affiliations, past and present, tying together in the process all of the novel's characters and settings where their paths have crossed. As she paints, Lily's "feeling" for those around her is "drawn out" and "elongated" even as she also limns a collective history by "tunneling her way into her picture, into the past" (Woolf *Lighthouse* 191, 173). Like Gibson's "footage," which links a privileged demographic of consumers in *Pattern Recognition*, Lily's painting organizes a local network in *To the Lighthouse*. Like the brands that trigger limbic responses in Gibson's novel, Lily says that "what she wished to get hold of" with her painting "was that very jar on the nerves," a reminder of those "moments when one can neither think or feel" (193). Where Cayce's labor is specifically geared to affect

---

[26] We know that it features a "triangular purple shape," "a line there, in the centre," "greens and blues," and "lines running up and across" (Woolf *Lighthouse* 52, 208–09).

(in contrast to feeling), Lily's still invokes the notion of deeply felt "sympathy," which ties it more closely to feminine strategies of empathetic organization (156, 208).[27] Mrs. Ramsay's influence haunts Lily's work, but that does not mean the two are allied in all matters: there will be none of Mrs. Ramsay's "mania ... for marriage" in the network that Lily's painting engenders (175). Instead, her friendship with the scientist William Bankes, admiration at a distance of the poet Carmichael, and careful handling of the philosopher Mr. Ramsay hints more at professional collegiality than heterosexual domesticity. *To the Lighthouse* suggests that an enterprising artist like Lily could preserve the affective emphasis of Victorian social life without reproducing its sexual division of labor.[28]

Both *To the Lighthouse* and *Pattern Recognition* encourage their readers to contemplate the continued influence of domestic femininity, but they describe its interface with expert authority differently. As Cayce moves from the world of work to the arms of her new boyfriend at the conclusion of *Pattern Recognition*, losing the very skill that made her so successful on the job, expert and domestic authority come to appear mutually exclusive components of surprisingly separate spheres. In *To the Lighthouse*, Lily seems rather more able to pick and choose. Her work combines a sympathy that recalls Mrs. Ramsay's maternal powers with an aesthetic that suggests the expertise of modernist abstraction. By telling the story of an artist who uses her talents

---

[27] Fluet observes that arguments about turning the empathetic work of social intervention into a more professional labor tend to "take for granted that responsible being-in-public for modern women has its origins in affect, emerging from the willed transformation of at-home, maternal feelings into public feelings" ("Hit-Man" 287).

[28] Banerjee foregrounds the "liminality" of such a project in her reading of Cornelia Sorabji's 1934 memoir, *India Calling*, which speaks in the "disembodied" voice of the "professional citizen" while simultaneously reminding her readers of the way gender difference structures the lives of women experts (*Imperial* 148).

to represent the heterosexual homestead, *To the Lighthouse* combines what *Pattern Recognition* keeps separate. Whatever the contrast between Lily's success and Cayce's removal, however, both novels imply that women's expert authority is most intelligible in its relationship – whether complementary or antagonistic – to domesticity. To suggest the primacy of this relationship is to beg questions about what it means for the circulation of expert knowledge between the workplace and the home, as well as about whether it makes sense to still think of domesticity as indicating a separate sphere.

In the London of Bowen's *The Heat of the Day*, war makes it challenging to imagine any domestic setting impermeable to the larger world.[29] For Stella Rodney and the men in her life, it seems clear that history is a more than allegorical force. "They were creatures of history," the narrator intones; history is a veritable physical presence sitting "in the third place at their table" (Bowen *Heat* 217).[30] Bowen treats the Blitz as an exemplary setting for fiction: *The Heat of the Day* employs this seemingly exceptional circumstance to establish the rule that historical conditions always constrain choice. Stella surmises: "At any time it may be your hour or mine – you or I may be learning some terrible human lesson which is to undo everything we had thought we had. It's that, not death, that we ought to live prepared for. – What shall we do?" (269). Preparing to calculate is what should drive us, according to Stella, which invokes the broader problem Bowen's novel considers – namely, how best to equip oneself to choose, given that decision-making often feels like no choice at all. "One cannot

---

[29] Ellmann describes the book as a "novel about leaks, about the porousness of architectural and psychic space, about the failure to keep secrets in, intruders out" (*Shadow* 153).
[30] "Indeed," Brook Miller argues, "the return to history is not ultimately just a 'third presence' or 'shadow across the page'; it is constitutive" ("Narrative" 144).

always choose" how one's lovers behave, Stella observes (268). Her lover, Robert Kelway, meanwhile, who has betrayed England to the Germans, contends that one cannot even choose one's ideas and ideals: "I didn't choose them: they marked me down. They are not mine anyhow; I am theirs" (306). *The Heat of the Day* is strict in enforcing the axiom that human action is shaped by larger forces, even as it dwells on the capacity of its characters to calculate under such constraints.

The Heat of the Day tests possibilities for such reasoning by narrating the decision-making processes of two women. Stella, the middle-class office worker, in love with Robert, the Nazi spy, shares space in the novel's plot with the working-class Louie. Stella frames her choices in terms on loan from the likes of Rhys and Woolf, which is to say that she presents the problem of being a woman shaped by the heritage of domesticity. "Ladies had gone not quite mad," she muses, "from in vain listening for meaning in the loudening ticking of the clock" (Bowen *Heat* 193). Possessors of "[v]irtue with nothing more to spend," domestic heroines "knew no choices, made no decisions – or, did they not?" (193). Domesticated femininity means life constrained, Stella thinks, but perhaps not life devoid of the information that would allow one to reason. "Everything spoke to" the women of the house; "knowledge was not to be kept from them; it sifted through to them, stole up behind them, reached them by intimation" (193). The house of domestic fiction resembles the house during wartime in this respect: its walls cannot keep the wider world out.

Well aware of this fact, Louie sets out to manage her relationship to that wider world through the aggressive reading of newspapers. She learns from her roommate to balance a "suspicious" reading practice with a more sympathetic approach that involves appreciating "the variety of true stories, which made the war seem human"

(Bowen *Heat* 170, 68). "Dark and rare were the days when she [Louie] failed to find on the inside of her paper an address to or else account of herself. Was she not a worker, a soldier's lonely wife, a war orphan, a pedestrian, a Londoner … a fuel-saver and a housewife?" (168). While a sympathetic approach domesticates news of the day – "War now made us one big family" (169) – Connie's "re-reading of everything" allows Louie to begin critically "reading between the lines" (170). When Louie gets pregnant, both skills come in useful. "Such a time to choose," Connie shakes her head, before calculating that the child is due at around the point when Britain "shall be having the Second Front" (366–67). This propitious beginning ends the novel, suggesting that even decisions that appear less than fully rational, like having a baby out of wedlock during wartime, can still sometimes work out.

Bowen's two deliberate, thoughtful, if not entirely reasonable women meet just once in *The Heat of the Day*, which has left readers not always fully sure how they are supposed to compare Stella and Louie's contemplation of calculation. The coincidence of their meeting emphasizes the difference between them as much as the novel's narrative structure insists upon their connection. Robert Caserio argues that the relationship between these two feels forced as a result, akin, he finds, to the equally insistent but difficult to articulate tie that Woolf establishes between Clarissa and Septimus in *Mrs. Dalloway*. In both cases, such linkage helps us to rethink trusted oppositions between bourgeois women and their others, which Caserio claims further helps to suggest that women's experiences in these novels come to stand in for human experience in general. He argues that "by virtue of being women [Bowen's] Stellas and Louies have led lives that make it hard to tell if activity and passivity, choice and no choice, are different or the same; but she also suggests that by virtue of being women her heroines represent what history and narrative are, in our century, for women and men alike" ("Modernism" 281). In presenting women's plots as if they could model the problems of calculative agency in general, *The Heat of the Day* anticipates what commentators think of as a dynamic emblematic of contemporary capitalism, after the feminization of labor. By suggesting through its parallel narratives that to understand women as calculative agents we need to think more about how to compare middle- and working-class women, *The Heat of the Day* anticipates the sort of narrative comparison engaged in by Monica Ali's contemporary novel, *Brick Lane*.

SISTERS AT WORK

Naila Kabeer's study *The Power to Choose* (2000) and Ali's novel *Brick Lane* treat the same raw material, Sylheti women's experiences in the garment trade in the United Kingdom and Bangladesh. Both books consider the possibility that by representing women at work, one can learn something about representing economic agency in general, not just about the limits of a feminine alternative to a still authoritative masculine economic subject. If Bowen's use of women to model a general condition of constrained choices anticipates this sort of reasoning, Kabeer and Ali are primed to consider a later moment when labor has been feminized and women at work are not a gendered exception but the new rule. To understand how *homo economicus* has been revised, these books suggest, one has but to ask what *she* can do.

Kabeer's study frames its methodological investigation with a counterintuitive observation about how work and home combine for two subject populations: "In Bangladesh, a country ... [with] strong norms of purdah ... women appeared to have abandoned old norms in response to new opportunities ... By contrast, in

Britain ... Bangladeshi women were largely found working from home, in apparent conformity with purdah norms" (*Power* viii).[31] This contrast leads Kabeer to evaluate her subjects' success in terms of the extent to which they are willing to challenge "patriarchal constraint head on" and turn accomplishment at work into the impetus for renovating their lives outside the factory (192). The most successful are nothing short of "pioneers," she argues, who by introducing "greater diversity into the social landscape in which women will be making their choices in the future" affect the economic landscape in which not only they but also their masculine fellows act (192, 361). Kabeer presents women as models for economic agency who are "neither the free-floating, atomised individuals of neo-classical analysis nor ... the 'structural dopes' of certain sociological portrayals" (327).[32] Instead, whether they are transporting purdah to England or renegotiating its strictures in Dhaka, Kabeer's laborers weigh decisions while well aware of the "social, rather than purely individual, implications of their choice" (334). Her Dhaka interviewees know, Kabeer argues, "that Bangladesh is undergoing a major social transformation in which they had played a part" (362). Instead of calculative agents driven by self-interest, Kabeer presents subjects who calculate with an eye to how their individual decisions enable wider change. These are

---

[31] Kabeer argues that despite the evident links between such places and the people who inhabit them, scholarship on the garment trade has persisted in approaching workers in Dhaka and London as if they were different species. "Women workers in Bangladesh were seen to be a legitimate focus for concern," she explains. "Bangladeshi women in Britain, on the other hand, were seen to be expressing their cultural preferences by opting to work from home, even if the conditions of work were equally exploitative" (364).

[32] Kabeer treats rational action as at best a useful myth, for actually to calculate would require "statistical analysis of information on a scale and complexity that is likely to defy the cognitive capacity and material resources of any human individual" (21). Put in these terms, Callon agrees, no one could possibly act rationally, for no one has "all the relevant information on different states of the world and on the consequences of all conceivable courses of action" ("Embeddedness" 4).

subjects who understand work rather than domestic sympathy as the basis of social reform.

Ali's novel also enables readers to indulge in the idea that when working women reflect on their choices they engage in a kind of analysis of social organization. *Brick Lane* focuses on two sisters. In London, Nazneen stitches blue jeans in her council flat before helping to found a small business while, in Dhaka, Hasina performs the "real woman job" of "machinist" in a garment factory before doing a stint as a sex worker, taking a longer-term position as a nanny, and then eloping with a colleague (103). Like Kabeer's study, from which Monica Ali readily acknowledges she "drew inspiration," *Brick Lane* spends considerable time weighing what its heroines think their actions mean to their families, to their neighbors, and to the communities in which they live (371). Like Kabeer, moreover, Ali presents women's economic agency as more befuddling to academics and labor activists than to the subjects they seek to analyze. "Understanding the possibilities that access to wage labor has opened up" is hard for many social scientists, Kabeer argues, because those possibilities typically fail to measure up to scholars' expectations for labor standards and lack any kind of safety net ("Globalization" 21). Kabeer quotes liberally from her subjects' "social science 'stories'" to explain why women "do not view their jobs in . . . [an] unequivocally negative light" (21). Ali's *Brick Lane* represents a kind of literary supplement to this compilation of working women's tales, but demonstrates that story-telling offers its own interpretative challenges.

Although the conclusion of *Brick Lane* portrays Nazneen happily engaged in launching her business, the novel relies on narrative sleight of hand to explain how she turned into such an enterprising type. There is a narrative caesura in *Brick Lane*'s tale that separates Nazneen's life as a bored housewife and piece-worker from her life as a clothing designer. Through much of the novel, Ali's migrant protagonist plays the part of an "unspoilt girl ... [f]rom the village" (9). She faces an array of predictable problems when her family arranges a marriage to an older man named Chanu, and he brings her to East London's Tower Hamlets. In a fashion the novel expects readers to recognize as conventional for immigrant fiction, Nazneen consoles herself by dreaming of the family she left behind in Bangladesh, learns to govern her eccentric husband, becomes a mother to two girls, and tries her best to do good in the community. Somewhat less conventionally, she punctuates her boredom by having a torrid affair. Even this divergence from the more usual immigrant plot offers barely a hint to suggest that Nazneen will end the novel by launching a start-up company.

Nazneen's first paying job is what the sociologist Kabeer depicts as stereotypic employment for Sylheti women in Tower Hamlets.[33] Within this ethnic category, piece work seems part and parcel of a story about family, community, and nation. This frame is paradoxically confirmed when Nazneen starts sleeping with Karim, a hunky middleman with a penchant for neighborhood activism and noticeably "broad shoulders" (Ali *Brick* 150). His appearance at her door with a bale of jeans signifies Nazneen's entry into the paid labor force, to be sure, but its more immediate narrative significance is the beginning of a romance "English style," as her friend Razia puts it (319). "Everything goes against it. Family, duty, everything,"

---

[33] The novel is largely composed of such typical situations, which has led to its status as a quasi-sociology text and to a less than favorable reputation among some reviewers for being a book "populated entirely by clichés, one-dimensional people taken straight from a textbook of Indo-Anglian Lit" (Aparisim Ghosh "Flavour" 51). Others have been more generous in their assessment of the novel's bent: "Indeed," Ali Ahmad notes, "one of *Brick Lane*'s most striking features is its power as a work of sociology, attributable, in some measure, to the rigour with which its author studied Naila Kabeer's magisterial survey of Bangladeshi women and the labour market in London and Dhaka" ("Note" 201).

which is precisely what makes it so appealing (319). Karim and Nazneen "play house" together, engage in bodice-ripping sex – "He pushed her onto the bed and tore at her blouse and pushed the skirt of her sari around her waist" – and muse over a relationship with no future: Nazneen chalks up Karim's talk of marriage to "the stupidity of youth" (218, 51). Provocative as this story may be, *Brick Lane* treats it as entailing little change of situation. Karim sees Nazneen as Chanu does, as "the real thing," a "Bengali wife," and – despite all of the sex – "[a]n unspoilt girl. From the village" (284, 339).[34]

There are hints of a competing narrative arc in Nazneen's story, however. Sewing at home leads to the discovery that "work in itself, performed with a desire for perfection, was capable of giving satisfaction" (Ali *Brick* 219). A marked contrast emerges between Nazneen the happy wage earner and Nazneen the young girl taught to "treat life with indifference," the wife performing chores as "[l]ife made its pattern around and beneath and through her," and the lover stereotyped as the very essence of Bengali womanhood (4, 23). Work liberates Ali's protagonist to dance and sing along with the radio in the novel's final pages, to go ice skating, and to endorse the possibilities available to her as an independent contractor. Razia observes, "You can do whatever you like" (369). "I will decide what to do," Nazneen agrees. "I will say what happens to me. I will be the one" (301). Given the scant precedence for such assertiveness, even Nazneen herself is "startled by her own agency" (4).

---

[34] Karim's appearance introduces another apparently dead-end genre as well, that of cultural politics: Nazneen's young lover chairs a group with the unfortunate name of the "Bengal Tigers," whose archenemies are the white working-class "Lion Hearts." He is also not above reading aloud an internet Hadith of the day that just happens to be about adultery, which leaves Nazneen cold (255).

A sequence of narrative bursts provides the transition from Nazneen's earlier life – during which she is guided by the belief that "since nothing could be changed, everything had to be borne" – to her later entrepreneurial success (Ali *Brick* 4). In this set of short passages, Nazneen designs, Razia walks into "Fusion Fashions, bold as a mynah bird," asks for work, and drums up business in "distant lands" from Tooting to Wembley (360). Nazneen experiences this transition as a *deus ex machina*: she had "prayed to God, but He had already given her what she needed: Razia" (363). That she might require divine intervention to become an entrepreneur is suggested by Nazneen's inability to fathom how rational actors do what they do. On an early walk through the neighborhood, she imagines that "[e]very person who brushed past her on the pavement, every back she saw, was on a private, urgent mission to execute a precise and demanding plan" (35). She marvels at the calculation involved in buying a newspaper with exact change "so that the exchange was swift and seamless" (35). She imagines engaging in such commerce, altering her costume, and adopting a new walk so as to mimic those around her: "If she wore a skirt and a jacket and a pair of high heels, then what else would she do but walk around the glass palaces on Bishopsgate and talk into a slim phone" (201). Nazneen is a keenly attentive and relentlessly curious ethnographer. "The way [a] woman walked was fascinating," she thinks, while following the strides of a commuter whose "footsteps rang like declarations" on the Tube platform (334). Nazneen treats those footsteps like a rich text, asking, "Could a walk tell lies?," "How much could it say?," "Could it change you?" (334). Although her elevation to businesswoman is a mysterious process, *Brick Lane* is consistent in its presentation of Nazneen as a budding expert in the manners and rituals of London's worldly women.

She is also an interpreter of her sister's contrasting narrative of work: Hasina's story appears in a series of letters sent to Nazneen in London. The content of those letters recalls the tales told by Kabeer's sources. Hasina is part of the generation of Bangladeshi women going to work, which as depicted in *Brick Lane* merits protest by local mullahs and by husbands who urge their "garment girls" to wear burkhas inside the factory (Ali *Brick* 107). Just as it does for Nazneen, work has an extraordinary effect on Hasina's sense of her place in the world. "Working is like [a] cure," she reports (107). Even the most dead-end job opens lines of flight, and Hasina lives life as an ongoing search for new opportunities. *Brick Lane* invites skepticism about whether her frequent changes constitute improvement when, in the novel's final chapters, Hasina abruptly quits her latest job as a nanny and "vanish[es] with the cook" (368). Although both experience the instability that commentators on contemporary economy think of as the hallmark of, in Bauman's term, "liquid life," Hasina distinguishes herself by remaining committed, or so it would seem, to the very domestic realm that Nazneen abandons.

Brick Lane prompts questions about whether this decision locates the two sisters on different rungs of some developmental ladder. The novel answers by way of a formal conceit that makes it clear that interpreting Hasina's choices is a literary matter: where the novel presents Nazneen speaking and thinking idiomatically, Hasina writes letters that though ostensibly in Bengali appear on the page as broken English.[35] In contrast to choppy syntax in which her tale appears, Nazneen's story unfolds in language that reviewers have found notable for its Dickensian description and

---

[35] Among the most egregious and pertinent examples is this passage: Hasina writes, "In London do roads ever melting? Aleya have cousin is Londoni. She tell me in London the people have no God. I keep quiet when she say" (Ali *Brick* 108).

"satirical detachment" reminiscent of "Thackeray in *Vanity Fair*" (MacDonald "Year").[36] Unevenness of presentation appears to confirm that a hierarchical arrangement elevates Nazneen's adventure in commerce while devaluing Hasina's romantic impulse. It also implies a predictable hierarchy between the Northern and Southern markets in which Nazneen and Hasina, respectively, labor. In the North, a narrative of economic progress still seems available to some, while in the South instability and rapid change is all that one can anticipate.

Lest we accuse Ali of endorsing such hierarchy, however, Nazneen undercuts it when she interprets her sister's elopement. "Why does she do these things?" Chanu asks. "Because," Nazneen answers, "she isn't going to give up" (Ali *Brick* 367). By treating Hasina's decision as a legitimate attempt to manage possibility, Nazneen suggests that it may not be so backward to still believe in love. With mundane job prospects, little indication that education is available, and the ever present possibility of falling back into the sex trade, who is to say that romancing the cook is an irrational choice? Nazneen's answer treats Hasina's transformation as akin to her own, inexplicable on its face and, therefore, not to be dismissed before further study. Nazneen leaves open the possibility, even, that Hasina has experienced a kind of upward mobility different, but every bit as significant, as hers. Or, equally, that what readers should learn from Hasina's life of change without certain progress is the lesson that for all of its momentum Nazneen's rise might result in a life no more stable than that of her sister. If this seems an

---

[36] Ali's novel invokes a realism that is as identifiably canonical – reviewers have placed *Brick Lane* alongside the works of Dickens, Dostoevsky, and Hardy (Kapoor "New"; Mishra "Enigmas" 42; Abu-Jaber "London" 25) – as it is canonically postcolonial – Selvon's *Lonely Londoners* and Naipaul's *A House for Mr. Biswas* are frequent comparisons as well (Gorra "East" 9).

unsatisfying narrative conclusion, it is worth noting that Kabeer's *The Power to Choose* leaves its readers in a similar place. Both novel and sociological investigation represent women who in moving "to a more central, better paid and more visible place in the economy" become interpretable as "an expression of a new, if problematic inclusion" (Kabeer *Power* 404).

Inclusion means women stand to lose their marginal status in the global economy and instead join the multifarious category of calculative-agents-in-training imagined by contemporary governmentality. In Nazneen's case, this means exemplifying the stereotype of the migrant as an "investor" who "incurs expenses" and endures hardship in order to "obtain some kind of improvement" (Foucault *Birth* 230).[37] Thus, the conclusion of *Brick Lane* with its excited description of Nazneen and Razia's new business may be read as folding two Sylheti women into a generic narrative of migration whose plot twists and turns are best understood in economic as opposed to political or cultural terms. *Brick Lane* identifies its economic leanings by providing an entrepreneurial denouement to the story of Nazneen overcoming cultural regulation. Hasina's story tests this economic framing, but only if we agree to treat her decision to run off with the cook as a different kind of decision than those she makes when switching jobs. Nazneen does not make this distinction: she neither understands Hasina's disappearance as permanent – she has run off with guys before – nor all that remarkable – when Chanu breaks the news to her over the phone she is almost relieved: "Oh," she says, "I thought something terrible [had happened]" (Ali *Brick* 367). Fleeing the workplace for the domestic realm is not an end point for Hasina any more than

---

[37] Migration, conceived in this manner, gets "brought back into economic analysis ... as behavior in terms of individual enterprise, of enterprise of oneself with investments and incomes" (230).

opening a shop resolves matters for Nazneen. Instead, *Brick Lane* concludes with both characters on the move, still learning what it means to calculate, to make educated decisions, and to behave like rational actors.

Pattern Recognition is not as easily interpreted as offering such an open ending. The appearance of sequels called *Spook Country* and *Zero History*, however, may encourage readers to reconsider the earlier novel's conclusion. Both novels reprise the character of Bigend, with *Spook Country* documenting the return of the footage, now packaged as a "viral pitchman platform" called "Trope Slope" (Gibson *Spook* 105). Most importantly, the novels feature a new "Cayce" embodied as a freelance writer and former member of cult band "The Curfew" named Hollis Henry.[38] Like Cayce, Hollis works for Bigend without knowing quite what she is doing. And, also, like her predecessor, Hollis's real work appears to involve building and extending a network among variously capitalized actors that interest Bigend. Hollis relies on a far-flung and very dedicated fan base that serves as the kind of support system Cayce found in the footage forums. She builds on her network as her precursor Cayce did, and she finds herself moving over the course of the two novels from the center (more or less) of a fringe group into the margins of a (more or less) professional marketing industry. The reproducibility of this trajectory suggests that Cayce's retirement is not the end of the story. Indeed, the final pages of *Pattern Recognition* itself – the very ones that detail Cayce's retreat to the home – may be said to confirm that her exit is not final. These last pages include a series of "where are they now?" emails about Stella still distributing the footage, Cayce's London contact Magda

---

[38] The first "Cayce" makes a pointed if brief return in *Zero History*, where she shares with Hollis a "sense of once having been where you are" (Gibson *Zero* 335).

working in the "viral marketing" wing of the industry, an acquaintance named Judy Tsuzuki finding a job in Bigend's Tokyo office, and so forth. Cayce's continued monitoring of this network from within her home tests the conclusiveness of the novel's "Reader, I married him" ending. As Annelise Riles allows, the "inherent recursivity" of networks makes them self-perpetuating, a point on which Gibson's ending and sequel elaborate (*Network* 172). The network of women in which Cayce participates appears almost by accident, a side effect of her main endeavor to track down the footage. It is as if that network is latent in her working environment – which itself has no boundaries, existing anywhere commodities are marketed: which is to say, everywhere.

Elaborating such complex arrangements of action and intention, subjectivity and social structure is a hobbyhorse of recent fiction, as Ali's novel also demonstrates. That said, there are differences: for instance, the international division of labor so forcefully represented in *Brick Lane* appears only fleetingly in *Pattern Recognition*. When reviewing a new candidate for a sneaker logo, Cayce briefly ponders "the countless Asian workers who might ... spend years of their lives applying versions of this symbol to an endless and unyielding flood of footwear. What would it mean to them, this bouncing sperm? Would it work its way into their dreams, eventually? Would their children chalk it in doorways before they knew its meaning as a trademark?" (Gibson *Pattern* 12). This series of questions clearly tests Cayce's ability to imagine the sublime numbers to whom the marketing industry connects her. *Brick Lane* also finds it difficult to neatly register connection across the borders geographic and economic that separate London from Dhaka. The novel's rendering of Hasina's prose in broken English suggests both proximity and distance. The dream of a network of women that cuts across such divides is, perhaps, the ultimate fantasy that *Pattern*

Recognition and *Brick Lane* share. By crediting these two novels with giving readers analytic purchase on this fantasy, I do not mean to endorse a narrative of progress for the novel as a genre so much as to espouse a genealogy for the genre's recent iterations. I think that *The Heat of the Day*, *To the Lighthouse*, and *Voyage in the Dark* help create the need for contemporary novels to renovate literary treatment of working women. As the open endings of *Brick Lane* and *Pattern Recognition* suggest, however, recent fictions are nowhere near to wrapping up this literary experiment.

Postscript

The literary politics of being well attached

As if responding to the generic dictates of the *Bildungsroman*, *Brick Lane* presents a woman whose life changes utterly when her network of interpersonal connections realigns. Nazneen discovers in Razia a business partner as well as a sustaining friend. This relationship leads to a variety of others, and the novel equates Nazneen's expanding circle with empowerment. Crucially, however, *Brick Lane* does not provide a typical narrative of development, for the novel declines to equate empowerment with independence. Nazneen's husband returns to Bangladesh and her boyfriend moves on, but the loosening of these ties does not so much make her self-reliant as enable her to link up with new people. Through its tale of a woman who learns which connections can fulfill her dreams, *Brick Lane* narrates less the development of an individual than the transformation of a group. Nazneen divides her life into before and after: "before I knew what I could do" and after she has learned what is possible when she has a fully functioning support system (Ali *Brick* 365). Like *Half of a Yellow Sun* or *Anil's Ghost* or *The Glass Palace*, *Brick Lane* embeds its characters' stories within what amounts to a narrative assessment of the productivity and flexibility of different kinds of social arrangements. What the nuclear family and the extramarital couple cannot do for Nazneen in Ali's novel, the friendship network and the business community can.

Instead of defining individual development as a process of liberation, *Brick Lane* promotes personal growth as a function of the quality Bruno Latour calls being "well-attached" (*Reassembling* 218). It is only by "multiplying the connections with the outside," Latour contends, "that there is some chance to grasp how the 'inside'" of the subject "is being furnished" (215–16). With this axiom, Latour finds a mission for social science and encourages his peers to speak of human actors only when describing "the large network of attachments" to subjects and objects animal, vegetable, and mineral that make their actions possible (217). "As [Gabriel de] Tarde insisted long ago," Latour writes, "the family of 'to have' is much richer than the family of 'to be' because, with the latter, you know neither the boundary nor the direction: to possess is also being possessed; to be attached is to hold and to be held" (217). Although fiction can be as curious as Latour about the agency of objects, my aim has been to clarify the novel's investment in how human subjects have and hold, how they associate and group. Fiction reveals this investment every time a work like *Brick Lane* supplements the novel's historical interest in the life of individuals with attention to the group dynamics that support them.

Earlier Victorian gothic fictions like *Dracula* offered "a glimpse of alternative kinship practices," Nancy Armstrong argues, but they did so "only to demonstrate spectacularly that such alternatives . . . produce monsters" (*Novels* 145–46). More recent experiments in altering interpersonal arrangements yield more varied results. These include the academic household modeled in *Half of a Yellow Sun*, the research team constructed in *Anil's Ghost*, and the highly mobile extended family described in *The Glass Palace*. If, as Armstrong argues, the nineteenth-century gothic propagated "the bone-chilling truth that . . . alternative kinship relations . . . may well mean our extinction as liberal individuals," twentieth-century fiction considers what happens next, after the liberal subject has ceased to define the limit of literary subjectivity (146, 52). Instead of lamenting the passing of an older aspiration of personal liberation, contemporary novels and their early twentieth-century predecessors just as often celebrate the competent management of populations, test the viability of flexible affiliations, and puzzle over the durability of trading clans.

Fiction's experiments in group dynamics stand ready to advance recent scholarship that bemoans the neoliberal transformation of "freedom" into "market freedom" and individuality into entrepreneurship. Fiction's contribution is all the greater because neoliberalism's most strident critics appear less convinced than ever that their analytic tricks of the trade are equipped to deal with state-of-the-art governmentality. Eva Cherniavsky questions "the abiding value of critical defamiliarization," that staple of social criticism, given the mutability of the entrepreneurial subject and the "ultra-rapid forms of free-floating control" through which governance quickly adjusts its tactics and strategies ("Neocitizenship" 2–3). Neoliberalism does not stay still long enough to critique. The paradox, Slavoj Žižek argues, is that amidst such instability, "[w]e find ourselves constantly in the position of having to decide about matters that will fatefully affect our lives" ("Some" 24). "Far from being experienced as liberating," he writes, "this compulsion freely to decide is … experienced as an anxiety-provoking obscene gamble" (24). Moreover, Žižek contends, there is "no guarantee that the democratic politicization of crucial decisions … will necessarily improve the quality and accuracy of decisions" (24–25). "Nothing can save us" from present conditions, proclaim Eric Cazdyn and Imre Szeman (*Globalization* 5). Neither education, nor morality. "Neither sudden scientific breakthroughs, nor technological marvels. Neither quick fixes, nor golden bullets" (5). To suggest that novels might offer recourse where science and morality fail would be ludicrous were it not for fiction's habituation to the mutability of social order and the crisis of individual agency these critics of neoliberalism ably describe.

Where F. R. Leavis sought to generate interest in literature's capacity to preserve minority culture, contemporary fiction invites us to think about how literature formulates social change in the context of state crisis, economic uncertainty, and all of the instability that appears constitutive of what it means to govern. There is no question that literature does so in a local and ad hoc fashion, which may make its solutions of reworked social networks and reimagined expert teams appear insufficient to address systemic crises that any number of commentators perceive as occurring globally. Where the fiction I have considered has an advantage, I believe, is in its predilection for working both within and against given administrative arrangements as opposed to demanding that we imagine a space "outside" governmentality.

The fiction I have presented does not reproduce the utopian imperative felt by, among others, Cazdyn and Szeman. These two scholars detect a collective sense of "something missing" from life as we know it, which for them constitutes "both the *nothing* to which we are alive again and the radical future that we miss despite being unable to expressly prescribe, imagine, or desire it" (*Globalization* 60). The dream of escape from governmentality can also be less grand, Lauren Berlant reminds us. Diagnosing a present in which "living increasingly becomes a scene of the administration, discipline, and recapitulation of what constitutes health," she affirms the "practical sovereignty" of people who take "small vacations" from governmental dictates by, among other tactics, eating "unhealthy" food ("Slow" 755–56, 779). Where Berlant's subjects momentarily interrupt their administered lives to make "a less bad experience," Cazdyn and Szeman look to the horizon and towards life "after globalization"

(Berlant "Slow" 779; Cazdyn and Szeman *Globalization* 60). Instead of escape, whether brief or enduring, much twentieth-century novelistic endeavor suggests the possibility for meaningful change without any promise of sovereignty regained or post-globalization achieved.

To say that contemporary fiction is often less than utopian is not to say that it fails to criticize current government. Far from it. The fiction I have considered regularly questions authority. But it does so less as a means of demonstrating that its characters are ungovernable than as a way of engaging in what Michel Foucault calls "the art of not being governed quite so much" ("Critique" 193). Fiction imagines the possibility of widening norms of accepted behavior and recalibrating expert influence. The novels I have considered do not seek to escape existing forms of government so much as to test them, to intervene in governmentality, and to renovate it.

I think Leavis was right: the "trained frequentation of literature" can give "the thinking that attends social and political studies" a certain "edge and force" ("Literature" 11). To this end, I have suggested ways that fiction attunes readers to new political possibilities and equips them to imagine alternative social arrangements. I have been guided by the idea that fictional tales of characters who strive to become well attached provide object lessons for readers in search of more satisfying models of association. This is thinking small, to be sure. As every novel I have treated in this book is convinced, however, small changes matter. To better understand large shifts – like the conquest of Burma depicted in *The Glass Palace* – fiction suggests that we focus on an interpersonal scale.

"Man is a political animal because he is a literary animal," Rancière affirms, "who lets himself be diverted from his 'natural' purpose by the power of words" (*Politics* 39). If we are used to thinking of novels as acclimating readers to their individual natures, surely it is not a stretch to think that fiction can teach us other ways of conceiving our social selves. Part of the project of reconfiguring government entails remembering that "personal liberty" was always a kind of shorthand, a way of describing attachment to a whole administrative network. To execute and guarantee the writ of habeas corpus requires a judge and a judicial system. The principle of natural right connotes a nation-state or an empire or a transnational non-governmental organization equipped to guarantee that right, while adjudicating precisely to whom it applies. The fictional elaboration and reproduction of individual agency is in no way exempt from this rule. As Mark McGurl explains in detail, in *The Program Era*, creative writing programs have institutionalized as "good writing" particular ways of generating characters and social worlds. As Sarah Brouillette shows, meanwhile, in *Postcolonial Writers in the Global Literary Marketplace*, publishing-house selections and marketing strategies habituate readers to the idea that novelists may speak with authority on any social matter their fiction can represent.

Ngũgĩ was as right as Leavis to argue on behalf of a "multi-disciplinary outlook" for literary study, for the only way to grapple with the novel's contribution to governance is by avoiding any inclination to read fiction in a disciplinary vacuum (Ngũgĩ "Abolition" 148). To understand the novel as a form of governmentality, finally, must mean that we cease to gnash our teeth over literature's social relevance and withstand lingering urges to rely upon acid tests of ideological complicity to guide our criticism. Literary scholarship might better think of itself as fiction's managerial collaborator and competitor than its judge and arbiter. When characters dream of being well attached, when plots stoke aspirations for responsible governance, we in the academy would do well to adapt our expectations about what novels can think. We will thereby be prepared to recognize how novels encourage their readers to rethink what government can do.

Bibliography

Abani, Chris. *Song for Night*. New York: Akashic Books, 2007.

Abbas, Ackbar. "Cosmopolitan De-Scriptions: Shanghai and Hong Kong." *Public Culture* 12.3 (2000): 769–86.

Abu-Jaber, Diana. "London Kills Me." *The Nation* October 20, 2003: 25–28.

Abu-Lughod, Janet. *Before European Hegemony: The World System, AD 1250–1350*. New York: Oxford University Press, 1989.

Achebe, Chinua. *The Trouble with Nigeria*. Portsmouth, NH: Heinemann, 1984. (Originally published 1983).

"The Writer and His Community." *Hopes and Impediments*. New York: Doubleday, 1988, pp. 47–61. (Original work published 1984).

Adichie, Chimamanda Ngozi. "African 'Authenticity' and the Biafran Experience." *Transition* 99 (2008): 42–53.

Half of a Yellow Sun. New York: Knopf, 2006.

Adichie, Chimamanda Ngozi, with Kera Bolonik. "Memory, Witness, and War: Chimamanda Ngozi Adichie Talks with Bookforum." *Bookforum* 14.4 (2008). www.bookforum.com/inprint/014_04/1403

Afigbo, A. E. *The Warrant Chiefs: Indirect Rule in Southeastern Nigeria, 1891–1929*. New York: Humanities Press, 1972.

Agamben, Giorgio. *Homo Sacer: Sovereign Power and Bare Life*. Trans. Heller-Roazen, Daniel. Stanford University Press, 1998.

Means Without End, Notes on Politics. Minneapolis: University of Minnesota Press, 2000.

State of Exception. Trans. Attell, Kevin. University of Chicago Press, 2005.

Agustín, Laura M. "A Migrant World of Services." *Social Politics* 10.3 (2003): 377–96.

Ahmad, Ali. "Brick Lane: A Note on the Politics of 'Good' Literary Production." *Third Text* 18.2 (2004): 199–205.

Ali, Monica. *Brick Lane: A Novel*. New York: Scribner, 2003.

Amin, Samir. *Re-Reading the Postwar Period*. New York: Monthly Review Press, 1994.

Appadurai, Arjun. *Fear of Small Numbers*. Durham, NC: Duke University Press, 2006.

Appiah, Kwame Anthony. "Cosmopolitan Reading." *Cosmopolitan Geographies: New Locations in Literature and Culture.* Ed. Dharwadker, Vinay. New York: Routledge, 2001, pp. 198–227.

The Ethics of Identity. Princeton University Press, 2005.

Apter, Emily. "On Translation in a Global Market." *Public Culture* 13.1 (2001): 1–12.

Ardis, Ann. *New Women, New Novels.* New Brunswick, NJ: Rutgers University Press, 1990.

Arendt, Hannah. *The Origins of Totalitarianism.* New York: Meridian, 1958. (Originally published 1951).

Armstrong, Nancy. *Desire and Domestic Fiction: A Political History of the Novel.* New York: Oxford University Press, 1987.

How Novels Think. New York: Columbia University Press, 2005.

Armstrong, Nancy, and Leonard Tennenhouse. "The Problem of Population and the Form of the American Novel." *American Literary History* 20.4 (2008): 1–19.

"Sovereignty and the Form of Formlessness." *differences* 20.2–3 (2009): 148–78.

Armstrong, Paul. "The Narrator in the Closet." *MFS: Modern Fiction Studies* 47.2 (2001): 306–28.

Arnold, Matthew. *Culture and Anarchy.* London: Smith, Elder and Co., 1869.

Arrighi, Giovanni. *Adam Smith in Beijing: Lineages of the Twenty-First Century.* London and New York: Verso, 2007.

The Long Twentieth Century. New York: Verso, 1994.

Auerbach, Erich. *Mimesis: The Representation of Reality in Western Literature.* Princeton University Press, 1953.

Aw, Tash. *The Harmony Silk Factory.* New York: Riverhead, 2005.

Badru, Pade. *Imperialism and Ethnic Politics in Nigeria.* Trenton, NJ: Africa World Press, 1998.

Banerjee, Sukanya. *Becoming Imperial Citizens: Indians in the Late-Victorian Empire.* Durham, NC: Duke University Press, 2010.

Banks, Iain. *The Business.* London: Little, Brown, 1999.

Bannon, Ian, and Paul Collier, eds. *Natural Resources and Violent Conflict.* Washington, DC: The World Bank, 2003.

Barlow, Tani E., Madeleine Yue Dong, Uta G. Poiger, Prita Ramamurthy, Lynn M. Thomas, and Alys Eve Weinbaum. "The Modern Girl around the World: A Research Agenda and Preliminary Findings." *Gender and History* 17.2 (2005): 245–94.

Barnard, Rita. *Apartheid and Beyond: South African Writers and the Politics of Place*. Oxford University Press, 2007.

Bates, Robert. "Political Insecurity and State Failure in Contemporary Africa." *CID Working Papers*. Cambridge, MA: Center for International Development at Harvard University, 2005: 1–53.

Bauman, Zygmunt. *Liquid Life*. Cambridge: Polity Press, 2005.

Liquid Modernity. Cambridge: Polity Press, 2000.

Bayart, Jean-Francois. *The Illusion of Cultural Identity*. London: Hurst & Co., 2005.

Bayly, C. A. *The Birth of the Modern World, 1780–1914: Global Connections and Comparisons*. Malden, MA: Blackwell, 2004.

Becker, Gary S., and Kevin M. Murphy. *Social Economics: Market Behavior in a Social Environment*. Cambridge, MA: Belknap Press of Harvard University Press, 2000.

Benería, Lourdes. *Gender, Development, and Globalization: Economics as if All People Mattered*. New York: Routledge, 2003.

Berlant, Lauren. "Intuitionists: History and the Affective Event." *American Literary History* 20.4 (2008): 845–60.

"Slow Death." *Critical Inquiry* 33.3 (2007): 754–80.

Bhabha, Homi K. *The Location of Culture*. New York: Routledge, 1994.

Bhattacharjea, Aditya, and Lola Chatterji. *The Fiction of St. Stephen's*. New Delhi: Ravi Dayal, 2000.

Bhuwania, Anuj. "The 'Law' of the Police." *Sarai Reader* 7 (2007): 134–43.

Boccardi, Mariadele. "History as Gynealogy." *Women: A Cultural Review* 15.2 (2004): 192–203.

Bodkin, Ronald G. "Women's Agency in Classical Economic Thought: Adam Smith, Harriet Taylor Mill, and J. S. Mill." *Feminist Economics* 5.1 (1999): 45–60.

Bose, Sugata. *A Hundred Horizons*. Cambridge, MA: Harvard University Press, 2006.

Bowen, Elizabeth. *The Heat of the Day*. New York: Anchor Books, 2002. (Originally published 1948).

Braudel, Fernand. *The Wheels of Commerce*. Trans. Reynolds, Siân. *Civilization and Capitalism*. Vol. 2. New York: Harper and Row, 1982. (Original work published 1979).

Brennan, Timothy. *At Home in the World*. Cambridge, MA: Harvard University Press, 1997.

Wars of Position. New York: Columbia University Press, 2006.

Brinks, Ellen. "Gendered Spaces in *Kamala: The Story of a Hindu Child-Wife*." *Nineteenth-Century Contexts* 30.2 (2008): 147–65.
Brouillette, Sarah. *Postcolonial Writers in the Global Literary Marketplace*. New York: Palgrave, 2007.
Brown, Nicholas. *Utopian Generations: The Political Horizon of Twentieth-Century Literature*. Princeton University Press, 2005.
Brown, Wendy. *Edgework: Critical Essays on Knowledge and Politics*. Princeton University Press, 2005.
States of Injury: Power and Freedom in Late Modernity. Princeton University Press, 1995.
Bull, Malcolm. "Vectors of the Biopolitical." *New Left Review* 45 (2007): 7–25.
Burchell, Graham. "Liberal Government and Techniques of the Self." *Economy and Society* 22.3 (1993): 267–82.
Burrows, Victoria. "The Heterotopic Spaces of Postcolonial Trauma in Michael Ondaatje's *Anil's Ghost*." *Studies in the Novel* 40.1–2 (2008): 161–77.
Burton, Antoinette. "Archive of Bones: *Anil's Ghost* and the Ends of History." *Journal of Commonwealth Literature* 38.1 (2004): 39–56.
Butler, Judith. "Critique, Dissent, Disciplinarity." *Critical Inquiry* 35.4 (2009): 773–95.
Butler, Judith, and Gayatri Chakravorty Spivak. *Who Sings the Nation-State?* New York: Seagull, 2007.
Callon, Michel. "The Embeddedness of Economic Markets in Economics." *The Laws of the Market*. Ed. Callon, Michel. Malden, MA: Blackwell, 1998, pp. 1–57.
Callon, Michel, Pierre Lascoumes, and Yannick Barthe. *Acting in an Uncertain World: An Essay on Technical Democracy*. Trans. Burchell, Graham. Cambridge, MA: MIT Press, 2009 (2001).
Caplan, Richard. "From Collapsing States to Neo-Trusteeship." *Third World Quarterly* 28.2 (2007): 231–44.
Caraway, Teri L. "The Political Economy of Feminization: From 'Cheap Labor' to Gendered Discourses of Work." *Politics and Gender* 1.3 (2005): 399–429.
Cardano, Marc, Robert F. Scherer, and Crystal Owen. "Attitudes towards Women as Managers: Sex Versus Culture." *Women in Management Review* 17.2 (2002): 51–60.

Casanova, Pascale. *The World Republic of Letters*. Cambridge, MA: Harvard University Press, 2004.

Caserio, Robert L. "The Heat of the Day: Modernism and Narrative in Paul De Man and Elizabeth Bowen." *Modern Language Quarterly* 54.2 (1993): 263–84.

Cazdyn, Eric M., and Imre Szeman. *After Globalization*. Malden, MA: Wiley-Blackwell, 2011.

Chakrabarty, Dipesh. *Habitations of Modernity: Essays in the Wake of Subaltern Studies*. University of Chicago Press, 2002.

—— "Legacies of Bandung." *Economic and Political Weekly* 40.46 (2005): 4812–18.

—— *Provincializing Europe: Postcolonial Thought and Historical Difference*. Princeton Studies in Culture/Power/History. Princeton University Press, 2000.

Chan, Stephen. "The Memory of Violence." *Third World Quarterly* 26.2 (2005): 369–82.

Chang, Leslie T. *Factory Girls: From Village to City in a Changing China*. New York: Spiegel & Grau, 2008.

Chatterjee, Partha. *The Nation and Its Fragments*. Princeton University Press, 1993.

—— *Nationalist Thought and the Colonial World: A Derivative Discourse*. Minneapolis: University of Minnesota Press, 1986.

—— *The Politics of the Governed: Reflections on Popular Politics in Most of the World*. New York: Columbia University Press, 2004.

Chatterjee, Upamanyu. *English, August: An Indian Story*. New York Review Books Classics. New York Review Books, 2006. (Originally published 1988).

Chaudhuri, Rosinka. "The Flute, Gerontion, and Subalternist Misreadings of Tagore." *Social Text* 22.1 (2004): 103–22.

Cheah, Pheng. "Cosmopolitanism." *Theory, Culture and Society* 23.2–3 (2005): 486–96.

—— *Spectral Nationality: Passages of Freedom from Kant to Postcolonial Literatures of Liberation*. New York: Columbia University Press, 2003.

Cherniavsky, Eva. "Neocitizenship and Critique." *Social Text* 27.2 (2009): 1–23.

Chesterman, Simon. "Transitional Administration, State-Building, and the United Nations." *Making States Work*. Ed. Chesterman, Simon, Michael Ignatieff, and Rames Thakur. New York: United Nations University Press, 2005, pp. 339–58.

Chesterman, Simon, Michael Ignatieff, and Ramesh Thakur. "Introduction: Making States Work." *Making States Work*. Ed. Chesterman, Simon, Michael Ignatieff, and Rames Thakur. New York: United Nations University Press, 2005, pp. 1–10.

Chitale, Venu. *In Transit: [Novel]*. Bombay: Hind Kitabs, 1950.

Chow, Rey. *The Age of the World Target: Self-Referentiality in War, Theory, and Comparative Work*. Durham, NC: Duke University Press, 2006.

— *The Protestant Ethnic and the Spirit of Capitalism*. New York: Columbia University Press, 2002.

Claybaugh, Amanda. "Government Is Good." *Minnesota Review* 70 (2008): 161–66.

Clough, Patricia Ticineto. "The Case of Sociology: Governmentality and Methodology." *Critical Inquiry* 36.4 (2010): 627–41.

Colquitt, Clare. "A Call to Arms." *South Atlantic Review* 51.2 (1986): 77–91.

Comaroff, Jean, and John Comaroff. "Millennial Capitalism: First Thoughts on a Second Coming." *Public Culture* 12.2 (2000): 291–343.

Comaroff, John. "The End of Neoliberalism?" *The Salon* 1 (2009): 46–49.

Conrad, Joseph. "Heart of Darkness." *Youth and Two Other Stories*. New York: Doubleday, 1903, pp. 45–164. (Originally published 1899).

— *Nostromo*. New York: Penguin, 1985. (Originally published 1904).

— *Typhoon and Other Tales*. New York: Oxford University Press, 1986. (Originally published 1902).

Cook, Victoria. "A Spectre of the Transnational: Exploring Identity as Process in Michael Ondaatje's Anil's Ghost." *Journal of Commonwealth Literature* 9.1 (2002): 105–17.

Crisis States Research Centre (CSRC). "Crisis, Fragile and Failed States: Definitions Used by the Crisis States Research Centre." CSRC, London School of Economics, 2006.

Cunningham, David. "Capitalist Epics." *Radical Philosophy* 163 (2010): 11–23.

Daiya, Kavita. *Violent Belongings: Partition, Gender, and National Culture in Postcolonial India*. Philadelphia: Temple University Press, 2008.

Damrosch, David. "Toward a History of World Literature." *New Literary History* 39.3 (2008): 481–95.

Dangarembga, Tsitsi. *Nervous Conditions*. Seattle, WA: Seal, 1988.

Das, Veena. *Life and Words: Violence and the Descent into the Ordinary*. Berkeley: University of California Press, 2007.

Das, Veena, and Ashis Nandy. "Violence, Victimhood, and the Language of Silence." *The Word and the World*. Ed. Das, Veena. New Delhi: Sage Publications, 1986, pp. 177–95.

de Soto, Hernando. *The Mystery of Capital*. New York: Basic Books, 2000.

de Waal, Alex. "Dollarised." *London Review of Books* 32.12 (2010): 38–41.

Dean, Mitchell. *Governmentality*. London: Sage, 1999.

"Liberal Government and Authoritarianism." *Economy and Society* 31.1 (2002): 37–61.

DeHart, Monica. "'Hermano Entrepreneurs!' Constructing a Latino Diaspora across the Digital Divide." *Diaspora* 13.2–3 (2004): 253–78.

Deleuze, Gilles. "Postscript on the Societies of Control." *October* 59 (1992): 3–7.

Deleuze, Gilles, with Antonio Negri. "Control and Becoming." 2010 (1990). www.generation-online.org/p/fpdeleuze3.htm#iframe_height =300

Derrickson, Teresa. "Will the Untruth Set You Free? A Critical Look at Global Human Rights Discourse in Michael Ondaatje's *Anil's Ghost*." *Lit: Literature, Interpretation, Theory* 15.2 (2004): 131–52.

Desai, Anita. "Introduction." *The Home and the World*. New York: Penguin, 1985, pp. 7–14.

Dickinson, Elizabeth. "Watch List." *Foreign Policy* 180 (2010): 84–85.

Dillon, Elizabeth Maddock. *The Gender of Freedom*. Stanford University Press, 2004.

Dimock, Wai-chee, and Lawrence Buell. "Introduction: Planet and America, Set and Subset." *Shades of the Planet: American Literature as World Literature*. Ed. Dimock, Wai-chee, and Lawrence Buell. Princeton University Press, 2007, pp. 1–16.

Diouf, Mamadou. "The Senegalese Murid Trade Diaspora and the Making of a Vernacular Cosmopolitanism." *Public Culture* 12.3 (2000): 679–702.

Donzelot, Jacques. "Michel Foucault and Liberal Intelligence." *Economy and Society* 37.1 (2008): 115–34.

"The Mobilization of Society." *The Foucault Effect*. Ed. Burchall, Graham, Colin Gordon, and Peter Miller. University of Chicago Press, 1991, pp. 169–79.

Donzelot, Jacques, and Colin Gordon. "Governing Liberal Societies: The Foucault Effect in the English-Speaking World." *Foucault Studies* 5 (2008): 48–62.

Doyle, Laura, and Laura A. Winkiel. *Geomodernisms: Race, Modernism, Modernity*. Bloomington: Indiana University Press, 2005.

Duncan, Ian. *Modern Romance and Transformations of the Nation.* New York: Cambridge University Press, 1992.
   Scott's Shadow: The Novel in Romantic Edinburgh. Princeton University Press, 2007.
Eagly, Alice Hendrickson, and Linda Lorene Carli. *Through the Labyrinth: The Truth about How Women Become Leaders. Leadership for the Common Good.* Boston, MA: Harvard Business School Press, 2007.
Eggers, Dave. *What Is the What.* New York: Vintage, 2006.
Ehrenreich, Barbara, and John Ehrenreich. "The Professional-Managerial Class." *Between Labor and Capital.* Ed. Walker, Pat. Boston, MA: South End Press, 1979 (1977), pp. 5–45.
Ehrenreich, Barbara, and Arlie Russell Hochschild. *Global Woman: Nannies, Maids, and Sex Workers in the New Economy.* New York: Metropolitan Books, 2003.
Ekechi, F. K. *Tradition and Transformation in Eastern Nigeria.* Kent State University Press, 1989.
Ekwe-Ekwe, Herbert. *Biafra Revisited.* Reading, England: Africa Renaissance, 2007.
Ellmann, Maud. *Elizabeth Bowen: The Shadow across the Page.* Edinburgh University Press, 2003.
Eng, Tan Twan. *The Gift of Rain.* New York: Weinstein Books, 2008.
Englebert, Pierre. "Why Congo Persists." *Globalization, Violent Conflict, and Self-Determination.* Ed. Fitzgerald, Valpy, Frances Stewart, and Rajesh Venugopal. London: Palgrave, 2006, pp. 119–46.
Esty, Joshua. "Virginia Woolf's Colony and the Adolescence of Modernist Fiction." *Modernism and Colonialism: British and Irish Literature, 1899–1939.* Ed. Begum, Richard, and Michael Valdez Moses. Durham, NC: Duke University Press, 2007, pp. 70–90.
Ewald, Francois. "Norms, Discipline, and the Law." *Representations* 30 (1990): 138–61.
"Failed States Index 2007." *Foreign Policy* 161 (2007): 54–63.
"Failed States Index 2008." *Foreign Policy* 167 (2008): 64–68.
"Failed States Index 2009." *Foreign Policy* 173 (2009): 80–93.
"Failed States Index 2010." *Foreign Policy* 180 (2010): 74–79.
"Failed States Index 2011." *Foreign Policy* 187 (2011): 48–57.
Fanon, Frantz. *The Wretched of the Earth.* New York: Grove, 1963.
Farred, Grant. "Leavisite Cool: The Organic Links between Cultural Studies and *Scrutiny*." *dispositio/n* 12.48 (1996): 1–19.

Farrier, David. "Gesturing towards the Local." *Journal of Postcolonial Writing* 41.1 (2005): 83–93.

Fassin, Didier. "Humanitarianism as a Politics of Life." *Public Culture* 19.3 (2007): 499–520.

Fearon, James, and David Laitin. "Ethnicity, Insurgency, and Civil War." *American Political Science Review* 97.1 (2003): 75–90.

Felski, Rita. *The Gender of Modernity*. Cambridge, MA: Harvard University Press, 1995.

Ferguson, Adam. *An Essay on the History of Civil Society*. Edinburgh: Printed for A. Millar and T. Caddel in the Strand, London, and A. Kincaid and J. Bell, Edinburgh, 1767.

Ferguson, James. "Decomposing Modernity: History and Hierarchy after Development." *Postcolonial Studies and Beyond*. Ed. Loomba, Ania, Suvir Kaul, Matti Bunzl, Antoinette Burton, and Jed Esty. Durham, NC: Duke University Press, 2005, pp. 166–82.

Global Shadows: Africa in the Neoliberal World Order. Durham, NC: Duke University Press, 2006.

Ferguson, Niall. *Empire: The Rise and Demise of the British World Order and the Lessons for Global Power*. New York: Basic Books, 2003.

Fluet, Lisa. "Hit-Man Modernism." *Bad Modernisms*. Ed. Mao, Douglas, and Rebecca L. Walkowitz. Durham, NC: Duke University Press, 2006, pp. 269–97.

Forna, Aminatta. *Ancestor Stones*. New York: Grove Press, 2006.

Forster, E. M. *Howards End*. New York: Bantam, 1985. (Originally published 1910).

Forsyth, Frederick. *The Biafra Story*. Baltimore, MD: Penguin, 1969.

Forter, Greg. "Barry Unsworth and the Arts of Power: Historical Memory, Utopian Fictions." *Contemporary Literature* 51.4 (2010): 777–809.

Fothergill, Anthony. "Connoisseurs of Terror and the Political Aesthetics of Anarchism." *Conrad in the Twenty-First Century: Contemporary Approaches and Perspectives*. Ed. Kaplan, Carola, Peter Mallios, and Andrea White. New York: Routledge, 2005, pp. 137–54.

Foucault, Michel. *Abnormal*. Trans. Burchell, Graham. New York: Palgrave, 2003.

The Birth of Biopolitics. Trans. Burchell, Graham. New York: Palgrave, 2008.

The History of Sexuality. Vol. 1. New York: Vintage, 1978.

Language, Counter-Memory, Practice. Trans. Bouchard, Donald. Ithaca, NY: Cornell University Press, 1977.

Security, Territory, Population. Trans. Burchell, Graham. New York: Palgrave, 2007.

"*Society Must Be Defended*." Trans. Macey, David. New York: Picador, 2003.

"What Is Critique?" *The Political*. Ed. Ingram, David. Malden, MA: Blackwell, 2002, pp. 191–211.

Frank, Andre Gunder. *ReOrient: Global Economy in the Asian Age*. Berkeley: University of California Press, 1998.

Freeman, Carla. *High Tech and High Heels in the Global Economy: Women, Work, and Pink-Collar Identities in the Caribbean*. Durham, NC: Duke University Press, 2000.

Friedman, Thomas. *The World Is Flat*. New York: Farrar, Straus, and Giroux, 2005.

Fund for Peace, The. "Failed States Index Scores 2008." Washington, DC, 2008. www.fundforpeace.org/web/index.php?option=com_content&task=view&id=292&Itemid=452

"Failed States Index Scores 2009." Washington, DC, 2009. www.fundforpeace.org/web/index.php?option=com_content&task=view&id=391&Itemid=549

"Failed States Index Scores 2010." Washington, DC, 2010. www.fundforpeace.org/web/index.php?option=com_content&task=view&id=452&Itemid=900

"Failed States Index Scores 2011." Washington, DC, 2011. www.fundforpeace.org/global/?q=fsi-grid2011

"Methodology Behind Cast (Conflict Assessment System Tool)." Washington, DC, 2006. www.fundforpeace.org/web/index.php?option=com_content&task=view&id=107&Itemid=145

Gallagher, Catherine. *The Body Economic: Life, Death, and Sensation in Political Economy, and the Victorian Novel*. Princeton University Press, 2006.

"The Body Versus the Social Body in the Works of Thomas Malthus and Henry Mayhew." *Representations* 14 (1986): 83–106.

Ganapathy-Doré, Geeta. "Fathoming Private Woes in a Public Story: A Study of Michael Ondaatje's *Anil's Ghost*." *Jouvert* 6.3 (2002). http://english.chass.ncsu.edu/jouvert/v6i3/anil.htm

Gandhi, Leela. *Affective Communities*. Chicago University Press, 2006.

Ganguly-Scrase, Ruchira. "Paradoxes of Globalization, Liberalization, and Gender Equality: The Worldviews of the Lower Middle Class in West Bengal, India." *Gender and Society* 17.4 (2003): 544–66.

George, Rosemary Marangoly. *The Politics of Home*. Cambridge University Press, 1996.
Ghosh, Amitav. *The Glass Palace*. New York: Random House, 2002. (Originally published 2000).
   The Hungry Tide. Boston, MA: Houghton Mifflin, 2005.
   Sea of Poppies. London: John Murray, 2008.
Ghosh, Aparisim. "Flavour of the Week." *Time International* July 14, 2009: 51.
Ghosh, Sarath Kumar. "Millionaires of the Orient." *New York Times* October 12, 1902: 11.
   Prince of Destiny. London: Rebman Ltd., 1909.
Gibson, William. *Pattern Recognition*. New York: G. P. Putnam's Sons, 2003.
   Spook Country. New York: G. P. Putnam's Sons, 2007.
   Zero History. New York: G. P. Putnam's Sons, 2010.
Gibson-Graham, J. K. *The End of Capitalism (as We Knew It): A Feminist Critique of Political Economy*. Oxford: Blackwell, 1996.
Gikandi, Simon. "Globalization and the Claims of Postcoloniality." *South Atlantic Quarterly* 100.3 (2001): 627–58.
   Ngũgĩ Wa Thiong'o. New York: Cambridge University Press, 2000.
Gillies, Mary Ann, Helen Sword, and Steven G. Yao. *Pacific Rim Modernisms*. University of Toronto Press, 2009.
Gilroy, Paul. *Postcolonial Melancholia*. New York: Columbia University Press, 2005.
Girard, Monique, and David Stark. "Heterarchies of Value." *Global Assemblages*. Ed. Ong, Aihwa, and Stephen J. Collier. Malden, MA: Blackwell, 2005, pp. 293–319.
Gladwell, Malcolm. "The Sure Thing." *The New Yorker* January 18, 2010: 24–29.
Goodlad, Lauren. "Is There a Pastor in the *House?*: Sanitary Reform, Professionalism, and Philanthropy in Dickens's Mid-Century Fiction." *Victorian Literature and Culture* 31 (2003): 525–53.
Gorra, Michael. "East Enders." *The New York Times Book Review* September 7, 2003: 9.
Grewal, Inderpal, and Caren Kaplan. *Scattered Hegemonies: Postmodernity, and Transnational Feminist Practices*. Minneapolis: University of Minnesota Press, 1994.
Grosz, Elizabeth. *Becomings: Explorations in Time, Memory, and Futures*. Ithaca, NY: Cornell University Press, 1999.

"Deleuze's Bergson: Duration, the Virtual and a Politics of the Future." *Deleuze and Feminist Theory*. Ed. Buchanan, Ian, and Claire Colebrook, Edinburgh University Press, 2000, pp. 214–34.

The Nick of Time: Politics, Evolution, and the Untimely. Durham, NC: Duke University Press, 2004.

Guha, Ranajit. *Dominance without Hegemony: History and Power in Colonial India*. Cambridge, MA: Harvard University Press, 1997.

Gurnah, Abdulrazak. *Desertion*. New York: Pantheon, 2005.

Habermas, Jürgen. *The Structural Transformation of the Public Sphere*. Trans. Burger, Thomas. Cambridge, MA: MIT Press, 1991. (Original work published 1962).

Hardt, Michael. "The Withering of Civil Society." *Deleuze and Guattari: New Mappings in Politics, Philosophy, and Culture*. Ed. Kaufman, Eleanor, and Kevin Jon Heller. Minneapolis: University of Minnesota Press, 1998, pp. 23–39.

Harootunian, Harry. "Postcoloniality's Unconscious/Area Studies' Desire." *Postcolonial Studies* 2.2 (2002): 127–48.

Hart, Matthew, and Jim Hansen. "Introduction: Contemporary Literature and the State." *Contemporary Literature* 49.4 (2008): 491–513.

Harvey, David. *A Brief History of Neoliberalism*. Oxford University Press, 2005.

"The Geography of Class Power." *Socialist Register* 34 (1998): 49–74.

Hassan, Waïl. "Agency and Translational Literature." *PMLA* 121.3 (2006): 753–68.

Hawkesworth, Mary E. *Globalization and Feminist Activism*. Lanham, MD: Rowman & Littlefield, 2006.

Hawley, John C. "Biafra as Heritage and Symbol: Adichie, Mbachu, and Iweala." *Research in African Literatures* 39.2 (2008): 15–26.

Hayford, J. E. Casely. *Ethiopia Unbound*. London: Frank Cass and Co., 1969. (Originally published 1911).

Hayles, N. Katherine. "Traumas of Code." *Critical Inquiry* 33.2 (2006): 136–57.

Hayot, Eric. "On Literary Worlds." *Modern Language Quarterly* 72.2 (2011): 129–61.

Hegel, G. W. F. *The Philosophy of Right*. Trans. Knox, T. M. Oxford University Press, 1967.

Helman, Gerald, and Steven Ratner. "Saving Failed States." *Foreign Policy* 89 (1992): 3–20.

Hindess, Barry. "The Liberal Government of Unfreedom." *Alternatives* 26.2 (2001): 93–111.
Hitchcock, Peter. "Postcolonial Failure and the Politics of the Nation." *South Atlantic Quarterly* 106.4 (2007): 727–52.
Ho, Engseng. *The Graves of Tarim: Genealogy and Mobility across the Indian Ocean.* Berkeley: University of California Press, 2006.
Hobson, John M. *The Eastern Origins of Western Civilization.* New York: Cambridge University Press, 2004.
Hosain, Attia. *Sunlight on a Broken Column.* London: Chatto & Windus, 1961.
Hussain, Nasser. "Beyond Norm and Exception: Guantánamo." *Critical Inquiry* 33.3 (2007): 734–53.
Hutcheon, Linda. "Crypto-Ethnicity." *PMLA* 113.1 (1998): 28–33.
Ike, Chukwuemeka. *Sunset at Dawn.* London: Collins and Harvill Press, 1976.
Ingrassia, Catherine. *Authorship, Commerce, and Gender in Early Eighteenth-Century England: A Culture of Paper Credit.* New York: Cambridge University Press, 1998.
International Monetary Fund. *World Economic Outlook: A Survey by the Staff of the International Monetary Fund.* Washington, DC: International Monetary Fund, 2010.
Isichei, Elizabeth. *A History of the Igbo People.* New York: St. Martin's Press, 1976.
Jameson, Fredric. "Fear and Loathing in Globalization." *New Left Review* 23 (2003): 105–14.
   "Modernism and Imperialism." *Nationalism, Colonialism, and Literature.* Minneapolis: University of Minnesota Press, 1990, pp. 43–68.
   The Political Unconscious. Ithaca, NY: Cornell University Press, 1981.
   A Singular Modernity: Essay on the Ontology of the Present. London and New York: Verso, 2002.
   "Third-World Literature in the Era of Multinational Capitalism." *Social Text* 15 (1986): 65–88.
Johnson, Claudia L. "F. R. Leavis: The 'Great Tradition' of the English Novel and Jewish Part." *Nineteenth-Century Literature* 56.2 (2001): 198–227.
Joseph, Jonathan. "Governmentality of What?" *Global Society* 23.4 (2009): 413–27.
Joshi, Priya. *In Another Country.* New York: Columbia University Press, 2002.
Judt, Tony. *Ill Fares the Land.* New York: Penguin, 2010.

Judt, Tony, and Kristina Božič. "The Way Things Are and How They Might Be." *London Review of Books* 32.6 (2010): 11–14.

Kabeer, Naila. "Globalization, Labor Standards, and Women's Rights: Dilemmas of Collective (in)Action in an Interdependent World." *Feminist Economics* 10.1 (2004): 3–35.

——. *The Power to Choose: Bangladeshi Women and Labour Market Decisions in London and Dhaka*. London: Verso, 2000.

Kabir, Ananya Jahanara. "Gender, Memory, Trauma: Women's Novels on the Partition of India." *Comparative Studies of South Asia, Africa, and the Middle East* 25.1 (2005): 177–90.

Kaletsky, Anatole. *Capitalism 4.0: The Birth of a New Economy in the Aftermath of Crisis*. New York: PublicAffairs, 2010.

Kanaganayakam, Chelva. "In Defense of *Anil's Ghost*." *Ariel: A Review of International English Literature* 37.1 (2006): 5–26.

Kapoor, Mini. "New Lonely Londoners." *Indian Express* May 25, 2003. www.indianexpress.com/res/web/pIe/print.php?content_id=24525

Kelman, James. *Translated Accounts*. New York: Doubleday, 2001.

Kidder, Deborah. "The Influence of Gender on the Performance of Organizational Citizenship Behaviors." *Journal of Management* 28.5 (2002): 629–48.

Kinicki, Angelo. "The New Hiring Standard: Adaptability." January 2, 2008. http://knowledge.wpcarey.asu.edu/article.cfm?articleid=1532

Koggel, Christine. "Globalization and Women's Paid Work: Expanding Freedom?" *Feminist Economics* 9.2 (2003): 163–84.

Kotkin, Joel. *Tribes*. New York: Random House, 1993.

Krishnan, Madhu. "Biafra and the Aesthetics of Closure in the Third Generation Nigerian Novel." *Rupkatha: A Journal on Interdisciplinary Studies in the Humanities* 2.2 (2010): 185–95.

Lalami, Laila. "Love and Betrayal in Colonial Africa." September 26, 2005. www.thenation.com/doc/20050926/lalami

Latour, Bruno. *Reassembling the Social: An Introduction to Actor-Network Theory. Clarendon Lectures in Management Studies*. Oxford University Press, 2005.

——. "Spheres and Networks: Two Ways to Reinterpret Globalization." *Harvard Design Magazine* 3 Spring/Summer (2009): 138–44.

——. "Why Has Critique Run out of Steam? From Matters of Fact to Matters of Concern." *Critical Inquiry* 30.2 (2004): 225–48.

Laurence, Patricia. *Lily Briscoe's Chinese Eyes: Bloomsbury, Modernism, and China*. Columbia: University of South Carolina Press, 2003.

Law, John, and Michel Callon. "The Life and Death of an Aircraft: A Network Analysis of Technical Change." *Shaping Technology/ Building Society: Studies in Sociotechnical Change*. Ed. Bijker, Wiebe, and John Law. Cambridge, MA: MIT Press, 1992, pp. 21–52.

le Carré, John. *The Constant Gardner*. New York: Scribner, 2001.

Leavis, F. R. *D. H. Lawrence: Novelist*. New York: Knopf, 1956.

Education and the University: A Sketch for An "English School." London: Chatto & Windus, 1948. (Originally published 1943).

The Great Tradition. New York: Penguin, 1993. (Originally published 1948).

"Literature and Society." *Scrutiny* 12.1 (1943): 2–11.

Li, Tania Murray. *The Will to Improve*. Durham, NC: Duke University Press, 2007.

Liu, Alan. *The Laws of Cool: Knowledge Work and the Culture of Information*. University of Chicago Press, 2004.

Lokugé, Chandani. "Introduction." *Kamala: The Story of a Hindu Child Wife*. New Delhi: Oxford University Press, 1998, pp. 1–18.

Luhrmann, T. M. *The Good Parsi: The Fate of a Colonial Elite in a Postcolonial Society*. Cambridge, MA: Harvard University Press, 1996.

Lukács, Georg. *The Historical Novel*. Trans. Mitchell, Hannah, and Stanley Mitchell. Lincoln: University of Nebraska Press, 1983. (Original work published 1937).

MacDonald, Marianne. "My Year as a Star." *The Telegraph* May 10, 2004. www.telegraph.co.uk/culture/books/3616570/My-year-as-a-star.html

Majumdar, Nivedita. "Nationalizing the Woman: Nation and Gender in Tagore's *The Home and the World*." *Journal of Commonwealth and Postcolonial Studies* 12.1 (2005): 24–41.

Mamdani, Mahmood. "African States, Citizenship and War: A Case-Study." *International Affairs* 78.3 (2002): 493–506.

"Blue-Hatting Darfur." *London Review of Books* 29.17 (2007): 18–20.

Citizen and Subject: Contemporary Africa and the Legacy of Late Colonialism. Princeton University Press, 1996.

"Letters." *London Review of Books* 29.8 (2007): 4.

"The Politics of Naming: Genocide, Civil War, Insurgency." *London Review of Books* 29.5 (2007): 5–8.

Saviors and Survivors: Darfur, Politics, and the War on Terror. New York: Pantheon Books, 2009.

Manto, Saadat Hasan. *Mottled Dawn*. Trans. Hasan, Khalid. New Delhi: Penguin, 1997.

Mao, Douglas. "Romances of the Central Committee." Modernist Studies Association Conference 12. University of Victoria, 2010: 1–11.

Solid Objects: Modernism and the Test of Production. Princeton University Press, 1998.

Marinkova, Milena. "'Perceiving [...] in One's Own Body' the Violence of History, Politics and Writing: *Anil's Ghost* and Witness Writing." *Journal of Commonwealth Literature* 44.3 (2009): 107–25.

Mars-Jones, Adam. "It Was All Going So Well." *The Observer* May 15, 2005. http://books.guardian.co.uk/reviews/generalfiction/0,1484042,00.html

Marx, John. "The Historical Novel after Lukács." *Georg Lukács: The Fundamental Dissonance of Existence*. Ed. Bewes, Timothy, and Timothy Hall. London: Continuum, 2011, pp. 188–202.

"Literature and Governmentality." *Literature Compass* 8.1 (2011): 66–79.

The Modernist Novel and the Decline of Empire. Cambridge University Press, 2005.

Marx, Karl. *Capital*. Vol. 1. New York: Vintage, 1977.

Selected Writings. Ed. Simon, Lawrence H. Indianapolis: Hackett, 1994.

Mason, Daniel. *The Piano Tuner*. New York: Knopf, 2002.

Massad, Joseph. "The Politics of Desire in the Writings of Ahdaf Soueif." *Journal of Palestine Studies* 28.4 (1999): 74–90.

Mazzarella, William. "The Myth of the Multitude, or, Who's Afraid of the Crowd?" *Critical Inquiry* 36.4 (2010): 697–727.

Mbembe, Achille. *On the Postcolony*. Berkeley: University of California Press, 2001.

McCann, Sean. *A Pinnacle of Feeling: American Literature and Presidential Government*. 20/21. Princeton University Press, 2008.

McGurl, Mark. *The Program Era: Postwar Fiction and the Rise of Creative Writing*. Cambridge, MA: Harvard University Press, 2009.

Meagher, Kate. "Hijacking Civil Society." *Journal of Modern African Studies* 45.1 (2007): 89–115.

Medovoi, Leerom. "Global Society Must Be Defended." *Social Text* 25.2 (2007): 53–79.

Metcalf, Thomas. *Imperial Connections*. Berkeley: University of California Press, 2007.

Mill, John Stuart. *On Liberty*. Indianapolis: Hackett, 1978. (Originally published 1859.)
Miller, Brook, with Luke Elward, Tessa Hempel, and Philip Kollar. "Narrative, Meaning and Agency in *The Heat of the Day*." *Elizabeth Bowen: New Critical Perspectives*. Ed. Osborne, Susan. Cork University Press, 2009, pp. 132–48.
Miller, C. Brook. "Holroyd's Men." *The Conradian* 29.2 (2004): 14–30.
Miller, Peter, and Nikolas Rose. *Governing the Present*. Cambridge: Polity Press, 2008.
Mishra, Pankaj. "Enigmas of Arrival." *New York Review of Books* December 18, 2003: 42–44.
Mitchell, Timothy. *Rule of Experts*. Berkeley: University of California Press, 2002.
Mo Ibrahim Foundation. *2011 Ibrahim Index of African Governance*. London: Mo Ibrahim Foundation, 2011.
Mo, Timothy. *The Redundancy of Courage*. London: Vintage, 1991.
Moghadam, Valentine. *Globalizing Women*. Baltimore, MD: Johns Hopkins University Press, 2005.
Mongia, Padmini. "Between Men: Conrad in the Fiction of Two Contemporary Indian Writers." *Conrad in the Twenty-First Century: Contemporary Approaches and Perspectives*. Ed. Kaplan, Carola, Peter Mallios, and Andrea White. New York: Routledge, 2005, pp. 85–99.
Moore-Gilbert, Bart. "Imagining Independent India: Japan as a Model for Indian Nationalism, 1895–1918." *Journal of Commonwealth and Postcolonial Studies* 9.2 (2002): 123–34.
Moretti, Franco. "Conjectures on World Literature." *New Left Review* 1 (2000): 54–68.
Morris, Rosalind. "Failures of Domestication: Speculations on Globality, Economy, and the Sex of Excess in Thailand." *differences* 13.1 (2002): 45–76.
Mufti, Aamir. *Enlightenment in the Colony*. Princeton University Press, 2007.
  "Orientalism and the Institution of World Literatures." *Critical Inquiry* 36.3 (2010): 458–93.
Mukherjee, Meenakshhi. "The Beginnings of the Indian Novel." *History of Indian Literature in English*. Ed. Mehrotra, Arvind Krishna. New York: Columbia University Press, 2003, pp. 92–102.
  The Perishable Empire. New Delhi: Oxford University Press, 2000.
Mulhern, Francis. "English Reading." *Nation and Narration*. Ed. Bhabha, Homi K. New York: Routledge, 1990, pp. 250–64.

The Moment of "Scrutiny." London: New Left Books, 1979.

Mullings, Beverly. "Women Rule? Globalization and the Feminization of Managerial and Professional Workspaces in the Caribbean." *Gender, Place and Culture* 12.1 (2005): 1–27.

Mundy, Jacob. "Performing the Nation, Pre-Figuring the State." *Journal of Modern African Studies* 45.2 (2007): 275–97.

Naipaul, V. S. *A Bend in the River.* New York: Vintage, 1989. (Originally published 1979).

Nandy, Ashis. *The Illegitimacy of Nationalism.* New Delhi: Oxford University Press, 1994.

Needham, Anuradha Dingwaney. "Multiple Forms of (National) Belonging." *MFS: Modern Fiction Studies* 39.1 (1993): 93–111.

Newsweek. 25 April 2011: cover page.

Ngũgĩ wa Thiong'o. "On the Abolition of the English Department." *Homecoming: Essays on African and Caribbean Literature, Culture, and Politics.* New York: Hill and Co., 1972, pp. 145–50.

Petals of Blood. London: Heinemann, 1977.

Niger-Thomas, Margaret. "Women and the Arts of Smuggling." *African Studies Review* 44.2 (2001): 43–70.

Niranjana, Tejaswini. *Mobilizing India: Women, Music, and Migration between India and Trinidad.* Durham, NC: Duke University Press, 2006.

Northrup, David. "Globalization and the Great Convergence." *Journal of World History* 16.3 (2005): 249–67.

Nugent, Paul. "States and Social Contracts in Africa." *New Left Review* 63 (2010): 35–68.

Nussbaum, Martha, ed. *For Love of Country.* Boston, MA: Beacon, 1996.

Ojakangas, Mika. "Impossible Dialogue on Bio-Power: Agamben and Foucault." *Foucault Studies* 2 (2005): 5–28.

Okunoye, Oyeniyi. "Captives of Empire: Early Ibadan Poets and Poetry." *Journal of Commonwealth Literature* 34 (1999): 105–16.

Ondaatje, Michael. *Anil's Ghost.* New York: Vintage, 2000.

Ong, Aihwa. *Flexible Citizenship: The Cultural Logics of Transnationality.* Durham, NC: Duke University Press, 1999.

Neoliberalism as Exception. Durham, NC: Duke University Press, 2006.

Outka, Elizabeth. "Buying Time: *Howards End* and Commodified Nostalgia." *Novel: A Forum on Fiction* 36.3 (2003): 330–50.

Padavic, Irene, and Barbara F. Reskin. *Women and Men at Work. Sociology for a New Century.* Thousand Oaks, CA: Pine Forge Press, 2002.

Pandey, Gyanendra. *Routine Violence: Nations, Fragments, Histories.* Stanford University Press, 2006.
Panitch, Leo, and Martijn Konings. "Myths of Neoliberal Deregulation." *New Left Review* 57 (2009): 67–83.
Parry, Benita. "Narrating Imperialism." *Cultural Readings of Imperialism: Edward Said and the Gravity of History.* Ed. Ansell-Pearson, Keith, Benita Parry, and Judith Squires. New York: St. Martin's Press, 1997, pp. 227–46.
Perkin, Harold. *The Rise of Professional Society: England since 1880.* New York: Routledge, 1989.
The Third Revolution: Professional Elites in the Modern World. New York: Routledge, 1996.
Perry, Mark. "The 2008 Male Recession? The Gender Jobs Gap." *Carpe Diem.* Ed. Perry, Mark. 2010 (Original work published 2008). http://mjperry.blogspot.com/2008/12/2008-male-recession-gender-jobs-gap.html
Peters, Krign, and Paul Richards. "'Why We Fight': Voices of Youth Combatants in Sierre Leone." *Africa* 68.2 (1998): 183–210.
Poovey, Mary. *A History of the Modern Fact.* University of Chicago Press, 1998.
"The Liberal Civil Subject and the Social in Eighteenth-Century British Moral Philosophy." *The Social in Question.* Ed. Joyce, Patrick. New York: Routledge, 2002, pp. 44–61.
Making a Social Body: British Cultural Formation, 1830–1864. University of Chicago Press, 1995.
Posner, Richard A. *The Crisis of Capitalist Democracy.* Cambridge, MA: Harvard University Press, 2010.
A Failure of Capitalism: The Crisis of '08 and the Descent into Depression. Cambridge, MA: Harvard University Press, 2009.
Prakash, Gyan. "Civil Society, Community, and the Nation in Colonial India." *Ethnographica* 6.1 (2002): 27–39.
Putzel, James. "War, State Collapse and Reconstruction: Phase 2 of the Crisis States Programme." *CSRC Working Paper 1 Series 2.* London School of Economics, 2006: 1–30.
Pykett, Lyn. *Engendering Fictions.* London: Edward Arnold, 1995.
Quiggin, John. *Zombie Economics: How Dead Ideas Still Walk among Us.* Princeton University Press, 2010.

Rai, Shirin. *Gender and the Political Economy of Development: From Nationalism to Globalization*. Malden, MA: Polity Press, 2002.

Rancière, Jacques. "The Aesthetic Dimension: Aesthetics, Politics, Knowledge." *Critical Inquiry* 36.1 (2009): 1–19.

The Politics of Aesthetics: The Distribution of the Sensible. Pbk. edn. Trans. Rockhill, Gabriel. London and New York: Continuum, 2006.

"The Politics of Literature." *SubStance* 33.1 (2004): 10–24.

Ray, Sangeeta. *En-Gendering India*. Durham, NC: Duke University Press, 2000.

Read, Jason. "A Genealogy of Homo-Economicus." *Foucault Studies* 6 (2009): 25–36.

Retort. *Afflicted Powers: Capital, and Spectacle in a New Age of War*. New York: Verso, 2005.

Rhys, Jean. *Voyage in the Dark*. Jean Rhys: The Complete Novels. New York: Norton, 1985. (Originally published 1934).

"Voyage in the Dark, Part 4 (Original Version)." *The Gender of Modernism*. Ed. Scott, Bonnie Kime. Bloomington: Indiana University Press, 1990, pp. 381–89.

Richardson, Samuel. *Pamela; or, Virtue Rewarded*. London: Penguin, 1980. (Originally published 1740).

Riles, Annelise. *The Network Inside Out*. Ann Arbor: University of Michigan Press, 2000.

Riley, Denise. *"Am I That Name?": Feminism and the Category of "Women" In History*. Minneapolis: University of Minnesota Press, 1988.

Robbins, Bruce. *Feeling Global*. New York University Press, 1999.

"The Smell of Infrastructure." *boundary 2* 34.1 (2007): 25–33.

"Very Busy Just Now: Globalization and Harriedness in Ishiguro's *The Unconsoled*." *Comparative Literature* 53.4 (2001): 426–41.

"Village of the Liberal Managerial Class." *Cosmopolitan Geographies: New Locations in Literature and Culture*. Ed. Dharwadker, Vinay. New York: Routledge, 2001, pp. 15–32.

Rosin, Hanna. "The End of Men." *The Atlantic* 2010: 56–72.

Roy, Parama. "Bhadralok/bhadramahila." *Keywords in South Asian Studies*. Ed. Dwyer, Rachel M. London: SOAS, 2006. www.soas.ac.uk/southasianstudies/keywords/

Rubenstein, Michael. *Public Works: Infrastructure, Irish Modernism, and the Postcolonial*. University of Notre Dame Press, 2010.

Safa, Helen. "Questioning Globalization: Gender and Export Processing in the Dominican Republic." *Journal of Developing Societies* 18.2–3 (2002): 11–31.
Said, Edward. *Culture and Imperialism*. New York: Knopf, 1993.
Salih, Tayeb. *Season of Migration to the North*. Trans. Johnson-Davis, Denys. Portsmouth, NH: Heinemann, 1969.
Sangari, Kumkum. *Politics of the Possible*. London: Anthem, 2002.
Sanghera, Sandeep. "Touching the Language of Citizenship in Ondaatje's *Anil's Ghost*." *CLCWeb: Comparative Literature and Culture: A WWWeb Journal* 6.3 (2004). http://clcwebjournal.lib.purdue.edu/clcweb04-3/sanghera04.html
Sarkar, Sumit. *Beyond Nationalist Frames*. New Delhi: Permanent Black, 2002.
Writing Social History. New Delhi: Oxford University Press, 1997.
Saro-Wiwa, Ken. *Sozaboy*. New York: Longman, 1994. (Originally published 1985).
Sassen, Saskia. *Territory, Authority, Rights*. Princeton University Press, 2006.
Satthianadhan, Krupabai. *Kamala: The Story of a Hindu Child-Wife*. New Delhi: Oxford University Press, 1998. (Originally published 1894).
Schoenbach, Lisi. "A Jamesian State: *The American Scene* and 'the Working of Democratic Institutions'." *The Henry James Review* 30.2 (2009): 162–79.
Schwarz, Daniel. "Conrad's Quarrel with Politics in Nostromo." *College English* 59.5 (1997): 548–68.
Scott, James C. *Seeing Like a State*. New Haven, CT: Yale University Press, 1998.
Scott, Walter. *Waverley*. New York: Penguin, 1985. (Originally published 1814).
Sen, Amartya. *Development as Freedom*. New York: Knopf, 1999.
Sennett, Richard. *The Culture of the New Capitalism*. New Haven, CT: Yale University Press, 2006.
Seshagiri, Urmila. "Modernist Ashes, Postcolonial Phoenix: Jean Rhys and the Evolution of the English Novel in the Twentieth Century." *Modernism/Modernity* 13.3 (2006): 487–505.
Shamsie, Muneeza. "Sunlight and Salt: The Literary Landscapes of a Divided Family." *Journal of Commonwealth Literature* 44.1 (2009): 135–53.
Shirkhani, Kim. "The Economy of Recognition in *Howards End*." *Twentieth Century Literature* 54.2 (2008): 193–216.

Siddiqi, Yumna. *Anxieties of Empire and the Fiction of Intrigue*. New York: Columbia University Press, 2008.

Simmel, Georg. "The Metropolis and Mental Life." *The City Cultures Reader*. Ed. Miles, Malcolm, Tim Hall, and Iain Borden. New York: Routledge, 2004, pp. 12–19. (Original work published 1903).

Simons, Anna, and David Tucker. "The Misleading Problem of Failed States." *Third World Quarterly* 28.2 (2007): 387–401.

Sklair, Leslie. *The Transnational Capitalist Class*. New York: Blackwell, 2001.

Slaughter, Joseph. "Enabling Fictions and Novel Subjects: The *Bildungsroman* and International Human Rights Law." *PMLA* 121.5 (2006): 1405–23.

Smith, Adam. *The Wealth of Nations*. 2 vols. Oxford University Press, 1976. (Originally published 1776).

Smith, Zadie. *White Teeth*. New York: Random House, 2000.

Soueif, Ahdaf. *The Map of Love*. New York: Anchor, 2000. (Originally published 1999).

"Talking About *The Map of Love*." *EnterText* 1.3 (2000): 97–112.

Spivak, Gayatri Chakravorty. "Diasporas Old and New: Women in the Transnational World." *Class Issues: Pedagogy, Cultural Studies, and the Public Sphere*. Ed. Kumar, Amitava. New York University Press, 1997, pp. 87–116.

"Ethics and Politics in Tagore, Coetzee, and Certain Scenes of Teaching." *Diacritics* 32.3–4 (2002): 17–31.

"Righting Wrongs." *South Atlantic Quarterly* 103.2/3 (2004): 523–81.

Stevens, Jacob. "Prisons of the Stateless." *New Left Review* 42 (2006): 42–67.

Stoler, Ann Laura. *Carnal Knowledge and Imperial Power*. Berkeley: University of California Press, 2002.

Stremlau, John. *The International Politics of the Nigerian Civil War*. Princeton University Press, 1977.

Suleri, Sara. *The Rhetoric of English India*. University of Chicago Press, 1992.

Sylvester, Christine. "Bare Life as a Development/Postcolonial Problematic." *The Geographical Journal* 172.1 (2006): 66–77.

Szalay, Michael. *New Deal Modernism: American Literature and the Invention of the Welfare State*. Durham, NC: Duke University Press, 2000.

Tagore, Rabindranath. *The Home and the World*. New York: Penguin, 1985. (Originally published 1915).

Tickell, Alex. "Writing the Nation's Destiny: Indian Fiction in English before 1910." *Third World Quarterly* 26.3 (2005): 525–41.
Tölölyan, Khachig. "Elites and Institutions in the Armenian Transnation." *Diaspora* 9.1 (2000): 107–36.
Trilling, Lionel. *E. M. Forster*. Norfolk: New Directions, 1943.
Trumpener, Katie. *Bardic Nationalism*. Princeton University Press, 1997.
Tsing, Anna Lowenhaupt. *Friction: An Ethnography of Global Connection*. Princeton University Press, 2005.
Unger, Roberto Mangabeira. *Free Trade Reimagined*. Princeton University Press, 2007.
UNIFEM (United Nations Development Fund for Women). *Progress of the World's Women 2002*. New York: United Nations, 2002.
United Nations. *World Survey on the Role of Women in Development*. New York: United Nations, 1999.
Vassanji, M. G. *The Gunny Sack*. Portsmouth, NH: Heinemann, 1989.
Vera, Yvonne. *The Stone Virgins*. New York: FSG, 2002.
von Einsiedel, Sebastian. "Policy Responses to State Failure." *Making States Work*. Ed. Chesterman, Simon, Michael Ignatieff, and Rames Thakur. New York: United Nations University Press, 2005, pp. 13–35.
Walkowitz, Daniel. *Working with Class*. Chapel Hill: University of North Carolina Press, 1999.
Walkowitz, Rebecca L. "Comparison Literature." *New Literary History* 40.3 (2009): 567–82.
   Cosmopolitan Style: Modernism beyond the Nation. New York: Columbia University Press, 2006.
Wegner, Phillip E. "Recognizing the Patterns." *New Literary History* 38 (2007): 183–200.
Wells, Vikki. "The Promise of Liberalism and the Performance of Freedom." *Foucault and Political Reason*. Ed. Barry, Andrew, Thomas Osborne, and Nikolas Rose. University of Chicago Press, 1996, pp. 81–97.
West, Rebecca. *Black Lamb and Grey Falcon: A Journey through Yugoslavia*. New York: Viking, 1941.
Wilkinson, Richard G., and Kate Pickett. *The Spirit Level: Why Greater Equality Makes Societies Stronger*. New York: Bloomsbury Press, 2010.
Williams, Raymond. *The Politics of Modernism*. New York: Verso, 1989.

Woolf, Virginia. "Character in Fiction." *The Essays of Virginia Woolf*. Vol. 3. Ed. McNeillie, Andrew. London: Hogarth Press, 1986, pp. 420–38. (Original work published 1924).
To the Lighthouse. New York Harcourt, 1981. (Originally published 1927).
Wren, Robert M. *Those Magical Years: The Making of Nigerian Literature at Ibadan, 1948–1966*. Washington, DC: Three Continents Press, 1991.
Wright, Melissa W. *Disposable Women and Other Myths of Global Capitalism*. New York: Routledge, 2006.
Yeo, Eileen Janes. "Conflicts between the Domestic and Market Economy in Britain: Past and Present." *Women and Market Societies: Crisis and Opportunity*. Ed. Einhorn, Barbara, and Eileen Janes Yeo. Brookfield, VT: Elgar, 1995, pp. 131–45.
Zaidi, S. Akbar. "A Failed State or Failure of Pakistan's Elite?" *Economic and Political Weekly* July 12, 2008: 10–11.
Zaman, Niaz. *A Divided Legacy*. New Delhi: Oxford University Press, 2001.
Zartman, William. *Collapsed States*. Boulder, CO: Lynne Rienner, 1995.
Zeleza, Paul Tiyambe. *Manufacturing African Studies and Crises*. Dakar: Codesria, 1997.
Žižek, Slavoj. *The Parallax View*. Cambridge, MA: MIT Press, 2006.
"Some Politically Incorrect Reflections on Urban Violence in Paris and New Orleans and Related Matters." *Urban Politics Now: Re-Imagining Democracy in the Neoliberal City*. Ed. BAVO and Jan van Eyck Akademie. Rotterdam: NAi Publishers, 2007, pp. 12–29.
Zwerdling, Alex. *Virginia Woolf and the Real World*. Berkeley: University of California Press, 1986.

Index

Abani, Chris
  Song for Night 78
Abbas, Ackbar 109, 133
Achebe, Chinua 42, 68
  Arrow of God 42
  "The Writer and His Community" 42
Adichie, Chimamanda Ngozi 9, 70
  Half of a Yellow Sun 10, 47–48, 49, 65–77
Administration 26, 56, 57, 58
  and fiction 1, 7, 8, 20, 37, 38, 87, 130, 216
  of populations 13, 20, 31, 55, 61, 62, 90, 127, 144
  see also meritocracy
Agamben, Giorgio 54, 58, 59
Ali, Monica 9
  Brick Lane 9, 201–10, 213
Appadurai, Arjun 134, 149
Armstrong, Nancy 140, 190, 214

Banks, Iain
  The Business 99
Bauman, Zygmunt 128, 154, 181
Berlant, Lauren 186, 216
Bhabha, Homi K. 162
Bowen, Elizabeth
  The Heat of the Day 198–201
Braudel, Fernand 149
Brennan, Timothy 92
Butler, Judith 20

Callon, Michel 185
Callon, Michel, Pierre Lascoumes, and Yannick Barthe
  Acting in an Uncertain World 91, 100–2, 105, 106
Cazdyn, Eric, and Imre Szeman 215, 216
Chakrabarty, Dipesh 33, 110, 122
Chang, Leslie 183

Chatterjee, Partha 33, 127, 163
Chatterjee, Upamanyu
  English, August 43
Chitale, Venu 159
Chow, Rey 5, 34, 35
civil society 61–62, 63, 125–28, 142, 143, 146, 153, 165, 168
civil war 55, 65, 70, 95
collaboration and collaborators 4, 24, 46, 105
  across disciplines 10, 13, 19, 47, 218
  as represented in novels 91, 94, 99, 100, 124, 142, 164, 167
colonial state 61, 144
community 31, 144, 146, 147, 149, 151, 156, 167
  and the novelist 42
Conrad, Joseph 1
  "Heart of Darkness" 1, 4
  Nostromo 160–63
  Typhoon 37–38
cosmopolitans and cosmopolitanism 6, 98, 100, 108, 110, 117, 123
Crisis States Research Centre (CSRC) 56
critique 20, 215

Dangarembga, Tsitsi
  Nervous Conditions 42
de Soto, Hernando 132, 135, 169
Dean, Mitchell 32, 127, 172
Deleuze, Gilles 56, 57, 128
Diouf, Mamadou 148
domesticity 66–69, 141, 197
  and domestic fiction 108, 111, 117, 189, 190, 199
  and education 73, 78
  and social order 64, 82, 84, 107
  and the workplace 177
Duncan, Ian 139, 150

243

Eggers, Dave
  What Is the What 76
Ehrenreich, Barbara 175
entrepreneurs and entrepreneurship 31, 128, 132, 154, 169, 206
ethnicity and race 33, 62, 68, 79, 144–45, 153
  and commercial organization 145
  see also trading diaspora
experts and expertise 65, 68, 81, 127, 141, 151, 187, 216
  and experience 70, 77
  and experts without accreditation 75, 81, 87, 102, 104, 126
  and femininity 107, 116, 197
  and laypeople 14, 19, 25, 90, 91, 100, 106
  and literature 23, 92, 123, 217
  see also cosmopolitans and cosmopolitanism; sentiment and sympathy

"Failed States Index" 51–54, 64, 81
Ferguson, Adam 126, 131
Forna, Aminatta 75
Forster, E. M.
  Howards End 116–21
Foucault, Michel 9, 31, 62, 128, 143, 172, 181, 217
  and liberalism 29, 59, 106, 134
  and norms 54–56
Friedman, Thomas 97

Ganguly-Scrase, Ruchira 182
George, Rosemary Marangoly 147
Ghosh, Amitav 3, 10
  The Glass Palace 4, 25, 136–44
  The Hungry Tide 99
  Sea of Poppies 10
Ghosh, Sarath Kumar 167
  Prince of Destiny 163–67
Gibson, William 12
  Pattern Recognition 184–91, 196, 210
  Spook Country 210
Gikandi, Simon 6, 40
Gilroy, Paul 154, 158
Gladwell, Malcolm 132
globalization 3, 6, 11, 89, 91, 109, 125, 132–36, 144, 145, 148, 154, 163, 169, 171, 174–76, 187, 216

governmentality 31, 59, 209
  and literature 8–9, 13, 20, 35, 49, 72, 215, 216, 218
Grosz, Elizabeth 180
Gurnah, Abdulrazak
  Desertion 154, 158

Habermas, Jürgen 69
Harvey, David 31
Hayford, J. E. Casely
  Ethiopia Unbound 44
historical fiction 129–31, 143, 150, 151, 153, 154, 158, 160, 166, 168
Hosain, Attia
  Sunlight on a Broken Column 158
humanitarian intervention 50, 60–61

immigration, immigrants, and immigrant fiction 146, 151, 193, 204
imperialism 33, 136–37, 160
  and literature 1, 2, 21
  and postcolonial literature 45
  and postcolonial scholarship 5–6, 40
  and the professional division of labor 109
Ingrassia, Catherine 189

Jameson, Fredric 8, 22, 66, 184
Joshi, Priya 113

Kabeer, Naila 9, 201–3, 209
Kelman, James
  Translated Accounts 80
Kotkin, Joel 144

Latour, Bruno 24–25, 104, 214
le Carré, John
  The Constant Gardener 99
Leavis, F. R. 22, 35–41, 43, 216, 217
  The Great Tradition 37–38
  "Literature and Society" 36
Li, Tania Murray 34
liberalism 13, 26–30, 32, 63, 89, 127, 154, 190
  see also neoliberalism; Foucault, Michel
literary education 6, 40–41, 43–44, 72, 110, 122
  see also Leavis, F. R.; Ngũgĩ wa Thiong'o
Lukács, Georg
  The Historical Novel 128, 130, 138, 168

Mamdani, Mahmood 60–63
Manto, Saadat Hasan 81
Mao, Douglas 8, 196
Marx, Karl 129, 161, 168
meritocracy 19, 25, 50, 88, 92, 97, 100, 123
  and democracy 81, 91, 100–7, 109
  see also sentiment and sympathy
migration
  see immigration, immigrants, and immigrant fiction
Mill, John Stuart 26–27, 28, 32
Miller, Peter, and Nikolas Rose
  Governing the Present 29, 31, 33, 34, 105
Mitchell, Timothy 27
Mo, Timothy
  The Redundancy of Courage 79
modernism and modernist fiction 23, 116, 192
  and literary periodization 22
Moretti, Franco 11
Mukherjee, Meenakshi 163
Mulhern, Francis 37, 39

Naipaul, V. S.
  A Bend in the River 86
nation and nationalism 44, 47, 85, 89, 138
  and literature 40, 79, 86, 110–11
neoliberalism 31, 105, 135, 169, 215
  see also liberalism
networks and networking 12, 28, 41, 134, 136, 144, 146, 159, 165, 187, 210, 213, 216
  see also collaboration and collaborators
New Woman 112–13, 116
Ngũgĩ wa Thiong'o 40, 218
  "On the Abolition of the English Department" 40, 218
  Petals of Blood 86
Nussbaum, Martha 110

Ondaatje, Michael
  Anil's Ghost 94–98, 99–100
Ong, Aihwa 34, 148

Pandey, Gyanendra 83
Parry, Benita 160
partition of India 81, 83, 158
Perkin, Harold 27, 97, 177
Poovey, Mary 26

postcolonial literature 5, 6, 22, 49, 66
postcolonial state 33, 61, 83, 84
postcolonial writer 5, 42, 43, 72, 75, 76
Prakash, Gyan 144
professionalism 24, 27–28, 97, 160
  and the novel 25, 90, 98
  and professional education/training 70, 78, 123
  and the professional-managerial class 14, 35, 169, 171, 175
  see also experts and expertise; meritocracy; women, professional

race *see* ethnicity and race
Rancière, Jacques 21–23, 25, 217
Rhys, Jean
  Voyage in the Dark 193–95
Richardson, Samuel
  Pamela 116, 189
Riley, Denise 180, 192
Robbins, Bruce 7, 91
Rose, Nikolas *see* Miller, Peter, and Nikolas Rose

Said, Edward W. 1, 3
Sarkar, Sumit 110
Saro-Wiwa, Ken
  Sozaboy 78
Sassen, Saskia 132
Satthianadhan, Krupabai
  Kamala 113–16
Scott, James C. 104
Scott, Sir Walter 129
  Waverley 138–41, 150
self-governance 2, 29, 32, 78, 83, 170, 172
Sennett, Richard 133
sentiment and sympathy 4
  and collaboration 19, 35, 91, 95–96, 99, 106, 108, 117, 120, 169
  and education 72, 77, 114
Smith, Adam 26, 89
Smith, Zadie
  White Teeth 99
Soueif, Ahdaf
  The Map of Love 4–5, 151–54
sovereignty 59
Spivak, Gayatri Chakravorty 175, 176

Tagore, Rabindranath
   The Home and the World (Ghare-Baire) 109–12, 113
teams and teamwork *see* collaboration and collaborators
terrorism 57
trading diaspora 145–50
   see also ethnicity and race
Tsing, Anna 102

utopia 8, 217

Vassanji, M. G.
   The Gunny Sack 145–48

Vera, Yvonne
   The Stone Virgins 77

West, Rebecca
   Black Lamb and Grey Falcon 83–86
women, professional 107, 176, 184, 191
women and education 114, 116, 176
women and work 170, 174–80, 182–84, 203
Woolf, Virginia 42
   "Character in Fiction" 42
   To The Lighthouse 116, 195
world literature 10–11, 12
Wright, Melissa 178, 179